# THE PARTY AND THE ARMY
IN THE SOVIET UNION

# THE PARTY AND THE ARMY
# IN THE SOVIET UNION

YOSEF AVIDAR

THE PENNSYLVANIA STATE UNIVERSITY PRESS
UNIVERSITY PARK

*Translated into English by*

## DAFNA ALLON

Copyright © 1983 by The Magnes Press,
The Hebrew University, Jerusalem

Published in Israel by The Magnes Press,
The Hebrew University, Jerusalem

Published in Great Britain and Europe by
Frank Cass & Co., Ltd.,
11 Gainsborough Road, London E11 1RS

Published in North and South America and the Pacific Area by
The Pennsylvania State University Press, University Park;
Penn State Press edition printed in the
United States of America

**Library of Congress Cataloging in Publication Data**

Avidar, Yosef, 1906-
The party and the army in the Soviet Union.
Translation of: ha-Yeḥasim ben ha-miflagah le-ven ha-tsava bi-Verit ha-Moʿ atsot, 1953 ʿad 1964.
Includes bibliography and index.
1. Soviet Union. Armiĩa — History. 2. Soviet Union. Armiĩa — Political activity. 3. Kommunisticheskaĩa partiĩa Sovetskogo Soĩuza — History. 4. Soviet Union — Politics and government — 1953-    . I. Title.
UA772.A9513   1985      322'.5'0947       84-43066
ISBN 0-271-00393-6

TO YEMIMA

# CONTENTS

Introduction   1
The Main Theme; Source Material; Structure of the Book

*PART I:* The Communist Conception of Armed Forces   7

CHAPTER I: The Need for an Army   9
The Theoretical Stance; The Pragmatic Solution; The Mission of the Armed Forces; Control of the Forces; Development of Party Supervision

*PART II:* Focal Centres of Political Power, 1953–1957   43

CHAPTER II: The Armed Forces and Political Rivalries   45
In the Service of the Party; Doctrine, Indoctrination and Changing Situations; The Break in Continuity — the Death of Stalin; The End of Beria; The Army Rewarded; "The Personality Cult and Its Consequences"; Poland and Hungary; Khrushchev and the "Anti-Party Group"

CHAPTER III: The Fight Over Military Doctrine   67
Stalin, The Expert; The Breaking of Images; The Debate; The Summing-Up

CHAPTER IV: The Fight for Greater Autonomy   92
The Role of the Main Political Administration; Day to Day Activity; "Unity of Command"; Historiography of the Great Patriotic War

CHAPTER V: The Rise of Marshal Zhukov   117
Childhood and Youth; 1941 — The German Invasion; 1946, End of the Chapter; Death of Stalin; Zhukov as Others Saw Him; Summing-up

*PART III:* Party Control Re-Imposed     145

CHAPTER VI: The Deposition of Marshal Zhukov     147
Background and Reasons; June 1957, Full Member of Central Committee Presidium; How It Was Done; Was There a Real Danger of Zhukov's Making a Bid for Personal Power?

CHAPTER VII: The October 1957 Plenary Resolutions     179
What Was in the Resolutions; Explaining the General Line; Reform of the Military Councils; The MPA Streamlined; A Year Later

CHAPTER VIII: Education and Political Supervision     201
The Main Political Administration of the Army and Navy; The Political Administrations and the Political Sections; The Party Organisations; Party-Political Education; Historiography; The Military Councils

*PART IV:* The Beginning of the 1960's     239

CHAPTER IX: The Impact of Strategic Weapons     241
The Khrushchev Doctrine; The Doctrine — and the Military Theoreticians; The Cuban Missile Crisis

CHAPTER X: The Armed Forces Re-Modelled     257
Khrushchev Reduces Armed Forces Effectives; The Reform Faces the Traditional Structures; The Web of Conflict; Tension Rises in the Aftermath of the XXII Congress; Cuba

CHAPTER XI: The Army Chiefs and Khrushchev     294
1953–1957, Honeymoon; Those October 1957 Plenary Resolutions; May 1960, a Watershed in Military Conceptions; Cuba — the Real Beginning of the End; Why Khrushchev Had to Go; Khrushchev Settles His Own Fate; The Role of the Army Chiefs; "As you Were!"; Summing-Up

BIBLIOGRAPHY     325

INDEX     331

# INTRODUCTION

## *The Main Theme*

In this book I present an analysis of the special relations between the Communist Party leadership and the Armed Forces in the Soviet Union in the period that opened with the death of Stalin and closed with Khrushchev's removal from power. On the disappearance of the tyrant whose terror had ruled everyone and everything, the reins were loosened at last. At once the struggle began for the succession among individuals and groups of the inner Party leadership. A very considerable role was played in the early stages by the Armed Forces, which constituted one of the main focal centres of power in the State. The period under review also saw recurrent disputes between the Party leadership and the Army heads over military doctrine, the structure of the forces and the allocation of resources between civilian and military needs. Relations between the Army and the Party should not, however, be thought of as an uninterrupted struggle preoccupying the high command and the officers' corps. In the nature of things, these bodies concerned themselves with their professional military duties and with personal worries over promotion, conditions of service and the like. It was not a permanent tug-of-war but rather a long, silent, see-saw struggle, influenced in its ups and downs by internal and external political developments, by the personalities of the leaders, military and civilian, and by technological progress that enormously enhanced the power of the Armed Forces and therewith magnified the problem of controlling them.

Our attention must be focussed on something which is specific to the Soviet Union, the supremacy of the Party in the system. This is the cardinal point in the relations between the Armed Forces and the State. The Soviet regime is built on the clear, basic principle that the ruling body which decides on State policy is the Party leadership and apparatus, and that they supervise the execution of that policy by the government machine. This one fundamental principle has been maintained (with changes of emphasis) throughout the entire period of Bolshevik rule and has operated on every level of the civilian and economic administration. The Party is the pivot of the whole structure, from the Party Congress, which determines the policy that will be formally adopted by the Supreme Soviet, up to the Central Committee and the Politburo, which lay down the line for the Presidium of the Supreme Soviet and the Government, and down to the District Committee of the Party, which supervises the District Soviet, and the Party Committees in the factories that supervise trade union representation in the factories.

The Army cannot be directed and supervised with the means that the Party uses for the civil administration, education, science and research and for the entire economy. These means cannot be applied to the Army, a finite, structured body with its own machinery of control: the ranks and hierarchy of command and the discipline vital to its functioning, *sine qua non* of all armies. The day-to-day functioning and activity of the Army are almost completely independent of all the rest of the bodies in the complex and complicated Soviet set-up.

In the Soviet economic system, Party organs coordinate the activities of the various industrial branches, balance the needs of supplier and customer, producer and consumer. Things are different in the military sphere. There is the unique importance of defence as such: there is the large share of power accruing to the Army from its control of production apparatuses and institutes of research and development, all working for defence. The special needs of defence and the Army's unique structure do not allow granting any Party Committee, whether of a District or a Republic, authority to "co-ordinate" the armed forces stationed within its borders.

A central problem facing the Party leadership in its relations with the Army is the formidable force placed in the hands of the military command. How to ensure that the Party leadership will not be deprived of its sole hold on the power to settle issues that the use of this force signifies? And how to ensure that the Army's primary loyalty will be to the regime and its ruling leadership?

The Communist Party heads exerted themselves without pause to instill loyalty to the regime in the Army and to nurture it. The means employed for this purpose were mainly constant and institutionalised Party-political indoctrination by a ramified political apparatus operating at all levels of command throughout the entire military organisation. The authority vested in this apparatus has at times come close to splitting the command between the military officer and the representative of the political apparatus.* The much-discussed conceptions, "unity of command" and "sole commander", were differently interpreted by the commanders and the political workers. A hidden contest, which at times became an open one, went on between the holders of opposing views. The commander would try to get himself as much authority as possible as "sole commander", while the political apparatus would endeavour to limit his authority. This contest has accompanied the development of the Soviet Army from the beginning to the present time, affecting military discipline and even battle preparedness: the Party was more than once faced with the choice between a better state of military preparedness and longer hours of Party-political education. We shall have to record and anatomise the minor clashes and the major campaigns in this lengthy struggle.

## Source Material

Everyone who studies internal relations within the Soviet system immediately comes up against the serious problem of source material. This is the unavoidable outcome of the absence of freedom of expression in the USSR and therefore of any Soviet material critical of the official "general line" as well as of material concerning Soviet decision-making — how decisions are presented for consideration, how taken and how justified. Moreover, quite a

---

\* The technical term for a representative of the political apparatus is "political worker" and it will be used henceforth in the text.

number of Soviet publications of merely "limited" circulation but not considered secret are not available to the researcher; these include, for example, the Army monthly, *Military Thought* (Voyenaya Misl), widely circulated among officers, but nevertheless not to be had. The "iron curtain" that still exists and the present-day absence of diplomatic relations between Israel and the USSR have also blocked access to theoretically "open" material which is to be found in libraries in the Soviet Union but which does not leave the country.

As partial compensation for the inaccessible source material, I have had the good fortune to be able to interview Soviet officers — for the most part Colonels and Lt.-Cols. — who left the USSR in the early 1970's and to be able to record their statements. Some of them served in field units and on the Staffs and some held posts in the political apparatus in the Army. They were of the greatest help to me in getting to know what went on in the Soviet forces.

My primary sources were Soviet publications: the CPSU programmatic "platforms"; Resolutions of Party Congresses and Central Committee sessions; the State Laws; Resolutions of the Supreme Soviet sessions and Decrees of the Supreme Soviet Presidium; Army Orders and Regulations; reports of discussions of Commissions, conventions and "consultations"*; Army and Party periodicals; published collections of articles; articles in the daily press; Party instructions and guide-lines for the Army; and the like. Secondary sources were research works and writing on this subject by researchers in the West and articles in Western periodicals. All these primary and secondary sources will of course be found listed in the Bibliography.

## *Structure of the Book*

This work is in four parts, divided into 11 chapters. Part I deals with the basic Communist conception of armed forces and their control, and constitutes a sort of prologue to the rest of the work.

---

* Technical term for formal, joint Party/Army sessions.

Introduction

Part II deals with the Army's place in the set of focal centres of political power in the years immediately after Stalin's death. It outlines the Army's struggle to secure greater professional and institutional autonomy, a struggle strikingly epitomised in the career of Marshal Zhukov, the much-admired Minister of Defence. Zhukov's rise in the military and Party-political hierarchy is recounted in the last chapter of Part II, and his deposition in the first chapter of Part III, which also discusses the question whether or not Zhukov was a potential Bonaparte, a danger to the regime.

The main theme of Part III is the detailed delineation of the educational and supervisory means by which the Party re-asserted its control of the Army after Zhukov's deposition.

Part IV deals with the effect of the introduction of nuclear weapons systems on the relations between the Party and the Army. It closes with a consideration of the Army's attitude to the deposition of Khrushchev.

*PART 1*

THE COMMUNIST CONCEPTION OF ARMED FORCES

## CHAPTER I

## THE NEED FOR AN ARMY

### *The Theoretical Stance*

Russian Marxist theorists gave no little thought over the years to defining their stand on the question of whether there ought to be regular, standing armies. They saw all existing armies as tools of reaction used against the workers and they wanted them abolished and their place taken by general arming of the people. From the beginning, the views of Lenin were predominant. His views changed in the course of time, and in the end they became the final, infallible authority. But we are still at the beginning.

In his speech to the III Congress of the Russian Workers' Social-Democratic Party in May 1905, Lenin said: "War, shameful and senseless, tightens the noose, and it offers an exceptional, convenient chance for the revolution to annihilate the military caste, for widespread agitation, for arming the people in place of regular armies and for doing so speedily with the support of the masses."[1]

Six months later, Lenin published an article in *Novaya Zhizn* on the Sevastopol mutiny and the prevailing spirit of revolt in the Army and the Navy. Lenin said of armies:

> In every State everywhere, a standing army serves as a tool against the internal enemy rather than against an external one. Everywhere it turns into a tool of reaction, serving capital against the toilers, a hangman strangling the liberty of the

---

1 *Collected Works of V.I. Lenin*, 5th Ed., Political Literature Publications (Gosizdat), Moscow, 1969, Vol. 10, p. 218 (Russian).

people on the gallows. ... We must destroy this evil and annihilate the standing army completely. The people in arms must absorb the army into itself; the soldiers must bring their military competence along with them to the people. The barracks must disappear, and in its place must be a free military school. No force in the world will dare to clash with a free Russia supported by the people in arms, when it has destroyed the military caste, turned all the soldiers into armed civilians and all citizens who are fit to bear arms into soldiers.[2]

Lenin's article in the next issue of the same paper a week later was entitled "Autocracy on its deathbed and the new institutions of rule by the people." With lapidary force he declared: "Only power can constitute authority. In present-day society only the people in arms, with the armed proletariat at its head, can constitute power."[3]

In the speech of May 1905 already cited and in another article, in *Proletary* of July 1905, Lenin still stressed abolishing the standing army and arming the people simply as part of carrying out the revolution, but an essential part. He re-stated the same ideas somewhat more fully in November of that year, in two articles in *Novaya Zhizn* on the institutions of the people's rule that would have to be set up after the revolution. In the following years Lenin did not give the subject much attention, but when the revolution broke out in February 1917 he immediately and inevitably reverted to the idea of the people in arms' taking the place of the regular forces, the idea of a militia. "What kind of militia do we need, we the proletariat and all the toilers?" he wrote in a letter from Switzerland. "It must be truly of the people, that is to say, first, it must really comprise the whole population — all the adult civilians of both sexes; secondly, the militia unites the tasks of a people's army with police functions and also with its functions as the main, basic instrument for maintaining order in the State and administering the State. ..." He then put forward what was not a considered

2 *Ibid.*, Vol. 12, pp. 113–4
3 *Ibid.*, Vol. 12, p. 127

## The Need for an Army

organisational programme but merely a rough sketch to exemplify his idea of how to build up a militia:

> Here is an example of militia organisation: the population of Petrograd numbers two million ..., 750,000 of them adults fit to serve; if they serve in the militia — say, one day every fortnight — and continue receiving their wages from their employers while they serve, they will constitute a militia of 50,000 strong. Here you are, this is the kind of State we need! Here you are, a militia like this will be a "people's militia" in practice and not only in theory. This is the path we must take in order to prevent the re-establishment of a special police and a special army distinct from the people.[4]

Apparently these were still his views and he really thought that a militia of men and women serving two days a month could carry out all the tasks he enumerated. Further on in the same letter he names a few more things the militia might handle, such as distributing bread and milk, supervising the allocation of apartments, public health inspection. This and another letter of his, written at the end of March 1917, dealt with planning the "second stage" of the revolution, when there might be reason to fear that the reaction would prevail. But he nowhere gives even the remotest hint that he thought of the militia as merely a short-term, transitional affair needed to complete the "second stage" of the revolution. Lenin defined this second stage as the transfer of rule from the hands of the capitalist government and the big land-owners — the Lvovs, the Milukovs, the Gutchkovs and the Kerenskys — to the government of the workers and poor peasants. Since it is clear that a violent revolution cannot very well be carried out by militiamen who replace each other for only two days a month, it seems reasonable to assume that what Lenin meant in these letters was a stable militia organization or longer service. Step by step and fairly speedily, Lenin's emphasis on the general arming of the people began to change in accordance with the new realities that were

---

4  *Ibid.,* Vol. 31, p. 42.

coming into being in Russia. On 10 April 1917, only a week after his return to Russia, Lenin published a long article entitled, "The problems of the proletariat in the Revolution", showing a different approach to the militia idea. Lenin spoke of "units of armed persons who have to maintain perfect order and forcibly repress all attempts at counter-revolution. ... These units of armed persons differ from the Army in that they are the masses of the people themselves — they are in fact the people, and not an army distinct from the people and raised above."[5]

The theoretical attitude of the Party on the standing army was still unchanged. Theoretical material prepared for the Party programme in May 1917 stated that the Constitution of a Russian democratic republic must replace the army and the police <u>by arming the entire people.</u>[6] The subject was closely analysed in Lenin's "State and Revolution", written in the stormy days of August and September 1917, after the failure of the attempted coup against the provisional government.

> "What is this force made up of?" Lenin asked. "From special units of people carrying arms, who have prisons and so forth under them ... "[7]

He was referring to the "democratic stage", after the overthrow of the autocracy.

> "In the democratic stage, which is only one of the different forms of the State", Lenin explained, "organised, systematic use of coercion exists. But when the democratic development reaches a certain level, the proletariat annihilates the bourgeois, republican State machine and its standing army as well as the police and the civil service. The proletariat replaces them with a different, more democratic machine" still a State machine, but manned by "masses of armed workers steadily organising themselves as a militia."[8]

5 *Ibid.*, Vol. 31, p. 180.
6 *Ibid.*, Vol. 32, p. 155.
7 *Ibid.*, Vol. 33, p. 9.
8 *Ibid.*, Vol. 33, p. 100.

## The Pragmatic Solution

The *Red Guard* was created in Petrograd in the summer of 1917 to stand guard in the factories. It was almost entirely a Bolshevik creation and it owed allegiance to the Party. In the "Kornilov crisis" the Petrograd Soviet recognised the Red Guard as the workers' militia, and the Guard played an important part in the October *coup*. It was thought to number 20,000 men in Petrograd and anything from ten to twenty thousand in Moscow.[9] At this point no armed force remained in being in Russia capable of resisting the Germans, and the leaders had no choice but to accept the German terms in the Treaty of Brest-Litovsk. The Bolshevik takeover of power in October was followed by civil war and foreign intervention. In the armed struggle to strengthen their slender hold on the power they had just seized, the Bolshevik leaders were faced with urgent practical problems. The new reality pushed aside the theories that the Party had brandished during its fight to overthrow the governments after February 1917. This reality imposed practical solutions even if they ran counter to the accepted theoretical attitude. As early as December 1917, the institutions of the new regime realised that the Red Guard units were not sufficient for all the tasks facing them, and a commission was appointed to prepare the establishment of a Red Army. Within a short space of time, as a result of the decision, decrees and actions of the new institutions, an army was organised and established with a structure like that of all other armies everywhere.

On 15 January 1918, the People's Council of Commissars issued a decree establishing the Red Army of Workers and Peasants, to be a volunteer force of organised elements of the toiling masses possessed of revolutionary consciousness.[10] This attempt at mobilisation was a failure, for only some 100,000 volunteers presented themselves. On 22 April 1918, a decree of the All-Russian Central

---

9 *Large Soviet Encyclopaedia*, 3rd Ed., Moscow, 1973, Vol. 13, p. 327 (Russian).
10 *Soviet Government Decrees* (Gosizdat), Moscow, Vol. I, p. 352 (Russian).

## The Communist Conception of Armed Forces

Executive Committee[10a] authorised the call-up of the entire adult population for the army and for labour, but specified that military training and military service were restricted to workers and peasants.[11] Finally there came the important edict of 29 May 1918, which announced the change from a volunteering basis of the Red Army to compulsory military service and compulsory call-up of workers and poor peasants.[12] The General Staff was also established in May, and a few months later Yehoakim Vatsetis was appointed the first Commander of the Red Army.[13] In July 1918, the V All-Russian Soviet Congress went a step further. It dropped the distinction between the workers and peasants and the rest of the population and decreed compulsory military service for every physically fit citizen with a clean record between the ages of 18 and 40. It was laid down that the Army was to be centralised, well-trained and equipped.[14] Former Czarist officers were now called up as "military experts" to help form the Red Army and to ensure an experienced command.

left-communists

These developments did not mean an end of Bolshevik theoretical doctrines on the militia. The so-called "left Communists" were the main opponents of an army organised like other armies. They saw Trotsky's policy of creating an army and mobilising officers from the old Army as violating pure Socialist doctrine. Less than two months after the decree establishing the Red Army, at the beginning of March 1918, the VII Party Congress adopted ten "theses" on strengthening and developing Soviet rule, and these included the

---

10a All Executive Committees were government organs and should not be confused with the Central Committee of the Communist Party.
11 *Protocols. All-Russian Central Executive Committee*, Moscow, 1920, pp. 176–7 (Russian).
12 *Decrees*, Vol. 2, p. 334.
13 Yehoakim Vatsetis was born in 1873. Served in the Czarist Army, rising to the rank of Colonel. Went over to the Bolsheviks when the Revolution broke out. Commanded on the eastern front from June 1918 to September 1918, and from then on to July 1919 was Commander-in-Chief of the Soviet Armed Forces.
14 *Congresses* of the Soviets of the RSFSR and Autonomous Republics, Moscow, 1959, Vol. 1, p. 74 (Russian).

The Need for an Army

decision to create an armed force of workers and peasants as the first organisational steps "towards arming the entire people".[15]

Trotsky took action in the course of 1918 to ensure centralised control of the military forces that sprang up sporadically as the civil war spread to different parts of the country. He met with strong opposition from faithful adherents of the original revolutionary principles. His policy was damaging to the local Party cells in the Army, now placed under the supervision of a central Party body and bound to follow its instructions. The policy was also offensive to commanders of the partisan units which were created almost independently in the course of the fighting and which now had the discipline of the central command imposed on them. These commanders formed the nucleus of what was called "the military opposition". At the VIII Party Congress in March 1919, the new pragmatic line adopted by the Party leadership was vigorously criticised by the "military opposition" group, mainly Red Army commanders from among former "left Communists" — Smirnov, Safronov and Yaroslavsky — and Voroshilov along with them.[16] They argued vehemently against the Army organisation and discipline demanded by Trotsky, against the increasingly large authority accruing to the military experts, the increasing centralisation and not least against the bureaucratic control of the new political body in the Army. They demanded that the doctrine of partisan warfare based on local leadership and organisation be upheld — the system which they claimed had reaped success in the Civil War. These opposition arguments and demands were rejected by the military section of the Congress. The Plenary ratified the theses of Trotsky, which were put forward in his absence by Sokolnikov and were

15 *Protocols,* Congresses of the All-Russian Communist Party Conferences, VII Congress (Gosizdat), Moscow, 1927, p. 184 (Russian).
16 In 1918 Voroshilov had organized the Fifth Ukrainian Red Army, which marched from Lugansk to defend Tsaritsyn against Denikin's White Russian Army. In command at Tsaritsyn, he opposed Trotsky's orders and was backed by Stalin, then Political Commissar on that front. Voroshilov's devotion to Stalin dated from this period. (Tsaritsyn was re-named Stalingrad.)

firmly backed by Lenin and Stalin. Sokolnikov admitted that a regular army was in the process of being established, an army for the transition period. Stalin was uncompromising in this debate:

> The facts show that the volunteer force does not stand up to criticism, and that we shall not be able to defend our Republic unless we set up another army, <u>a different one</u>, imbued with a sense of discipline and where there is a properly organised political section, an army that will rise up at the first order and attack the enemy... I have to say that the non-proletarian elements constituting the majority in our army do not want to fight as volunteers for communism.[17]

The VIII Congress therewith interred the theses of the previous year about "organising towards a future arming of the entire people" with the philosophical Marxist epitaph that only with the abolition of classes would the "class army" become "the socialist militia of the entire people."[18]

### Transition to the Peace-Time Army

When the Civil War and the war with Poland were over, the debate flared up again in the military leadership over the correct doctrine and structure of forces for the Red Army, a debate that stemmed among other things from the growing opposition to Trotsky as Commissar for War and to the line of his Army Command.

The Head of the Army Political Administration, Gusiev, and one of the Army heads, Frunze, prepared a 21-point plan for re-organising the Army to be submitted to the X Congress in March 1921.[19] The emphasis was on the need for a "unified military doc-

---

17 Y. Stalin, *Works* (Gosizdat), Moscow, 1950. Vol. I, pp. 249–50 (Russian).
18 *Programmes and Standing Orders of the Communist Party of the Soviet Union* (Politizdat), Moscow, 1969, p. 42 (Russian).
19 Frunze was born in 1885; completed his higher education at the Polytechnical Institute of Petersburg; joined the Bolshevik wing of the Social-Democratic Party in 1904; was active as a professional revolu-

## The Need for an Army

trine", to be put into practice in a monolithic army under a military and political Command formed by Civil War experience. The programme opposed the militia as likely not to be collectively loyal to the regime.[20] Trotsky prevented the programme's being presented to the Congress, but the debate between the two camps turned into a serious contest for nothing less than the control of the Red Army. Trotsky relied in part on the views of men of the old military school, officers in the pre-Revolutionary Army who had served on the General Staff and in the military academies.

> tionary in 1905 and 1917. He was one of the organisers of the Army in the Civil War and served as senior Commander on various fronts. He wrote on military subjects and propounded his so-called "unified military doctrine". Succeeded Trotsky as Commissar for War and reorganised the Red Army. In the abortive 21-point plan referred to above, the first 15 points were prepared by Gusiev and the other six by Frunze.
>
> 20 Arguments for and against a militia of "the people in arms" kept cropping up without any directly visible relevance to specific political or military events. We have already referred to the Resolution proposed by Trotsky and passed by the IX Congress (1920) in favour of a gradual change-over to militia-type organisation for the army of the dictatorship of the proletariat. In their 1921 programme, Gusiev and Frunze opposed this change-over in the conditions then prevailing. In November 1921 Trotsky said: "I do not agree with Tukhachevsky in thinking that a change-over to a militia army would be mistaken. True, there are difficulties in such a change-over, but all the same we are making a transition to militia-type forms. We are doing it cautiously because of the difficulties in relations between the peasant and the worker." (L. Trotsky, *How the Revolution was carried out*, Revolutionary Supreme Military Council, Moscow, 1925, 3 Vols.; Vol. 2, pp. 206–7. Russian). This is what Frunze had to say on the subject in March 1922: "From the political point of view, it must be stated that there are now no special obstacles to changing over to organisation on militia-type lines; this transition must of course be a gradual one. ... In the conditions of our Soviet State, the pre-conditions exist for applying a militia system; from the point of view of military qualities, we have solved the problem of bringing the qualities of the militia-type arms more nearly up to those of the best regular units," (M. V. Frunze, *Selected Works*, Voyenizdat, Moscow, 1957, 2 Vols.; Vol. 2, pp. 68–77 Russian).

Gusiev and Frunze were supported by many of the Red Army Commanders who had come up during the Civil War, pre-eminent among them Voroshilov and Tukhachevsky.

This bitter, damaging dispute went on long after the Congress, its arrows envenomed by personal rivalries and sharpened by the instinct for a fight and the will to win. High-spirited, self-confident "Red Commanders" were bent on imposing their views and leaving their imprint on the army of the future. In theory the differences between the two sides were wide and deep, but in practice the views were not so diametrically opposed as their proponents made them appear. Frunze contended that the Red Army had no doctrine whatsover,[21] and Trotsky riposted that it was in no need of one. On 21 December 1921, Trotsky said:

> In our State we have principles of class orientation and international orientation that indicate possible theatres of war; we have principles of the composition and structure of the forces in harmony with the worker-and-peasant character of the State and in harmony with the strategy and tactics taught in the Red Army. If some people want to call these principles and the practical methods of the Red Army a "military doctrine", I shall not go to war with them, but if anyone dares to contend that we have no theory and practice at all, I shall tell him: "What you are saying is not true — you are intoxicated with empty phrases and you are intoxicating others."[22]

---

21  Frunze explained his "unified" doctrine in cloudy formulae, stressing the "class" nature of the Red Army. "It (the unified doctrine) expresses the sole will of the class that maintains the ruling authority in power. ... It (the doctrine) is accepted in the Army of the State. On the basis of the views ruling in the State concerning the nature of the military problems that it (the State) has to face — problems that stem from the class nature of the regime — and concerning the way to solve these problems, the unified doctrine determines the character of the structure of the Armed Forces, the methods of training for battle preparedness and the leadership." *Op. cit.,* Vol. 2, pp. 7–8.

22  Trotsky, *op. cit.,* Vol. 2, p. 219.

## The Need for an Army

On the famous question of the offensive in strategy *versus* the defensive, the positions taken by the two sides were again not such poles apart as they were stated to be. The supposedly "correct" line was that the only appropriate approach for the worker-and-peasant Army in the proletarian State was the offensive and nothing else. In fact all sides converged towards the more balanced notion of a combined defensive and offensive approach. Trotsky's opponents accused him of being against offensive tactics and in favour of fighting from fortified positions, but his views were not really so cut and dried. In an address to the Society of Military Science in the Military Academy in November 1921, Trotsky launched a trenchant attack on Tukhachevsky for contending that the Red Army must be a purely offensive one:

> Comrade Tukhachevsky is of the opinion that the day of positional warfare is over, but this is entirely mistaken. ... Idealisation of manoeuvre could be very dangerous. Only a dashing cavalryman thinks that one must always attack! Only a superficial thinker believes that retreat is fatal. Attack and retreat can both be part of manoeuvre and can lead equally to victory. There are wars ahead of us, and we must teach the General Staff to weigh up different situations, to judge when to attack and when to withdraw. What is needed is a doctrine of complete flexibility.[23]

Frunze for his part did not discount all possibility of retreat on condition that the capacity to continue fighting was preserved.[24] By March 1922 he had come close to Trotsky's views:

> Manoeuvre is not an end in itself but a means for reaching the main aim — victory by destruction of the enemy's milit-

---

23 *Ibid.*, pp. 205–6.
24 As early as July 1921, Frunze already considered a defensive stand in appropriate conditions of the terrain as a way of active support for a war of movement and manoeuvre, and he endorsed large-scale entrenchments and fortifications for temporary defence lines. *Op. cit.*, pp. 18–19.

ary power and capture of his principal bases. Manoeuvre does not rule out warfare from fortified positions; on the contrary, there can be no proper manoeuvre without exploiting entrenchment fully and waging a positional battle in some of the most important sectors. ... The fundamental character of a strategy of movement does not have to be formally offensive. Initiative and action will ensure a successful outcome if the campaign is conducted as fundamentally offensive in character. In our military education we must instill the idea that to withdraw is not to flee, that there is also strategic withdrawal when needed to preserve one's forces or shorten a front or entice the enemy to advance in depth and thus make it possible for us to cut his forces in two.[25]

Though Tukhachevsky's views were more uncompromising than those of Frunze, the contest between the rival camps was not really about formulae or the Army's aims, structure and composition or over strategy but over who was to control the Army. Lenin's decline and the struggle for the succession brought this issue to the fore. Stalin weaved his web of intrigue, and the contest ended with Trotsky's defeat by Frunze and his supporters.

In March 1924, Frunze was appointed Deputy Commissar for War with wide powers to carry out his proposed military reforms. On Trotsky's fall, Frunze moved up to take his place as Commissar for War and became Chief of General Staff. Frunze's reforms effected the transition from the mass army created in the Civil War days to a peace-time army in its aims, structure, composition and technical level. The reforms constituted a compromise in the matter of territorial structure: an expanded corps of the regular army was added to some of the territorial Divisions created by Trotsky in 1923, and all the cavalry units except one were put on a full-strength, regular basis in order to maintain a mobile spearhead for attack.

While the doctrinaire debates over "the people in arms", "military doctrine" and war of movement as against positional warfare

25 *Ibid.*, pp. 59–60.

had been, as we have stated, a cloak for the struggle over who was to control the Armed Forces and as that struggle had been decided with the defeat of Trotsky in 1924, the existence of a regular army was by then taken for granted. The USSR Constitution of 1924 laid down: "The organisation and administration of the Armed Forces are the responsibility of the supreme institutions of the USSR."[26] The 1936 (Stalin) Constitution stated: "General compulsory service is the law."[27] The Party programme adopted at the XXII Congress in October 1961 struck a note, however, that echoed the old debates. In the section headed, "Strengthening the Armed Forces and USSR defensive power", we find:

> The imperialist camp refuses to acquiesce in the existence of the world socialist system. The imperialists openly declare their insane plans for annihilating the USSR and the other Socialist States by means of war. This obliges the Party, the Armed Forces, the State Security institutions and all the peoples of the USSR to exercise constant vigilance. From the viewpoint of internal conditions, the USSR does not need an army. But as long as there is the danger that war can originate in the imperialist camp, and as long as general disarmament is not secured, the Communist Party of the Soviet Union finds it necessary to maintain USSR defensive might and the battle preparedness of the USSR Armed Forces.[28]

Thus a solution was found to the problem of explaining the need for the existence of an army even in the period of "full-scale Communist construction". The army is clearly needed to defend "the Socialist system" from imperialist plots and not at all for the purpose of ensuring that the Socialist States are kept within the Soviet bloc. The fact remains that the regular army exists in the USSR and grows ever bigger and stronger. Its disappearance has been postponed to the sweet by-and-by.

26 *Foundation and Development of the USSR,* Legal Literature, Moscow, 1973, p. 319 (Russian).
27 *Ibid.,* p. 467.
28 *Programmes ... of the CPSU,* pp. 187–88.

## The Mission of the Armed Forces

*The Stance of the Soviet Regime.* When the Red Army was created early in 1918, its purpose was stated to be defence of the regime and support for the social revolution in Europe. The Party leadership wanted an Army that would safeguard the interests of the Bolshevik Party above all else. Accordingly the make-up of its manpower had to be such as to ensure that the Army could serve as an instrument for the exercise of force in the hands of the dictatorship of the proletariat. It followed automatically that safeguarding the political interest which the Army was meant to serve mattered more than purely military efficiency.

The Russian Social-Democratic Workers' Party — the Bolsheviks — and the Council of Commissars[28a] which the Party set up on its seizure of power already stated this outlook clearly and unequivocally in the Decree issued by the Council on 15 January 1918 establishing the Red Army of Workers and Peasants:

> The old Army served as an instrument of class warfare in the hands of the bourgeoisie for the repression of the class of the toilers by the bourgeoisie. With the transfer of power to the proletariat and the poor peasantry and the classes of the exploited toilers, the need has arisen to create a new Army which the Soviet regime can rely on now in the present and which will serve in the near future as the basis for the replacement of the permanent Army by the entire people in arms as well as a support for the imminent social revolution in Europe. The Red Army will accept everyone ready to offer his strength and his life to defend the achievements of the October Revolution, the rule of the Soviets and socialism.[29]

The Decree of the All-Russian Central Executive Committee[29a]

---

[28a] Equivalent of Ministers of State. Hence the Council was equivalent to the Government or Cabinet.

[29] *Decrees*, p. 352.

[29a] The All-Russian Central Executive Committee, The "VTSIK" — the

## The Need for an Army

issued on 22 April 1918 gave the text of the oath to be taken by the recruits. Its content was in accord with the purpose for which the Red Army was established:

> As a son of the toiling people and as a citizen of the Soviet Republic, I hereby swear before the working classes of Russia and of the whole world to dedicate my actions and my thoughts to the great aim of freeing all the workers, and to fight for the Soviet Republic, for the aims of socialism and for the brotherhood of nations.[30]

Not long after the Decree was issued that established the Army, the deteriorating military situation led to the first, insistent demands for better organisation in the Army so as to improve its effectiveness in defence of the State. For all that, a constant effort was made not to permit any erosion of the awareness that the Army's principal task was to secure the political interests of the Communist Party in power and of international proletarian socialism.

In the first week of March 1918 Trotsky was appointed head of the Supreme Military Council and a little later People's Commissar for the Army as well. On 19 March he addressed a meeting in Moscow of the Council of Delegates of Workers, Soldiers and Peasants on the Army, its organisation and its mission:

> As long as we were fighting against Kaledin[30a] we could make do with units organised in haste, but now these do not suffice for the creative action that awaits us, which is to bring our country back to life and to safeguard the Soviet Republic under conditions of international counter-revolutionary siege. What is needed now is an organised Army, built up afresh in the right way. ...We need an Army that will make us a tremendous force for the sake of the struggle that is ahead of us against international imperialism. With the help of this

---

supreme legislature, acting on the basis of the 1918 Constitution, up until the establishment of the Supreme Soviet in 1938.
30  *Protocols of the All-Russian Central Executive Committee*, pp. 176–77.
30a  A "White" Russian Commander.

Army, we shall not only be able to defend ourselves but we shall also be able to play our part in the struggle of the international proletariat.[31]

Lenin even put the Army's international revolutionary role ahead of the defence of the regime — in his speeches at least. In an address on foreign policy to a joint session of the All-Russian Central Executive Committee and the Moscow Soviet on 14 May 1918, Lenin said:

> We who defended ourselves on 25 October 1917 won for ourselves the right to defend the fatherland. ... We are not defending the principle of a great Power nor are we defending national interests. We state openly that the interests of socialism and of world socialism are more important than national interests and the interests of the State. We are the defenders of the socialist fatherland.[32]

A special committee was set up at the 1918 VII Congress of the party to work out a new Party "platform"[32a] to be put to the next Congress, and this new programme was accepted at the March 1919 VIII Congress of the Party.[32b] It included a seven-clause section, "Regarding the Military Sphere", which stated flatly that the Army was an instrument of the dictatorship of the proletariat. It should be noted that this was not a pronouncement of the Council of Commissars (that is to say, of the Government) but was affirmed by the highest and most authoritative institution of the Party as part of its formal, binding programme and remained in force, at least formally, until October 1961.

The text was clear and concise:

> The Red Army, as an instrument of the proletarian dictatorship, must necessarily have a clear class character, that is to

---

31 Trotsky, *op. cit.*, Vol. I, pp. 26–27.
32 Lenin, *op. cit.*, Vol. 36, pp. 341–42.
32a A programmatic statement of principles.
32b The Party had in the meantime changed its name to the Russian (Bolshevik) Communist Party.

say, it must be recruited solely from the proletariat and the strata close to it of the semi-proletarian peasantry.[33]

Those who drafted the programme and those who ratified it at the Congress made not the slightest attempt to define even in general terms the task of the Red Army in defence of the fatherland. The designation of the Army as an instrument in the hands of the proleterian dictatorship exhausted the subject and marked the essential: the Army was intended to serve the regime and the State only when this was under the dictatorship of the proletariat.

The Constitution of the Soviet Union passed in 1924 made no reference at all to the aim of the Armed Forces, but the Constitution of 1936 (the "Stalin Constitution") reflected the period of "Socialism in One Country" in its concise designation of service in the Armed Forces:

> Section 132: Military service in the ranks of the Armed Forces of the Soviet Union is a binding obligation of honour of the citizen of the Union.
> Section 133: Defence of the fatherland is the sacred duty of every citizen of the Soviet Union.[34]

The difference is striking between this formulation and the Party programme. There is no mention of the dictatorship of the proletariat or international socialism and no trace of any need to justify the defence of the fatherland.

In the aftermath of the Second World War, the formation of a bloc of socialist countries in the Soviet sphere of influence made it necessary to re-define the aim of the Armed Forces. The Party programme adopted in 1961, in the section already referred to, "Strengthening the Armed Forces and USSR defensive power", stated *inter alia*:

> The Party sees as its sacred duty and that of the entire Soviet people and as the most important task of the Socialist State

---

33 *Programmes ... of the CPSU*, p. 42.
34 *Constitution, Basic Law of the Soviet Union*, Gosizdat, Legal Literature, Moscow 1957, p. 27.

the defence of the Socialist fatherland, the strengthening of the defence of the Soviet Union and the power of the Armed Forces. The Soviet Union sees as its international obligation together with the other socialist States to ensure the certain defence and security of the whole Socialist camp.[35]

This programme too does not define the Army as an instrument in the hands of the dictatorship of the proletariat, but it does refer to the matter:

> The Party considers that the dictatorship of the working class will cease to be necessary before the withering-away of the State, while the State as the organisation of the whole people will continue to exist until the complete victory of Communism.[36]

According to this programme, not only will the State continue to exist, as "the organisation of the whole people", but so will the Communist Party of the working class: this Party, which has already become the Party "of the whole people" as a result of the victory of socialism, will not only continue to exist but its task and its value will grow.[37]

A study of the paragraphs concerning Party rule over the Armed Forces shows that even if this is not stated directly the Army is seen as an instrument in the hands of the Communist Party leadership in the period of "full-scale Communist construction".

### Control of the Forces

Immediately after the February 1917 Revolution, when the Russian Army was still a tremendous size owing to mobilisation for war, the soldiers everywhere began to elect committees from their units and formations. There was also a general move to elect the officers, who were in fact subordinate to the Committees, which

---

35 *Programmes ... of the CPSU*, p. 188.
36 *Ibid.*, p. 176.
37 *Ibid.*, p. 217.

could replace them if they were dissatisfied with them. The whole Army was in an extraordinary state of ferment: discipline was seriously weakened, officers began to lose control of their units, and the damage went on spreading wider and wider. The vast majority of the soldiers were peasants and they were unspeakably weary of the war. They wanted to go back to their villages and be given a plot of land. Carried on the wave of unrest, the Bolsheviks encouraged the process. Fomenting the spirit of revolt, they did their best to capture the soldiers' committees. They wanted to bring about the disintegration of the army in the field, where most of the officers were not numbered among their supporters. The system of committees and election of Commanding Officers was effective in achieving this end, but it went absolutely counter to the new needs that arose with the seizure of power in October — the absolute and pressing need to create an efficient fighting force to repulse the assaults on the Soviet regime.

The principle of elections in the Army was abolished by an Order of the All-Russian Central Executive Committee of 22 April 1918[38] but instructions to do away with the elections had in fact been issued even earlier, shortly after the first Decree on the establishment of the Red Army.

In the Party programme adopted by the VIII Congress in March 1919, the "military sphere" paragraph affirmed:

> The demand for election of the officers' corps completely loses its value as a principle with regard to a class army of workers and peasants.[39]

Trotsky treated this subject very forthrightly in an article of his, "The Red Army Path", published on 22 May 1922:

> The sharp psychological turn-about from destruction of the old Army to creation of the new Army was achieved at the cost of constant internal friction and quarrels. The old Army had put itself under elected committees and under an elected

38 *Decrees,* Vol. 2, pp. 153–55.
39 *Programmes ... of the CPSU,* p. 44.

command which was in fact under the committees. This path was of course a politically revolutionary one, but it was not a military means for commanding troops in combat and preparing troops for combat. It was weird, unthinkable, ruinous. There was not nor could there be any possible way to command troops by means of elected committees and commanding officers, subordinate to the committees, who could be replaced at any minute. These political, organisational actions were right and necessary in order to disrupt the old Army but they were not at all conducive to the establishment of a new Army ready to fight. ... A revolutionary, fighting Army is not a propaganda platform and it does not fit into a system of elected committees.[40]

Control of the Red Army was decentralised in the beginning, and in fact the local Commissariats controlled the troops in their area. Then the leadership decided to concentrate control of the Army in the hands of a supreme body in order to secure Party control guided by over-all, central considerations and thus to exclude any risk of regionalist tendencies. The changeover to centralism in the Army units was, as Trotsky said, mainly a matter of psychological readjustment, but in the higher Party echelons there were many who had been trained in clandestine conditions and had trained others on the doctrine of negating the Army and on the doctrine of "the people in arms" and armed Guard forces subordinate to local workers' councils. These men found the sharp ideological reversal hard to accept. Not all the veteran activists were endowed with the pragmatism of Lenin, Trotsky, Stalin and others, brazen-faced men capable of making a complete about-face unhesitatingly when pushed to it by the needs of the rule they had seized.

The constant friction and the internal disputes recalled by Trotsky found trenchant expression at the Fifth Soviet Congress that convened in Moscow in July 1918 and they reached their climax and their defeat at the VIII Party Congress in 1919. The views of the

40 Trotsky, *op. cit.*, pp. 15–16.

## The Need for an Army

so-called "military opposition" that opposed the regular Army and the abolition of "democracy" in the Army were rejected and Trotsky's line was accepted of an Army established from above and kept under firm discipline and centralised control. This line, supported as we have already said by Lenin and Stalin, became the fixed and unchallenged position of the Party.

### Development of Party Supervision

If the Army was to carry out the tasks intended for it by the Party, from the very outset as a matter of course there had to be close, centralised Party supervision over all the Army's actions, in order to see to it that what had been created should not turn against its creator and serve some other political force.

With the decision to establish the Red Army and almost simultaneously with the process of demobilising the old, large Army, the Bolshevik Party faced an extremely difficult problem: the forces opposed to the regime and fighting to end it were grouped round a number of Tsarist Generals and included plenty of war-tried officers. To withstand these forces and wipe them out, the Bolshevik regime needed an organised, well-armed, disciplined army, led by able commanders loyal to the regime. The practical solution found was very characteristic of the Bolshevik leadership. In the absence of a reserve of its own or of other sources, it called on tens of thousands of Tsarist officers to join the Red Army, so as to use their military knowledge and experience on the various Staffs, in operational planning, and in command in the field, in logistic organisation and troop training.[41]

These officers were termed "military experts". They constituted the backbone of the officers' corps and functioned with considerable efficiency in the Red Army. Nevertheless, in order to ensure the loyalty of the units and formations to the regime, Political Commissars were appointed "on top of" the officers to supervise them

---

[41] D. Fedotoff White, *The Growth of the Red Army*, Princeton University Press, 1944, p. 37.

in taking political decisions — and purely military ones as well. Military operation orders had to be counter-signed by the Political Commissar in order to ensure that they were dictated by purely operative considerations and not by some dark, counter-revolutionary design. In case of a clash between the two interests, precedence was explicitly given to political security and the loyalty of the troops over military effectiveness.[42] Thus was born the institution of Political Commissars in the Red Army.

*Political Commissars*

The first Order defining the tasks and duties of the Political Commissars and of the Military Councils was issued on 6 April 1918, signed by Trotsky. The Order laid down, *inter alia*:

> The Military Commissar constitutes the political institution of Soviet authority attached to the Army. The personality of the Commissar is protected by immunity. ... The Commissar must exercise supervision so that the Army should not dissociate itself from the Soviet regime and that no cells should be created of conspiracy against the regime. ... The Commissar participates in all actions by the military leaders, receives reports along with them and confirms orders given. ... If the Commissar reaches the conclusion that a certain order is dictated by counter-revolutionary motives, it is incumbent on him to suspend the order.[43]

Putting so many former Tsarist officers, including Generals, into various posts in the Red Army was strongly resisted by those who considered themselves more devout followers of Party principles. As already related, they urged continuation of a system of local partisan-type units instead of the establishment of a regular army necessarily relying on Tsarist officers. Trotsky vigorously defended

---

42 John Erickson, *The Soviet High Command,* MacMillan and Company, Ltd., New York, 1962, p. 22.
43 Trotsky, *op. cit.,* Vol. 1, p. 406.

his policy and exerted himself to soften the opposition in the Party and the ranks of the Army to the "military experts". On 22 April 1918, he issued a "necessary clarification": He quoted the decision of the Central Executive Committee on this issue, and went on:

> We have to have a regular armed force, based on military science, and the cooperation of military experts is therefore a vital necessity. They must be enabled to devote themselves honourably and conscientiously to the work of building up the Army. We have to have a Soviet Army ... that will suit the over-all character of workers' and peasants' rule. To ensure this suitability is the basic aim of the institution of the Commissars for Military Affairs. ... Former Generals, working conscientiously in spite of their conservative outlook, are entitled to more respect than sham socialists.[44]

Trotsky continued this defence at a Central Executive Committee meeting in July 1918:

> The old officers' corps received its education at the people's expense. Those who served under Nikolai will also serve under orders from the working class ... The servants of the enemy, those who fight against the Revolution — we shall exterminate.[45]

Endless serious difficulties and complications resulted from the duplication of command and from inexpertness and inexperience on the part of the Commissars bordering on plain ignorance. Later in 1918, Trotsky was obliged to give a further "clarification" in an attempt to define more precisely the powers of the Commissars, in spite, as he acknowledged, of the difficulty in doing so:

> The Commissar has very limited powers in the operational-command sphere. It is clear to any knowledgeable person that there cannot be two Commanding Officers at one and the same time, especially in combat conditions; but there is

44 *Ibid.*, p. 135.
45 *Ibid.*, p. 145.

no bar to the Commissar's giving his opinion on operational problems, making suggestions, examining the execution of the operational orders and so on. ... On organisational-administrative questions in the rear, the Commanding Officers and the Commissars have equal authority.[46]

The regime was hampered by its very considerable dependence on these former Tsarist officers and concerned over the dangers involved. The leadership therefore made great efforts to prepare a reliable new corps of commanders, mainly from among the non-commissioned officers, most of whom were not of bourgeois origin and who were more likely to be loyal to the regime. In August 1918, Trotsky proclaimed:

> Non-Commissioned Officers: The Soviet Government summons you to take up posts of Commanding Officers. ... The Workers' and Peasants' Army is your Army.... Every N.C.O. serving in the Red Army is hereby promoted to the rank of Platoon Commander; the Soviet Government offers you the opportunity to rise to the top in the art of war.[47]

The military experts were playing a vital part in the meantime in building up the Red Army and waging the Civil War, and Lenin came to Trotsky's help against the "military opposition" in the Party. On the eve of the VIII Party Congress in March 1919, Lenin argued: "We have no experience or scientific training like the bourgeois experts have and we shan't be able to manage without them."[48] At the Congress itself he said: "None of the teachers of socialism dealt with this subject, and we only realised this when we came to build up the Red Army[49] — somewhat cavalier treatment of the revered "teachers of socialism".[50]

---

46 *Ibid.*, pp. 183–84.
47 *Ibid.*, Vol. 1, p. 174.
48 *Lenin*, op. cit., Vol. 38, p. 6.
49 *Ibid.*, pp. 139–40.
50 In the writings of Friedrich Engels there is a wealth of comment on historical and military affairs, on the course of the wars of his day, on

## The Need for an Army

The military section of the Party programme already referred to also dwelt on the need for Political Commissars:

> Red Army military training and education are carried out on the basis of class solidarity and socialist enlightenment. For this purpose there is need for Political Commissars from among reliable Communists who are ready to sacrifice themselves alongside the combat Commanding Officers, and it is therefore necessary to set up Communist cells in every unit in order to maintain contact internally [i.e., within each unit] with the way the men are thinking and to introduce the discipline that is its conscious product [i.e. of correct thinking].[51]

The debate did not die down after the VIII Congress, and Lenin went on defending the use of the military experts. In a special Circular of the Central Committee of June 1919 distributed to all Party organisations, "Everything for the Fight Against Denikin", Lenin wrote:

> Hundreds and hundreds of military experts have turned traitor against us — we shall hunt them down and shoot them. But there are thousands and thousands of military experts working with us without whom there could not arise the Red Army that has emerged from the accursed past of partisan warfare. The traces and vestiges of partisan warfare in our Army have been the cause of disintegration, defeats, disasters, losses of men and equipment, they have done

---

the value of different weapons and on the structure of troops in order of battle. On the problem under discussion here, Engels wrote that the emancipation of the proletariat would create new forms of warfare. He warned that the new methods of warfare that the proletarian State would have to make use of at its inception would be very different from the methods that the proletariat would practice once it was really emancipated. *The Possibilities and Prospects of War Between the Holy Alliance and France in 1852* (in Russian), Gosizdat Political Literature, 2nd ed., Moscow 1956, Vol. 7, p. 509.

51 *Programmes ... of the CPSU*, p. 43.

more harm than all the treacheries of military experts. What needs to be done is to examine the activity of the Commissars in the Army, improve their composition and carry out what it says in our programme: "Concentration of over-all supervision of the Army Command corps in the hands of the working class."[52]

At a meeting of the Moscow Soviet in March 1920, when the Civil War was coming to an end with the victory of the Soviet regime, Lenin admitted that it had only been with the help of the military experts, the former Tsarist officers, that the Red Army had won its victories.[53]

The Political Commissars were not put there as a façade just to appease the "military opposition". They and the members of the Military Council were under orders to supervise not only the former Tsarist officers but all Commanding Officers, including loyal Communists — and even the Commander-in-Chief himself. Here is a paragraph from a letter of Lenin's of 1 August 1918 to his representatives Kubuzov, Danishevsky, Makhonoshin and Raskolnikov, who were in Kazan at the time on the staff of the C.-in-C., Vatsetis:

Are the Army leaders and Vatsetis too doing their job energetically enough? Are the Commissars supervising them properly? I request an answer by telegraph.[54]

Political supervision was not all, as we have already shown. The Commissars were also under orders to encourage and urge on the Commanding Officers and the troops to keep on fighting, and to see to it that the troops should not disperse and melt away after setbacks. The numerous telegrams which Lenin sent to Commanding Officers and to members of the Revolutionary Military Council when matters were going badly for the Red Army on a given front testify to what was wanted of the Commissars. Lenin demanded

---

52 Lenin, *op. cit.*, Vol. 39, pp. 56–58.
53 *Ibid.*, Vol. 40, p. 199.
54 *Ibid.*, Vol. 50, p. 133.

## The Need for an Army

that better Commanders be sent out and principally stronger-minded Commissars.[55]

In cases of lack of success, defeats, withdrawals and desertions, the Commissars had to assume special powers. Thus Trotsky as Head of the Revolutionary Military Council and Commisar [Minister of State] for the Army and Navy wrote to the Eighth Army on 20 November 1918:

> If there is panic and confusion, the Commanding Officers and the Commissars are responsible. ... The Commissar must find out who is chiefly to blame and if necessary he must on the spot arrest the Commanding Officer responsible for the retreat ... and see to it that the Revolutionary Tribunal condemns the scoundrel to be shot.[56]

The VII Congress created a Political Section of the Revolutionary Military Council to run the political institutions attached to the Armed Forces. (Its name was changed two months later to 'Political Administration'.) This Administration was headed by a member of the Central Committee but remained under the Revolutionary Military Council (*Revvoyensoviet*). In the years that followed all the links in the chain of organisation and of this supervisory machinery of the Party within the Army were strengthened simultaneously and equally, from the Party cell in the unit all the way up to the representatives of the Political Administration and of the Party on the Military Council of the Military Districts.

This double-headed system of command in the units and even on the Staff, with all its drawbacks from the point of view of military efficiency, was a very substantial, practical reality.[57] Inevitably there was recurrent friction between the Commissars and

---

55 *Ibid.*, Vol. 51, pp. 49–50. E.g. telegram of Lenin's of 16 September 1919.
56 Trotsky, *op cit.*, Vol. 1, p. 355.
57 The finding that political considerations overrode purely military ones is a major theme of Erickson's in his entire work. See, e.g., *op. cit.*, p. 40.

the Commanding Officers, mainly those from the old Army. The Party leadership for its part and the Army Supreme Command were of course alive to the problems involved. The discussion of the pros and cons, the arguments back and forth over the need for an efficient single channel of command weighed against the basic awareness that political supervision with wide powers was a necessity — this controversy began with the birth of the Red Army and accompanied the relations between the Party and the Army Command long after the end of the Civil War, when there were no longer any ex-Tsarist officers in the Red Army. The numerous disputes on the subject were influenced in no small measure by the internal struggle within the Party, which revolved — among other issues — around control of the Army

*"Unity of Command"*

In June 1924 the Central Committee ratified the principle of "unity of command". In simple terms this meant that Commanding Officers were henceforth to be vested with both military and political authority. This would seem to signify the automatic disappearance of the Commissars — but only in principle. "Unity of command", it was stated from the outset, must be introduced cautiously and gradually. Political authority was accorded only to given individual officers, who were not only reliable Communist Party members but were considered suitable by higher Party echelon. When Frunze expatiated on what was new about "unity of command", he emphasised the need for gradualness, saying, "Frequently, not all the qualities and talents needed for carrying out both military and political tasks are to be found combined in a Commanding Officer who is a member of the Party."[58]

Against the background of the struggle in the Party leadership and parallel with the first steps to implement "unity of command" in the Army, the XIV Party Congress of December 1925 took a decision on a system of political leadership in the Armed Forces. A

---

58 Frunze, *op. cit.*, Vol. 2, p. 157.

## The Need for an Army

section was introduced into Party regulations concerning Party organisations in the Red Army and Navy. It laid down as follows:

> The over-all conduct of political action in the Red Army and Navy will be executed by the Political Administration of the Red Army of Workers and Peasants. The Administration will function as a Section of the Central Committee.[59]

This decision laying down that the Political Administration would function as a Section of the Central Committee transferred the supreme centralised institution of political supervision over the Red Army to the Party, thus rendering the Political Administration independent of the Army leadership and of the Commissariat [Government Ministry] for Defence.

The Political Administration later became the Red Army and Navy Main Political Administration. With the implementation of "unity of command", the title of the Military Commissar was changed to *Politruk;* he had concentrated in his hands the functions of political leadership on behalf of the Party. Some years later still, the Commissar became the Commanding Officer's ('Deputy for Political Affairs') — *Zampolit*, directly and simultaneously subordinate to the political official in the next highest Army unit or formation.

Not unnaturally, implementation of "unity of command" met with opposition from the Commissars and others in political posts in the Army. In fact, "unity of command" was never implemented more than partially, both as regards the number of officers affected and the powers exercised.[60] The formal situation regarding "unity

---

59 *Resolutions and Decisions of the Congresses, Conferences and the Plenaries of the Communist Party of the Soviet Union*, Moscow 1970, Polizdat, 8th ed., Vol. 3, p. 308.

60 Fedotoff White states that it is clear that the political bodies won in their fight against the principle of "unity of command". Full powers in political affairs were given the Commanders in appearance only. Not only were the *Zampolits* authorised to go directly to the highest political levels and also to the political corps in the secondary units, but a dispute with the commander on a subject touching political

of command" underwent successive changes in accordance with the Party leadership's wish or need to tighten up supervision and control. At the time of the appalling purges in the Army's high echelons, in May 1937, Commissars were appointed in all branches of the Army, including the Staffs and Military Colleges. The Party Secretaries of the Republic or the Province were attached to the Military Councils in the Military Districts. The authority of the military Commanders was of course considerably reduced.

Then, in August 1940, the institution of Military Commissars was abolished and "unity of command" re-introduced. This was apparently done for a number of reasons: the shock dealt the Army by the purges had gradually subsided; the winter war in Finland had revealed not a few inadequacies; Marshal Timoshenko had been appointed Minister of Defence to replace Voroshilov; and last but not least, preparations were in hand for the inevitable coming war. Yet the newly restored "unity of command" did not last for long; on 16 July 1941, shortly after the German invasion of the USSR, Military Commissars were appointed again in all battalions and formations. Like much else at the time, this move was generated by the military defeats and withdrawals and the disastrous drop in Army morale. The Commissars were supposed to encourage the fighting men, supervise the execution of all orders of the Supreme Command and report any Commanding Officer unworthy of his command. All orders on Battalion and Division level had to be counter-signed by the Military Commissar together with the Commander. The *Politruks* came under the Brigade Commissar and after him the Divisional Commander, and the Divisional Commissar was subordinate to the Military Council in the Army and to the Head of the Main Political Administration.[61]

---

activity was brought before the political institutions and not before any Army instance. *Op. cit.*, p. 240.
61 *The Communist Party of the Soviet Union on the Armed Forces of the Soviet Union.* Cospolizdat, Moscow, 1958, pp. 360–361.

## "Full Unity of Command"

The institution of Military Commissar was abolished again in October 1942 and "unity of command" restored. The relevant Order stated:

> A devoted corps of Commanding Officers has distinguished itself in the fighting. There is therefore no longer any need for the existence of the system of Commissars. Moreover, the continuance of the institution of Commissars is liable to put a brake on the improvement of the command of the troops.[62]

This time, "unity of command" was designated "full unity of command", and it also applied to Commanders who were not Party members. The Military Commissars in all Army branches once again became *Zampolits*. As the Order hinted, this measure was a result of "Needs must when the devil drives" — the dangers of disintegration, disaffection and lost battles. It was imperative to give the Commanding Officer more power and responsibility in leading the troops into battle and give him the status to enable him to restore discipline. The Soviet historian, Petrov, gives the credit for what he calls "this tremendous deed" — the introduction of "full unity of command" — to the Party political machine itself and the Komsomol, and he intimates in veiled terms that it "contributed" to the Commanders' "many-sided development" and to "an increase in the fighting capacity and offensive capacity of the troops."[63] In the dark hours of October 1942, Stalin put the Party political machine to work to support the Commanders and not to harrass them.

In May 1943, the State Council of Defence abolished the *Zampolits* in the companies and batteries. As a result, some 30,000 "political workers" were taken out and sent to military schools

---

62 *Ibid.*, pp. 370–71.
63 V.P. Petrov, *Party Organisation and Development in the Soviet Army and Navy,* Voyenizdat, Moscow, 1964, p. 378.

to be trained for armoured units and the mechanized infantry.[64] (From then on until 1950, there was no change in the powers of the Military Councils in the Armies and on the Fronts.) This further partial loosening of the reins of Party supervision met the needs and demands of the lower echelon fighting command in the field. It was made possible by the rise in the morale of the fighting men, who had passed over from withdrawals and holding battles to attacks on a large scale.

During the war, the network of political-military schools was greatly expanded, and the number of graduates reached some 300,000. A parallel effort was made to train "political workers" for positions of military command at different levels in the schools of the different arms.[65]

When the war was over, with mass demobilisation and the transition to a peace-time Army, there was once more a drive on the part of the authorities to strengthen Party control over the Commanding Officers and particularly over the higher ranks. The conditions that had called for full powers for Commanders in the field in time of war had disappeared and Stalin felt it was now necessary to take steps to limit those powers again. In February 1946, when the Commissariat of Defence was turned into the Commissariat of the Armed Forces, the political Administration was again set up in the three arms, land, air and sea. In July 1947, the Main Political Administration became the institution determining and controlling all Party political action in the Armed Forces.[66]

The desire to strengthen political supervision and training in the Armed Forces came up against the obstacle of the low level of the "political workers", a state of affairs that was increasingly evident in peacetime and which could no longer easily be blamed on the "Fascist enemy, invader of the fatherland". The "political workers" had not been exactly popular in wartime either, and now

---

64 *The Communist Party of the USSR and the Development of the Soviet Armed Forces,* Voyenizdat, Moscow, 1965, p. 300.
65 Petrov, *op. cit.,* p. 303.
66 *Ibid., pp.* 444–45.

## The Need for an Army

their standing reached its nadir in the eyes of the Army officers. In mid-1946 the Central Committee set up a special commission to examine the situation of the political workers corps, which by then numbered some 73,000. The commission found that the majority were not suited to their job, due to insufficient general and political schooling. When this commission reported in mid-1947, the Central Committee ordered the re-establishment of the Lenin Military-Political Academy, to prepare political workers with higher education for various positions in political institutions and as *Zampolits* in Army formations. New conditions in the peacetime Army called for a re-definition of the tasks imposed on the apparatus, and at the beginning of 1947 the Central Committee re-stated these principal tasks. Stress was laid on political and military education to strengthen the power of the Armed Forces;[67] political studies were re-introduced in the forces in training hours (during the war they had been replaced by talks after training hours only); and regular Leninist-Marxist training courses for the officer corps were also re-introduced.

In the last years of Stalin's rule, Party-political supervision over the Armed Forces was visibly tightened up. Two outstanding decisions in this direction were taken by the Central Committee in 1950: at the beginning of the year it was decided to re-introduce *Zampolits* in the companies and parallel units, something that certainly affected the status of the lower echelon commanders and made it harder for them to carry out their duties. It is worth remarking that the *Zampolits* were first appointed to units stationed outside or near the borders of the USSR, and only a year later in the rest of the units as well.

In mid-1950 the Central Committee decided to raise the status of the Military Councils in the Military Districts and in the Armies: from being advisory bodies alongside the Commanders, the Councils were now turned into "responsible, collective institutions", designated to "implement all sides of Army life and activity". At the same time, the post was restored of "Member of the

---

67 *Ibid.*, p. 445.

Military Council" in the "political workers" apparatus, a change directed to strengthening the Party leadership in the Army and Navy.[68] A Commander of a Military District or of an Army thereby lost a considerable part of his authority and became more dependent on the consent of the "Comrade" Zampolit for every important decision he had to take.

---

68   *Ibid.*, pp. 452–53.

*PART II*

FOCAL CENTRES OF POLITICAL POWER, 1953–1957

## CHAPTER II

## THE ARMED FORCES AND POLITICAL RIVALRIES

### In the Service of the Party

The absolute hold of the Party leadership over the Armed Forces is the cornerstone of Communist theory and practice in the USSR. From the very beginning, the Communist Party leaders were constantly haunted by the danger that the Army might become a focus of power over which they would have less than absolute control, and they felt themselves compelled to take extreme measures to prevent this from happening. The 1921 Kronstadt mutiny showed signs of becoming an attempt to impose the will of an armed body on the leadership at a moment of serious crisis in the State. The leadership also felt itself endangered by the attempt made to combine the mutiny with a revolt of the peasants. Accordingly very drastic repressive measures were taken, regardless of the mutineers' far more fanatical dedication to Communist principles than that of the leadership itself.

Frunze, who replaced Trotsky and became head of the Soviet Union Army in 1925, had political ambitions of his own. In the situation that prevailed in the leadership in 1925, Frunze's command of the Army constituted a threat to Stalin in his fight to gain supreme control. His enemies and detractors have contended that Stalin shrank from nothing to attain his ends and that Frunze was poisoned while undergoing medical treatment. There is no proof of this specific accusation but, be that as it may, Stalin was ever on the alert to stamp out any sparks of independence in the Army.

The serious international developments of the mid-1930's spurred the Soviets to great exertions and very considerable investment of resources in order to expand the Armed Forces and improve their performance. The senior command in the Forces attempted to close ranks and shoulder aside the political apparatus, in order to free itself to concentrate on raising the technical level of the troops. The whole process was reflected, among much else, in the re-introduction of military titles of rank in September 1935, when the first Marshals were appointed and the higher ranks were accorded various privileges. The Head of the Political Administration, Camarnik, may have decided to let Commanders have more extensive powers, both in order to increase military efficiency and also to reduce the tension between the Commanding Officers and the political workers, but in so doing he may have misjudged Stalin's intentions in the matter.[1]

A crucial confrontation took place between the political leadership and the military heads late in 1936. At a Central Committee session, all the senior commanders, members of the Committee, are believed to have supported Bukharin against Stalin, except for Voroshilov and Budienny. This was the session when Bukharin was accused by Yezhov, Head of the People's Commissariat for Internal Affairs (the NKVD), of being an agent of the German Gestapo. Bukharin spontaneously reacted by attacking Stalin for having seized power and made himself an autocrat with Yezhov's help.[2] If in fact this is what happened, it is understandable that such an attitude on the part of military men on the Central Committee added fuel to the flames of Stalin's determination to destroy all his adversaries, proved or potential, in the Armed Forces.

The causes that climaxed in the appalling purges of the senior command were many and complex, and we shall indicate only some of them here. Stalin (ably assisted by the NKVD) wanted to wipe out his opponents. Hitler was seeking to weaken the Soviet Army, which was seen to be gaining in strength. Heydrich, head

---

[1] This is Erickson's view. *Op. cit.*, p. 423.
[2] See L. Schapiro, "The Great Purge", in *The Red Army* (ed.) B. H. Liddell Hart, Peter Smith, Gloucester, Mass., 1968, pp. 67–68.

of the German State Secret Service, was working to undermine the heads of Intelligence in the Reichswehr Oberkommando. Thus various political and personal interests concurred to produce a catastrophic chain reaction. Heydrich had documents forged to make up a substantial dossier alleging secret contacts of Soviet Marshal Tukhachevsky and his comrades with German Reichswehr heads, unknown to their respective leaders, Stalin and Hitler. In April 1937, it seems, the dossier was transmitted to Stalin through the NKVD and simultaneously, by other channels, to Hitler. Beneš, President of Czechoslovakia, also passed information to Stalin through the Soviet Embassy in Prague to the effect that contacts had been established between Berlin and Red Army Commanders. The full details have never been disclosed, but it is clear that behind the intrigue to decimate the Soviet senior command, woven with the help of the NKVD, there stood Stalin himself.

## Doctrine, Indoctrination and Changing Situations

The principle that Party leadership of the Armed Forces was the rock on which the Forces were built has been the central theme of the indoctrination of the officer corps from the time of Lenin to the present. Even in the periods when "unity of command" in Army units was introduced or re-introduced, the watchword always was that the Party leads and builds up the Army and sees to its constant strengthening. Throughout the years from Frunze down to Malinovsky and Gretchko, the High Command has reiterated this line over and over again. As Malinovsky formulated it: "With us, unity of command develops and gains in strength on the Party basis and this is what characterises it."[3]

Continual and extensive information and propaganda efforts have been invested in the Army all along in order to convince officers and men alike that these principles are absolute — they are re-

---

[3] R.Y. Malinovsky, "Standing Vigilantly on Guard for Peace", *apud The Party and the Development of the Armed Forces*, Voyenizdat, Moscow, 1965, p. 424 (Russian).

peated over and over like a catechism by the propagandists, and other political workers. In periods of internal political struggle, when the political leadership is not united and cohesive, and when individuals within it are engaged in a struggle for power, or at times when the leadership as a whole is weakened and its grip on the Party itself and on other Communist Parties is slackened, then there is a rise in the relative importance of the main elements subordinate to the central power and, first and foremost among them, the Armed Forces. In such situations the Armed Forces may play a fairly independent role and sometimes the outcome of the whole struggle actually depends on them, for they can help one of the factions or one of the personalities to win the contest for power. Thus, contrary to their basic conception of the absolute subordination of the Army to the political leadership and perhaps even against their will, members of the political leadership fighting for power have been forced to accord a temporary recognition to the professional autonomy of the Army, to loosen the reins of Party-political control and to grant powers and privileges to the officer corps.[4]

## *The Break in Continuity — the Death of Stalin*

Stalin concentrated in his own hands undisputed control over all the elements of power and all the supreme institutions in the USSR. His death in March 1953 suddenly produced a confused situation, in the absence of any constitutional method for securing continuity of rule. The vacuum thus created summoned the various power foci to mobilise and prepare to fight for the hegemony in the State. At this juncture, the four main focal centres of power were: (1) the Government; (2) the Party; (3) the Armed Forces; and (4) the MGB (Ministry of State Security) and the armed forces of the Ministry of the Interior.

The personal fight for the succession was engaged alongside the

---

4 Roman Kolkovicz, *The Soviet Military and the Communist Party*, Princeton University Press, 1967, p. 33.

confrontation among the power foci. Less than twenty-four hours after the announcement of Stalin's death, a series of decisions was reached and made public on new appointments and institutional organisation. The decisions were taken, the public statements emphasised, at a special joint session of the Central Committee, the Council of Ministers and the Presidium of the Supreme Soviet. The number of members of the Party Presidium was reduced from 25 to 10 and 4 alternates. Other decisions signalled the trend to divide up and distribute the ruling power in the State so as to prevent the concentration of all the power in the hands of one man: Secretary of the Party Malenkov, viewed as the senior figure among Stalin's heirs and successors, was appointed Head of Government; Khrushchev was to concentrate on work in the Central Committee. Only a week later, however, Malenkov lost his position as Secretary of the Party, and in September 1953 the Central Committee Plenary elected Khrushchev as First Secretary of the Central Committee. This appointment of Khrushchev's marked the beginning of a gradual decline in the status of the government among the foci of power. The status of Malenkov as head of the government declined still further in the course of this process. He gradually stopped being thought of as the senior successor to Stalin and became instead a senior member of the collective leadership. Khrushchev on the other hand gradually became the central and most influential figure in the Party machine, and there was a simultaneous rise in the status of the Party among the foci of power.

When we come to assess the weight of the Armed Forces among the power foci, we have to note that right away in March 1953 the Ministry of the Army (which included the Air Force) was joined up with the Navy into one Ministry of Defence, headed by Marshal N. Bulganin, a "political Marshal" and a member of the Presidium. This combination was almost certainly created as a practical necessity, in order to counterbalance another focus of power, the Ministry of Internal Security, the coercive power headed by Beria, who had united the MGB and the internal armed forces of the Interior Ministry in his own hands. Marshals A. Vasilevsky and G. Zhukov were appointed First Deputies to Defence Minister

49

Bulganin. Zhukov, the greatest popular figure in the Army, the victorious hero of the war to defend the fatherland, also served as Commander of the Land Forces. Admiral N. Kuznetsov, till then Minister of the Navy, was appointed Commander of the Navy in the now unified Defence Ministry. Marshal Zhygarov remained Commander of the Air Force.

In Stalin's day, the MGB (under its different names — NKVD, KGB and the rest) had been the main instrument of coercion, repression and terror, notorious for terrible interrogations and the executions of opponents of Stalin, particularly among the leaders. Wielded by Beria, one of Stalin's most powerful minions, this was the instrument which in large measure helped institute and maintain the tyrannical dictatorship. When the inheritance was divided up, Beria received two posts, now combined in one, Minister of the Interior and Head of Internal Security, besides being a full member of the Party Presidium and Deputy Prime Minister. He therefore disposed of the very respectable military force under the Interior Ministry and of the Chekists, experts in tracking, investigating and liquidating individuals from a wide swathe of the population, including persons in the highest ranks of the hierarchy. It is hardly surprising that this concentration of power in Beria's hands produced a certain sense of insecurity in the bosoms of his nine colleagues. They feared that Beria might turn his machine against them in an attempt to take over the leadership or at least secure the decisive place in this arena where the contest for hegemony was being fought out between the power foci and the various leading personalities.

## The End of Beria

In June 1953 fear of Beria led the other members of the leadership, including those at the centre of the other power foci, to join together in self-defence and get ready to take the initiative themselves — in short, to liquidate Beria before he liquidated them, and to cut the claws of the MGB. To do this they had to turn for help to the Armed Forces heads, who controlled the only coercive force capable of counterbalancing the Chekists and the internal army at Beria's disposal and of mounting a conspiracy against Beria and his people.

The Khrushchev memoirs[5] relate how it was agreed to convene a meeting of the Presidium of the Council of Ministers, to which all the members of the Central Committee would also be invited, and to call in the Army to help in this situation where the Presidium bodyguard was under Beria's orders and his Chekists would be sitting in the next room during the meeting. The circle that was brought together eventually included eleven marshals and generals.

> In those days, explains Khrushchev, all military personnel were required to check their weapons when coming into the Kremlin, so Comrade Bulganin was instructed to see that the marshals and generals were allowed to bring their guns with them. We arranged for Moskalenko's group to wait for a summons in a separate room while the session was taking place. ...
> I requested the floor from Chairman Malenkov and proposed that we discuss the matter of Beria. ... I reviewed the moves (he) had made since Stalin's death ... stressing that (he) was trying to legalize arbitrary rule. ... Bulganin said something very much along the same lines. ... The other comrades stressed the same principles. ... I proposed that the Central Committee Presidium should release Beria from his duties as Deputy Chairman of the Council of Ministers and Minister of Internal Affairs and from all the other government positions he held. ... Malenkov ... pressed a secret button which gave the signal to the generals who were waiting in the next room. Zhukov was the first to appear. ... Malenkov said in a faint voice to Comrade Zhukov, "As Chairman of the Council of Ministers of the USSR, I request that you take Beria into custody pending investigation of charges made against him."

5 *Khrushchev Remembers,* translated and edited by Strobe Talbott, Bantam Books, New York, London, Toronto, October 1971 (by arrangement with Little, Brown and Company, (Boston), pp. 364–67.

"Handsup!" Zhukov commanded Beria.

Moskalenko and the others unbuckled their holsters in case Beria tried anything. Beria seemed to reach for his briefcase which was lying behind him on the windowsill. I seized his arm to prevent him from grabbing a weapon from the briefcase. We searched him later and found he had no gun ... (It) had simply been a reflex action. (He) was immediately put under armed guard. ... We agreed to entrust him to the air defense commander, Comrade Moskalenko.

At the time of the arrest it was also necessary to neutralise Beria's forces outside the Kremlin. A number of army units were moved up to the capital for this purpose. A reliable informant gives this description:[6]

> The Kantomirov Armoured Division was on divisional exercises at the time, some 20 kilometres from Moscow. It was supposed to advance 20 kilometres in the direction of Leningrad and carry out a certain manoeuvre.
>
> The pupils and instructors in the Frunze Military Academy were supposed to go out there in order to watch the exercise. Suddenly, this outing for the course was cancelled, the instructors and pupils were issued with their personal arms (usually kept in the Academy arsenal), and they were ordered to maintain a state of readiness.
>
> The Commander of the Kantomirov Division received an order not to move as planned but to be ready to move towards Moscow. Immediately after this, he was ordered — not by the Military District Commander but directly by Zhukov — to move to Moscow, proceed through the main streets (which armoured units usually did not do, because of the damage to the road surface) and deploy in the environs of the Kremlin.

6 Major Y. B., a cadet in the Frunze Military Academy at the time of Beria's arrest, cited as completely reliable by N.A. in a taped interview with me. N.A. served in the Soviet Army for 35 years, reaching the rank of Colonel.

Zhukov further told the Divisional Commander that he was henceforth to take his orders direct from him, Zhukov personally and from no-one else.

### The Army Rewarded

The fact that the Army was thus called in to help in the matter of arresting Beria raised its relative status among the instruments of coercive power available in the State and, as we shall see, MGB control over the Army was correspondingly weakened. Senior Commanders Koniev and Moskalenko were among Beria's judges, with Koniev presiding at the trial. When the Central Committee Plenary ratified the arrest, it at once made Deputy Minister of Defence Zhukov a full member of the Central Committee and no longer a mere alternate. Moskalenko was promoted to the rank of General of an Army and also made Commander of the sensitive Military District of Moscow. In mid-July 1953, the Party had the Army heads publicly endorse the action against Beria: for the Party to get the Army to endorse a political move was absolutely unprecedented.[7] From then on the regime was based internally on the Armed Forces to a greater degree than formerly, and there clearly had to be fitting recompense and recognition. In the three months after Beria's arrest there were ten promotions to the ranks of General, Admiral and Marshal.

In 1954 command of the internal army was transferred from an MVD (Ministry of the Interior) General to a military Commander, General Polkovnik S. Perevetkin. This put the Armed Forces still further ahead of any possible rival focus of power, and it considerably reduced the officer corps' fear of the internal security service. This service was detached from the Interior Ministry in April 1954

---

7 See Malcolm Mackintosh, *Juggernaut*, Secker & Warburg, London, 1967, p. 287. Mackintoch considers this a turning-point for the Army. He says that this very unusual step was clearly interpreted in Army circles as recognition of the Army's special status and of the value of Army backing for any ambitious Party leader working to achieve supreme power.

and became the independent body under the Council of Ministers better known by its Russian acronym, the KGB (Committee of State Security).

The struggle for dominance among the heads of the power foci still went on in the leadership, but the lines along which they were grouped had changed. At this stage in 1954 the main contest was without question the one between individual personalities fighting to take the lead. On the one hand there was Malenkov, head of Government, and against him there concentrated the forces represented by Khrushchev. This situation again meant an opportunity for the Armed Forces to throw their might into the balance. Malenkov strongly supported the development of light industry (or consumer industries) at the expense of heavy industry, while Khrushchev and his supporters could expect backing from the Army heads, who naturally urged preference for heavy industry, traditionally identified with strengthening the defence of the fatherland. In his efforts to mobilise resources for the consumption industries, Malenkov had reduced the defence budget for 1954 from 110.2 milliard rubles to 100.3 milliards.[8] The Army heads felt this as a serious blow and were driven into Khrushchev's camp. A link was forged between two of the main foci of power, the Party machine round Khrushchev and the Army command round Bulganin and Zhukov, as against the third focus, the government machine round Malenkov.

At the end of January 1955, an article appeared in *Red Star* headlined, "Heavy Industry is the Basis of the Strength of the Soviet State". The article affirmed that heavy industry always had been and still was the material basis of the defence capacity of the Soviet State and the guarantee of the integrity of its borders.[9] This was just some ten days before the Central Committee decided to depose Malenkov from the Premiership. The contest of wills

---

8 R. Garthoff, *The Role of the Military in Recent Soviet Politics*, Rand Corporation, RM-1638, March 1956, p. 9, *apud* Kolkovicz, *op. cit.*, p. 113.
9 *Krasnaya Zvozda*, 15 January 1955.

# The Armed Forces and Political Rivalries

with the government apparatus was in fact decided from the start by the community of interest at this stage between the two power foci which between them controlled the Party machine and the military force. On 8 February the Supreme Soviet unanimously elected Bulganin head of Government in place of Malenkov, as proposed by Khrushchev on behalf of the Central Committee.[10] The Army was soon recompensed for its support: Deputy Defence Minister Marshal Zhukov became Defence Minister, and the Armed Forces were apparently promised an increase in the budget reserves that Malenkov had thinned out, besides increased direct budget allocations to the Army and Navy.

Bulganin's speech to the Supreme Soviet when he was appointed was published two days later, and it made no secret of the point at issue:

> The material reserves of our country constitute one of the conditions for building up its economy successfully. These reserves are our strength. This is what strengthens the country's defence capacity. It would therefore be an unforgivable mistake to pay less attention than before to this important subject or to be tempted to solve current problems at the expense of the country's reserves.[11]

In the State budget as published the defence allocations were increased by over 10% and reached a sum of over 112 milliard rubles.[12] On the issue of whether to give precedence to heavy industry, the balance was of course now in favour of the Army's demands,[13] which continued to carry weight after Malenkov's depo-

---

10   *Izvestia*, 9 February 1955.
11   *Ibid.*, 10 February 1955.
12   *Ibid.*, 11 February 1955.
13   Minister of the Treasury A.G. Zveryev, summing up the Budget debate in the Supreme Soviet said:
> In January 1955 the Central Committee stressed that the Communist Party sees its primary mission as the furthering of development of heavy industry, which constitutes the solid foundation of the entire economy of the State and its unconquered defence

sition. Among the articles published for the 17th anniversary of the Army and Navy (23 February 1955), the one by the Chief of General Staff Marshal Sokolovsky affirmed: "Heavy industry is the foundation of the unconquered defence capacity of our country and we must carry on and strengthen it."[14] This was now the consecrated formula. The long article by Marshal Koniev (one of the two Deputy Defence Ministers) also had it: "The Communist Party and the Government devote their best attention to developing heavy industry, which was, is and will be the foundation of the unconquered defensive capacity of the State and of the strength of our splendid Armed Forces."[15]

In contrast to the general preference accorded the Army, a very large cut was made in effectives in August 1955.[16] There is, however, reason to think that this measure had been decided on earlier, as a result of the lessening of tension between the USSR and the West — the so-called "thaw" that started early in 1955. Notwithstanding the decision to reduce effectives, promotions were still generously distributed. About a month after Malenkov's deposition, some twelve Marshals and Generals were promoted, six of them receiving the highest rank of all, Marshal of the Soviet Union, doubtless as additional recompense for having supported the winners in the leadership contest. Another six Generals were promoted to the rank of General of an Army before the end of 1955.

The political status of the Army went on getting steadily stronger, and external symbols were not lacking. At the First of May parade, Armed Forces officers appeared for the first time in their fine, new dress uniforms, glittering with decorations and gold-braided shoulder-boards, all described in detail in the newspapers. A large share was allotted to the top echelons in the celebrations of the tenth anniversary of the victory over Germany, and addi-

> power. ... By far the greater part of the Budget allocations for economic development are destined for our heavy industry.
> *Izvestia*, 8 February 1955.

14  *Ibid.*, 23 February 1955.
15  *Pravda*, 23 February 1955.
16  Petrov, *op. cit.*, p. 457.

tional evidence of their enhanced status was provided by the long articles in the press by Minister of Defence Marshal Zhukov (in *Pravda*) and by his First Deputy, Marshal Vasilevsky (in *Izvestia*). The big assembly in the Bolshoi theatre of representatives of public organisations and of the Army and Navy had seven members of the Party Presidium and seven Marshals and Admirals on the dais. The Commander of Land Forces, Marshal Koniev, delivered the key address, which was printed in full in the main papers and, most unusual of all, was accompanied by a large photograph of the speaker. Unquestionably, the Army chiefs displayed a new self-assurance on these occasions. There was no obsequious fawning on the Party leaders. Stalin was still referred to, but without the stock flatteries or stereotyped praise. Self-assurance was not untinged with self-congratulation, each Marshal did what he could — by implication, it is true — to emphasise his particular share in the great victory—Koniev stressed the role of the Commands and Commanders of the Armies and Fronts.[17] Zhukov the role of the High Command, ignoring the early defeats;[18] while Vasilevsky expatiated on how the High Command took control of the very dangerous situation that was created at the start of the war.[19]

The improvement in the Armed Forces' status continued in 1956. In his famous secret speech to the XX Congress in February of that year, Khrushchev paid elaborate tribute to the Commanders and to their professional competence as compared with Stalin, the military ignoramus. The Congress elected six Army heads members of the Central Committee and 12 more commanders as alterate members, a relatively small number compared with the Army heads elected to the Central Committee at the XIX Congress in 1952, but these appointments strengthened the standing of the professional officers as against the political ones — two senior MPA officers were not re-elected.

---

17 *Pravda*, 9 May 1955.
18 *Ibid.*, 8 May 1955.
19 *Izvestia*, 3 May 1955.

## "The Personality Cult and Its Consequences"

The political leadership needed help from the Army and the Army heads in another direction — in its moves to overcome difficulties in relations with some East European States resulting from Khrushchev's revelations at the XX Congress. The Central Committee Plenary held an extraordinary session in the last week of June 1956, and on 30 June a Resolution was adopted "on overcoming the cult of personality and its consequences". The shaken self-confidence of the leadership *vis-à-vis* the Party activists at home and in the world Communist movement can be clearly discerned between the lines of this document, with its lame justifications of the leadership's failure to prevent Stalin's illegal and damaging actions in both internal and external affairs. If they had tried to stop him, they said, the people would not have supported them. And at the same time they produced the excuse, "We didn't know" — it was only after Stalin's death that they had learned of his many and grave misdeeds.

I see these contentions as testimony to the leaders' weakness and lack of backbone. They tried to wriggle out of responsibility and at the same time to prove that in fact they had acted under the autocracy, had "done things". The document, it should also be noted, carried on an argument with heads of other Communist Parties who sought the roots of the personality cult and its consequences in the Soviet social system itself.[20]

The decisions of the June 1956 Central Committee Plenary clearly betray grave concern over the Soviet Party's loss of prestige in the eyes of the other Communist Parties as guide and leader of the world Communist movement.

## Poland and Hungary

In the second half of July 1956 a delegation from Moscow went to Warsaw to represent the USSR at the 12th anniversary celebra-

---

20  *Resolutions and Decision* ... Vol. 7, pp. 208–9.

tions of the "re-birth of Poland" and at the session of the Polish Party Central Committee. This was the official story, but there is no doubt that the real aim was to settle the problems that had arisen in relations with the Polish leadership. Besides Bulganin, Ponomarenko and others, Defence Minister Zhukov was also on the delegation,[21] a fact that calls for comment: it was not at all usual for a Marshal, a professional soldier and not a political figure, to be present on a Party-political mission. In my judgement, Zhukov's presence was needed to improve the somewhat battered image of the Soviet political leadership, the past partners of Stalin. The appearance on the scene of the war hero whom Stalin had relegated to obscurity after the victory, a prestigious figure to be admired and honoured, was certainly also intended to remind the Poles of the presence of Soviet forces on their soil. The military weight thereby added to the delegation would, as it were, counterbalance the devaluation of the political members of the Soviet leadership.

Relations with the Poles reached a crisis in October 1956. On 19 October a large Soviet delegation headed by Khrushchev appeared in Warsaw uninvited. The intention was to get the Poles to come to heel — with the help of a movement of Soviet forces stationed in Poland in the direction of Warsaw. This delegation too included Marshal Zhukov; it is possible that Zhukov himself took over command of the Soviet forces in Poland at the time.[22]

Shortly thereafter the Soviet Army was called upon not only to threaten but to act, this time in Hungary.[22a]

21 *Pravda*, 22 July 1956.
22 Otto Preston Chaney, *Zhukov*, University of Oklahoma Press, 1971, p. 374.
22a On my return to Moscow in the second half of November (after my stay in Israel at the time of the Sinai campaign), I heard a great deal from my colleagues in the diplomatic corps — and mainly from U.S. Ambassador Charles Bohlen and British Ambassador Sir William Hayter — about the forceful and extremist pronouncements of Zhukov at the time of the Hungarian crisis, and especially in the last days of October. Bohlen interpreted Zhukov's remarks of 30 October 1956 as show-

Khrushchev and Molotov came incognito, with no aids, on the evening of November 2 to the Island of Brioni to consult with Tito about the situation in Hungary, or rather to inform him about what they were preparing to do.

Micunovic, the Yugoslav ambassador to Moscow, who was at that time in Belgrade, took part in the talks together with Kardelj and Rankovic. In his book *Moskow Diary* Micunovic writes: "Khrushchev turned again to the question of intervention by the Soviet Army. He said that there were also internal reasons in the Soviet Union why they could not permit the restoration of capitalism in Hungary. There were people in the Soviet Union who would say that as long as Stalin was in command everybody obeyed and there were no big shocks. But that now, ever since *they* had come to power, Russia had suffered the defeat and loss of Hugary. Khrushchev said this might be said primarily by the Soviet Army, which was one of the reasons why they were intervening in Hungary."[23]

### Khrushchev and the "Anti-Party Group"

After the XX Congress a situation once more developed within the leadership where a contender for power looked to the Army for support. This Congress and the Central Committee Plenary that followed on its heels ended not with a complete victory for Khrushchev but with a victory of sorts for the principle of collective leadership. As time passed there were clear signs that Khrushchev's opponents on the Presidium were gaining strength. It was not until the February 1957 Plenary that Khrushchev's position inside the leadership was seen to be improving. The following months witnessed a confrontation between Khrushchev and his opponents. A central issue was Khrushchev's project for reorganising the economy: he wanted to have a some 40 Ministries suppressed and to decentralise

---

ing his dissatisfaction with the decision to withdraw the troops from Budapest. Hayter summed it up that Zhukov had demanded strong action to repress the Hungarian rising and had got what he wanted.

23  Veljko Micunovic, *Moscow Diary*, Doubleday and Co., Inc., New York, 1980, pp. 133–34.

## The Armed Forces and Political Rivalries

the direction of the economy among regional economic Councils (*Sovnarkhoz*). He also intended to give more power to the different Republics and the large Districts through the appropriate Party Committees. Khrushchev's following was strong in the Party Secretariat and the Party machine and was growing stronger, while this time too his opponents were entrenched in the government and its apparatus. True, the reorganisation was intended to improve the functioning of the economy and reduce bureaucratic interference and excessive centralisation, but it would also buttress Khrushchev's position at a time of weakness in the leadership. It was clear that an aim and a result of the re-organisation would be to give the Party instances subordinate to Khrushchev increased powers to supervise and coordinate the economy, thereby automatically curbing the authority of the government machine, while Khrushchev would of course be personally strengthened as against his opponents. He was conducting a sustained campaign to extend and institutionalise the predominance of the Party over the other forces in the system.

The economic reorganisation was introduced on 1 July 1957. Interestingly enough, the numerous central Ministries for the industrial branches that were now replaced by regional bodies did not include the Ministries for military industry, which continued to function Union-wide, responsible to the central government only. This deviation from the original plan was almost certainly due to Zhukov,[24] who may even have got Khrushchev to make the military industries even more centralised than they had been until then.[25] Here was further testimony to the changed standing of the Armed Forces.

At this stage many members of the Presidium, probably the majority, were feeling concern over the accumulation of power in Khrushchev's hands and his hold on the Party machine. He had been First Secretary since 1953, and the collective leadership was

---

24  Chaney, *op. cit.*, p. 402.
25  Garthoff, *Soviet Strategy in the Nuclear Age*, New York, Frederick and Praeger, 1962, p. 30.

no longer so "collective" — in fact, its existence was endangered. The Presidium majority felt it desirable, even necessary, to depose Khrushchev, but all the indications are that not everyone concerned was sufficiently determined to see the matter through and that no-one made the necessary preparations for organising Khrushchev's deposition properly.

The Party Presidium at which the decision was supposed to be taken lasted from 18 June to 22 June, when a Central Committee Plenary session was to open, which would continue until 29 June. If a vote against Khrushchev was carried by all or most of the eleven members of the Presidium and officially published, it would almost certainly be automatically endorsed by the Plenary, which was far from being all Khrushchev "territory".

The facts are not certainly known, but the best conjectures put Khrushchev in the minority of the eight Presidium members present at the opening of the session (and of all the eleven members).[26] There were also four alternates present, one of whom was Zhukov. They could take part in the discussion but not vote. Another opinion is that Khrushchev never had more than three supporters in the whole Presidium — Kirichenko, Mikoyan and Suslov, and that while Suslov may have been for him he did not exert himself very energetically to save him.[27] Against Khrushchev and these three were arrayed in the first place Molotov, Malenkov, Kaganovich, later dubbed the "anti-Party group", and Shepilov — this last an alternate member, who was tacked on as it were. This group had the support of another four — the veteran Voroshilov, now serving as Chairman of the Supreme Soviet Presidium, Bulganin, Head of Government and the minor personages, Saburov and

---

26 R. Conquest, *Power and Policy in the USSR,* New York, San Martin's Press, 1961, p. 312. Conquest gives the figures of five against Khrushchev and three for (besides Khrushchev himself) in the limited group, and six against Khrushchev and five for him of the full 11 members.

27 Michel Tatu, *Le pouvoir en U.R.S.S.,* Editions Bernard Grasset, Paris, 1967, p. 30.

Pervuhin[28] — who were not however solidly united in their opposition to Khrushchev. It may very well be that if all Khrushchev's opponents on the Presidium had been more determined, if they had acted with speed and firmness, made their decision public and submitted it to the Plenary, their plan could have succeeded. But they did none of these things.

The clear and pressing problem for Khrushchev and his supporters was to prevent publication of a hostile decision or recommendation of the Presidium, if necessary by force or by the threat of force, until the Plenary convened, so as to give Khrushchev time to fight to get the decision changed. The weak point of those conspiring against Khrushchev was that they could not mobilise the support of those who controlled the forces of physical coercion (the Army and the KGB). This may well explain their indecisiveness and their failing to act with the necessary boldness. Khrushchev was able to threaten the use of force because he was backed by two powerful personalities who were "his men", Defence Minister Zhukov and General Serov, in charge of the KGB. Presumably what happened in the course of the Presidium meeting was that the infirm of purpose were deterred by implicit or explicit pressures involved in the knowledge that Khrushchev could call on "his men" if necessary and that they therefore began to propose compromises, until in the end all except Molotov, Kaganovich and Malenkov abstained from voting and accepted defeat.[29]

The failure of the plan to depose Khrushchev should perhaps be read as a *coup* — or counter-*coup* — by the Army, the KGB and Khrushchev's Party machine against the Presidium majority, which would otherwise have carried the Plenary with it. Even be-

---

28 In the official announcement of the composition of the Presidium (*Pravda*, 15 March 1953), ten names appear in order of importance: Malenkov first, Beria second, Molotov third, and so on. Saburov and Pervuhin were numbers nine and ten.

29 This is Conquest's reading of the events at the end of June. *Op. cit.*, pp. 312–13. To the best of my recollection, Conquest's view of the course of events is entirely in accordance with the opinions widely held by diplomatic observers in Moscow in July 1957.

fore the Plenary convened, the Presidium majority apparently disintegrated under combined threats and inducements.[30] It would seem, however, that Khrushchev was not inclined to leave the Plenary's moves to chance. Very precise rumours, citing "trustworthy sources", were rife in Moscow at the beginning of July to the effect that part of the Central Committee members and alternates had been brought to the Plenary session in military planes on Zhukov's order. Be this as it may, of all the 309 participants in the special Plenary — Central Committee members and alternates plus the members of the Control Committee — not one supported what was afterwards called the "anti-Party group". At this Plenary session, Minister of Defence Zhukov, who had been an important factor in the failure of the group, was elected a full member of the Presidium. Four of the eleven members were turned out of it, and a fifth was demoted to the status of alternate. The Presidium itself, which was the most important body in the decision-making institutions, was enlarged to fifteen members, and it was chiefly Presidium alternates and Party Secretariat members, Khrushchev's main lieges, who were now appointed.

Khrushchev's victory was real, yet not complete, for those who were deposed were not expelled from the Party. (According to a Resolution of the X Congress, a decision to expel a Central Committee member from the Party needed a two-thirds vote, and it would seem that no such proposal was brought before the 151 members of the enlarged Central Committee.)

In this serious crisis in the leadership in June 1957, the interaction of the forces at play raised the Army to the zenith of its political power. Under Zhukov's leadership the Army was able to turn the scales in favour of given groups and individuals in the Party leadership. What should not be lost sight of is that this special status of the Armed Forces came about as a consequence of the struggle in the leadership and depended on the existence of the crisis itself, on the conflicting groups and individuals' continuing to need their support. It was the need of the hour, but when the

---

30 *Ibid.,* p. 318.

## The Armed Forces and Political Rivalries

peak of the crisis was over and the new Presidium headed by Khrushchev settled down to a stable existence, the Army's support was no longer so vitally necessary. In my opinion it is reasonable to assume that the new leadership would be of one mind over the need to proceed at once to reduce the Army's special political status, tighten up Party control and return the Armed Forces to their proper place — complete subordination to the Party machine. The highest position of all was held by Marshal Zhukov, full Presidium member and Minister of Defence, openly fighting for professional autonomy for the Army and taking every advantage of the special influence he had acquired. The first and decisive step towards getting the Army into line with the Party again was therefore necessarily to condemn Zhukov and depose him.

It will be worth our while to pause over Zhukov's deposition,[30a] providing as it does an excellent demonstration of the functioning of the Party in its relations with the Army.

On 26 October 1957, only four months after the installation of the new Presidium, a simply worded announcement informed the public of the appointment of Marshal R. Malinovsky to replace Marshal Zhukov as Minister of Defence, and on 3 November the Supreme Soviet decision to this effect was made public.

The appointment of Marshal Malinovsky in preference to Marshal Koniev, his senior, and to Marshal Moskalenko, needs explaining. The opinions that I heard voiced in Moscow at the time depicted Malinovsky as a brave soldier in the field but as lacking in civic courage, a view of him that is shared by Soviet ex-officers who emigrated to Israel.[31] Khrushchev and his fellows on the Presidium would prefer a man not so obstinate in defence of the professional autonomy of the Army and not armoured in popular glory as a hero of the great victory—in short, a Marshal who would be easier to control. With Zhukov's deposition, the Armed Forces lost their defender on the body that took all the most important

---

30a Details of the manner and technique of Zhukov's deposition are given in Chapter 6 below.
31 According to the testimony of N.A.

decisions on Soviet policy, internal and foreign. When the Army heads publicly endorsed Zhukov's condemnation by the 1957 October Plenary, <u>the Party was restored to full predominance</u>. Marshals and Generals once more recited set declarations on the necessity of Party supremacy and repeated the clauses in the Plenary's decision on improving Party-political activity in the Armed Forces. The key verse in the credo was: "The main source of the strength of the Army and the Navy is that they are organised and educated by the Communist Party, the leader and guide of all Soviet society."[32]

---

32  *Izvestia*, 3 November 1957.

## CHAPTER III

## THE FIGHT OVER MILITARY DOCTRINE

Soviet military doctrines were influenced by Communist social theory and by Communist political designs. The work of the men who formed and fixed Soviet military doctrine was affected by their Marxist thinking and by their belief in the mission of the USSR and its armed forces to afford aid and assistance in revolutionary wars.

The Frunze-Gusiev team explicitly based its "unified military doctrine" on the teachings of Marx and Engels and constantly stressed the part to be played in revolutionary wars. Frunze took his stand on the special role of the offensive in Soviet military doctrine as a necessary corollary to the revolutionary-dynamic character of Bolshevik ideology. Trotsky — Frunze's main opponent — was also of the opinion that the fundamental class orientation of the State in its internal policies and its international orientation as the Workers' State were two main components of Soviet military doctrine.

The internal struggles within the Party leadership also left their mark on military doctrine; thus, as we have seen, in the twilight of Lenin's rule and after his death, the struggle for the succession was fought out, on the surface at least, in protracted debates on issues of military doctrines.

The rigid doctrinairism of the Soviet regime demanded an implicit belief on the part of the people in the indefectible wisdom of the Party leaders' decisions: "the only correct path" in military affairs as in all else is that of the Party. The Party exacts absolute obedience to the "general line" that it lays down — true, a line that changes direction sometimes, as dictated by internal and external circumstances. Any attempt to question the sacrosanctity of the "general line" would be sheer heresy. It follows as a matter of course that a rigid regime like this will not encourage critical and fruitful military thinking. Throughout the whole of Stalin's rule, there was no public discussion whatsoever over military doctrine like the debates that had gone on in the early years, from 1921 to 1924. Nevertheless it is possible to discern a more flexible attitude on criticism of military doctrine by the senior command than on purely ideological issues. Imposition of absolutely rigid military theories would seem to have reached its peak during World War II and after it, till Stalin's death.

## Stalin, The Expert

Stalin considered himself an expert authority, qualified to settle things in every field of science, thought and action. Naturally, he felt qualified to lay down the law for the military profession. The set of principles and rules called "military science" in the USSR was defined thus:

> Scientific knowledge of the laws that govern warfare; ways of preparing for war and conducting it in given historical circumstances. Military science also embraces the art of war, the problems of organising and training the Armed Forces, the problems of the economic and moral capabilities of the State and of enemy States.[1]

The military art is seen as one component of military science. It includes tactics, operations and strategy. Tactics covers ways of preparing for and conducting the battle; operational art lays down ways of preparing for and conducting an operation directed towards securing the strategic aims of the war, strategy lays down the way of organising, training and arming the Armed Forces, on the basis of the policy of the State, for the purpose of overcoming the enemy

---

1 *The Big Soviet Encyclopaedia*, 2nd ed., 1951, Vol. 8, p. 406.

## The Fight over Military Doctrine

in military campaigns and strategic operations in the war as a whole.[2]

A distinction is made in the USSR between authentic-Soviet military science and "pseudo-scientific", "bourgeois" doctrines: "bourgeois" military science is a function of the ideological and metaphysical world-outlook of the bourgeois military ideologists who believe in eternal, unchanging principles of warfare and are incapable of discovering and correctly defining the laws governing the content of authentic military science. Only Soviet military science is an original creation, built on the solid basis of Marxism-Leninism and resting on Leninist-Stalinist theory of warfare.[3]

After the grave defeats at the beginning of the war, when the Red Army finally succeeded in blocking the advance of the German forces at the approaches to Moscow, Stalin it appears felt the need to define the principles of warfare in order to give encouragement to the combatants and even more so to the command. In February 1943 Stalin felt able to affirm:

> From now on the fate of the war will not be decided by a transitory factor like surprise but by permanently operating factors: the stability of the rear, the morale of the Army, the quantity and quality of the Divisions, the armament of the Army and the organisational qualifications of the Army Commanders.[4]

---

2 *Ibid.*, p. 346.
3 Stalin was of course credited throughout his rule with the major contribution to Soviet military science. Everyone who wrote anything on the subject scattered lavish quotations from his writings on the subject in the 1920's and after. "In creating Soviet military science, Stalin also set the direction for future development in accordance with the growing political, economic and moral capabilities of the Soviet State under conditions of capitalist siege and constant threat of war. Stalin laid down the methods for the military-strategic and operational-tactical conduct of the Armed Forces and for analysing the strategic and tactical-operational situation in time of war." *Ibid*, p. 406.
4 Y. Stalin, *The Great Patriotic War of the USSR*, Gosizdat, Moscow, 1943, p. 40 (Russian).

These five principles — or, as they were called, the "five permanently operating factors" — became the five sacrosanct commandments of the next decade, repeated in the military literature as if they had been handed down on Mount Sinai, accepted without debate or question, without development or change, as defining the whole essence of warfare. Against the background of the early defeats and the relative stabilisation of the fronts later on at the time when these "five principles" were formulated and publicised, it is understandable that Stalin wanted to impose his view that the factor of surprise was a transitory one, the effect of which was now passing over.

I hold firmly to the opinion that the Army morale — the second of the "permanent" decisive factors according to Stalin's doctrine — was due not to Soviet revolutionary fervour but to the fighting qualities of the Russian soldier, qualities proved in many a war; they include love of the Russian fatherland — in a word, patriotism, as well as physical courage, a deep-rooted tradition of obedience to superiors, and an almost limitless capacity to face suffering and withstand the worst imaginable conditions of terrain, weather and short supplies. It is worth remarking that Stalin's first factor — stability of the rear — was also based on these essentially Russian qualities. It is true that these qualities were not always in evidence at the front — or in the rear — in the first phase of the war. There is testimony to the fact that during the retreats in the Kiev region and elsewhere, soldiers were prepared to shoot their Commanding Officers; the Russians themselves contend that these were mainly soldiers from the western regions annexed to the USSR in 1939. The unplanned, hurried withdrawal had caused the collapse of the administrative and Party machine in the rear, but the noteworthy thing is that the rot stopped very soon, thanks mainly to the Russians' patriotism. The line taken by official propaganda was the result of this rather than the cause: more and more all the stress was on defence of the fatherland against the German invader rather than defence of the Revolution against imperialists. Heroic figures of Russian history were praised to the skies. At the Red Army parade in Red Square on 7 November 1941, Stalin said:

> Soldiers of the Red Army and Navy, Commanders, partisans, political workers, the whole world is watching you. The war is a war of liberation, a just war ... Your inspiration in this war must be the bravery of our great soldiers — Alexander Nevsky, Demitrij Donskoy, Kuzma Minin, Dimitrij Pojarsky, Alexander Suvorov and Mikhail Kutuzov. Over you flies the victorious, inspiring flag of the great Lenin.[5]

On 1 May 1942, Order of the Day No. 130 of Minister of Defence Stalin read:

> Comrades! We are fighting a just war for the liberation of the fatherland. ... We are out to free our Soviet soil of the German-Fascist scoundrels.[6]

The third and fourth of Stalin's "permanent factors" — the quantity and quality of the Divisions, and the armament of the Forces — were also formulated, it is reasonable to assume, in view of the conditions in the first stage of the war, the relation of forces prejudicial to the Russians and the forced retreats deep into the interior of the USSR. The question of the relation of forces held a large place in post-war Soviet military literature.

As for the fifth "permanent factor" — the organisational qualifications of the Army commanders, the choice of this point not only indicated the general need to have officers qualified for their posts but also the special need to overcome officers' reluctance in taking the initiative. In the literature, the terms "leadership", "high degree of military knowledge" and even plain "military qualifications" do not come under the head of "organisational qualifications", which means only one thing: the officer's capacity to ensure that his orders will be carried out.[7]

---

5 *Ibid.*, pp. 35–36.
6 *Ibid.*, p. 53.
7 Garthoff, *Soviet Military Doctrine*, The Free Press, Illinois, 1953, p. 35.

When World War II ended and the Army began the transition to peace-time, it was gradually reduced in size — both in the number of Divisions and the number of recruits, and it was finally left at about a third of its wartime strength. Improvements were introduced in the structure and mechanisation of the forces. In March 1946, Stalin passed the reins to Bulganin, who was appointed Minister of War, and the titles "Red Army" and "Red Navy" were changed to "Soviet Army" and "Soviet Navy". Many changes were made in appointments to senior commands on the General Staff and in the commands of the various arms of the Armed Forces and also in the commands of the Military Districts and of the forces outside the borders of the USSR. The Command of the Moscow MD and of the city of Moscow remained in the hands of the MVD Generals under Beria.

Marshal Zhukov was demoted from the post he had held for a short time of Commander of the Land Forces. Novikov was demoted from the command of the Air Force (and apparently arrested). By these and other demotions, depositions and arrests of senior commanders and also by increased MVD surveillance over the cadres of commanders, which meant the threat of possible demotion, deposition and even arrest, Stalin curbed and subdued the senior command into absolute subservience. These actions were crowned with success from Stalin's point of view. From 1946 to 1953, the senior command was paralysed by fear. This led to the paralysis of all basic, new military thinking, in spite of the enormous changes that were then taking place in the development of weapons systems, and chiefly the beginning of the era of atomic and hydrogen arms.

At this stage, it should be remembered, atomic arms were not yet seen as decisive. Stalin was certainly not blind to the effect of their use for the first time against Japan nor to their continued development into still more destructive arms. Nevertheless, the grave prospect of atomic weaponry development did not lead him to make the slightest alteration in his much-trumpeted principles concerning "permanently operating factors" and the transitory nature of the factor of surprise. Thus in September 1946, at the beginning of the atomic era, Stalin declared, "The atom bomb does not constitute a serious force."[8]

There was even aggravation in the rigidity of military doctrine in the years 1946 and '47. Stalin reverted to the subject of the opening phase of World War II in order to minimise the importance of the German successes at that stage and to exalt the counter-attack. In 1947, in reply to a letter from the Soviet historian, Y.A. Razin, Stalin wrote:

> I am not referring to a counter-blow but to the counter-attack after an enemy attack which was successful but nevertheless did not achieve decisive results, an attack in the course of which the defender concentrates his forces, passes over to the counter-attack and delivers a decisive blow against the enemy. It is my opinion that a properly organised counter-attack represents a most interesting form of attack. This was already well-known in ancient times. ... Our own Commander Kutuzov, too, was well aware of this and wiped out Napoleon and his Army with the help of a well-prepared counter-attack.[9]

The paralysis that Stalin's rule imposed on new military thinking did not prevent fairly thorough discussion of theoretical military problems concerning certain subjects only. Just as Stalin himself did not pay serious heed to the necessary impact of atomic arms on military thinking, so in all the discussions, articles and essays of this period, there was nothing at all on the changes called for by the atomic era. The *Journal of Military History* later listed the subjects discussed and written about in this period and also criticised the way they were dealt with:

> The content and the periodisation of the military art; the place in military science of Soviet military economy; Soviet

---

8 Col. Y. Korotkov, *The Development of Soviet Military Theory in the Post-War Years*, Journal of Military History, *Krasnaya Zvezda* publication, Moscow, 1964, p. 40 (Russian).
9 *Bolshevik, Pravda* publication, Moscow, 1947, No. 3, p. 8 (Russian).

military geography; manoeuvre in battle and in the campaign. The paper affirmed that these discussions were of assistance to N.V. Tukhovsky in writing his work on Soviet military science in 1953. Clearly, the paper went on, the writings of this period bore the mark of the cult of personality. Quite a few studies also appeared on the battles of World War II and reviewed the role of the different arms, but the writers' hands were tied by Stalin's subjective evaluations of the events of the war and there was no room for critical analysis. As a result, the members of the military-science corps stopped thinking critically.[10]

## The Breaking of Images

The editors of *The Communist Party of the USSR and the Development of the Armed Forces,* published in Moscow in 1965, have this to say on the character of the period from 1945 to 1953:[11]

> In the first post-war period, the years 1946 to '53, there was an improvement in the structure of the forces, the motorisation of the Army was completed ... the level of Party-political military training was raised. However, Stalin's personality cult had an unfavourable effect on solving the problem of military development. By remaining *de facto* head of the Armed Forces after the war too, Stalin arrested the development of Soviet military science and blocked the advancement

---

10  Korotkov, *op. cit.,* pp. 41–42.
11  Soviet military literature divides the post-war period into two different sub-periods as regards build-up of the forces and development of military theory and thinking. The years from 1945 to 1953 are generally regarded as one period with clearly defined characteristics. As for the years after that, one school takes the years 1954 to '58 as a well-defined second post-war period, with the years from 1959 on as a third period. Another school sees the years after 1954 up to the mid-'60's as the second period (with a sub-division: 1954–'56), and the third period after this. A third school cuts off the second period at the year 1960 and puts the third period from 1961 on.

of talented young officers to positions of leadership in the Army and Navy.[12]

Marshal V. Sokolovsky and Major-General Cherdnichenko wrote as follows on the achievements and shortcomings of the post-war period in an article of theirs in the *Journal of Military History*, also published in 1965:

> In the 1945 to '53 stage, atomic arms were created, the air force developed swiftly and adopted long-range aircraft, the first models appeared of missiles, and the experience of the war just ended was learnt and digested. ...[13] In August 1949, only four years after the first atomic explosion in the USA, the first experimental atomic explosion was carried out in the USSR.[14]

The writers went on to use the by now consecrated phrases on "errors connected with the Stalin personality cult" and "insufficient appraisal" of the possibilities involved in atomic armament and its influence on the art of war. "The experience of past wars and mainly the lessons of the Great Patriotic War were interpreted in a one-sided and subjective manner: Stalin's mistakes over preparing the country to repel Fascist aggression and in the conduct of the fighting itself were passed over in silence or else excused. ... The theory appeared of "active defence"; counter-attack was adjudged an effective means of seizing the strategic initiative. Stalin alone had the right to elaborate theoretical-military problems and especially in the sphere of strategy. The personality cult fettered the creative initiative of the military; dogmatism and the citing of authorities continued to be rife in military-theoretical activity; groundless harassing of Generals and officers did not stop, which

---

12 *The Communist Party of the USSR and the Development of the Soviet Armed Forces, 1917–1964*. Voyenizdat, Moscow, 1965, p. 340 (Russian).
13 Marshal V. Sokolovsky and Maj.-Gen. M. Cherdnichenko, *Some Problems in Military Development in the Post-War Years*, Journal of Military History, March 1965, pp. 3–5.
14 *Ibid.*, p. 5.

engendered insecurity, suspiciousness and mutual distrust among the military."[15] Special weight attaches to this searching criticism, coming as it did from Marshal Sokolovsky, Chief of Staff during Stalin's last years and not one of the commanders deposed by him.

Serious theoretical discussion on military doctrine began at last in September 1953, some six months after Stalin's death. Part of the senior command and some of the military theory people had certainly been long aware of the need for this discussion, but as we have seen there was nothing they could do about it. Three things seem to have combined to set off discussion: the first and most important was of course the emergence of atomic arms, which meant that military doctrine must be got to take this formidable, new destructive force into account. It can be assumed that even if Stalin had gone on ruling, he would have had to allow or even initiate innovations and changes. As we have said, he did realise that atomic and hydrogen arms were important and did not altogether neglect their development. What he refused to recognise was that arming the Forces with this revolutionary new weapon called for bringing military doctrine into line with its power and its characteristics and for reaching a great number of conclusions on the structure of the forces and their preparation for war.

The second thing was the fact itself of Stalin's death. The paralysing fear that had gripped the senior command and the military theoreticians gradually dwindled. After some hesitancy, they started to challenge the frozen certainties of the dead leader.

The third factor was the enhanced status of the army chiefs among the focal centres of power in the USSR. It must be remembered that in late 1953 the new leadership, which had not yet settled in, was still supported in no small measure by the prestige of Stalin the beloved leader and did not dare to attack that prestige for several years more. It is also important to note that even after Stalin's death — and indeed up to the present — settling military doctrine or altering it has always been a clear prerogative of the

---

15  *Ibid.*, p. 7.

## The Fight over Military Doctrine

Party: officially at least, not only Stalin but the entire Party leadership stood behind the existing doctrines. The Soviet Encyclopaedia (the 1970 edition) quotes the official definition of Soviet military doctrine as follows:

> The set of official views and positions that determines the orientation of military organisation and development, the preparation for war of the State and the Armed Forces, the methods and forms of the conduct of the war. Military doctrine is elaborated and laid down by the political leadership of the Central Committee and of the Soviet Government, on the basis of the data of military science, resting on the political and economic strength of the USSR and the other States of the Socialist fraternity.[16]

It is my opinion that the process of challenging and changing military theory could not have started, let alone developed, had it not been for the third factor cited above, the enhanced status of the Army chiefs. True, as we have just stated, the Party leadership itself was supposed to initiate a discussion of this kind or at least to authorise it beforehand. At this stage, the Party leadership was apparently not strong enough or united enough to make a stand on its rights in this field over against the Army chiefs. This does not mean that the discussion that now began and the summing up of military doctrine that was reached were done against the will of the entire Party leadership or without backing from some at least of its members, but the internal struggle in the Party leadership and differing attitudes on the danger of war or the possibility of preventing war render it dubious whether the Army chiefs' public discussion and public summing up was actually done on the basis of instructions of the Central Committee and the Government, as called for by the official definition of powers. It is of course possible that the hydrogen bomb experiments in the USA in March 1952 and in the USSR in August 1953 panicked the Party leader-

---

16 *The Big Soviet Encyclopaedia*, 3rd ed., Moscow, Vol. 5, p. 205.

ship into giving the Army senior command the green light to go ahead with the necessary preparations to prevent the possibility of military surprise attack.[17]

The independence displayed by the Army heads who set about re-examining military doctrine — and thereby dared to publicly question Stalin's monopoly of military genius — stands out in even sharper relief when considered in the light of its timing. As we shall see, the summing up they reached was published as early as the spring of 1955, that is to say, nearly a year *before* the XX Congress and Khrushchev's famous speech there. Awe of Stalin's greatness was still very strong in the people, the Party and the leadership. In the ideological sphere, Stalin was considered Lenin's disciple, but in the military sphere according to Soviet propaganda he was the creator of military theory and not just a follower of Lenin. In his reply to Col. Razin in 1947, already referred to, Stalin wrote, *inter alia*:

> Unlike Engels, Lenin did not consider himself an expert on things military. He left the study of this subject to us, his juniors. We, Lenin's heirs, are not fettered in criticising Clausewitz' military doctrine by any directives of Lenin's, since he did not concern himself with this matter.[18]

The Army chiefs could not have begun revising Stalin's theory without openly disavowing belief in his military genius. This began to surface late in 1953, more than two years before the Party heads publicly challenged Stalin's image as leader and genius. It is the timing that testifies to the Army heads' special prestige in this period. The new trends emerged gradually and cautiously, but the first official article published on the subject already marked a breakthrough, signalling escape from the rigid framework in which military theory had for long been confined. Published in the theo-

---

17 Sokolovsky, Cherdnichenko, *op. cit.*, p. 5. The USSR indeed claims that it carried out an experimental H-bomb explosion before the USA, and that the USA did its experiment in 1954 and not in 1952.
18 *Bolshevik, loc. cit.*, pp. 6–7.

retical review of the Defence Ministry, *Military Thought*,[19] in the September 1953 issue, it was by the editor himself, A. Talensky,[20] and was entitled, "The Problem of the Nature and the Laws of Military Science." Talensky began by repeating the accepted axiom that the socialist laws governing society are the only objective and factual ones and that it was on this basis that Marxism-Leninism construed laws of warfare that only Socialist States are capable of utilising to their own advantage. At the same time, Talensky gave it as his opinion that it is possible to arrive at a general, basic law of war, and that the "permanently operating factors" accepted in Soviet doctrine as decisive for the outcome of a war, important though they are, are not basic and do not suffice to constitute such a basic law. Only one general, basic law of war can exist and it must deal with armed conflict. Thus Talensky did not throw out Stalin's "permanent factors" but argued that the theory did not constitute the law of war. Talensky's theory of armed conflict did not bar the possibility of a swift, decisive defeat of one of the warring sides and implied that this possibility was connected with surprise. Without his saying so openly, it emerges from his exposition that a surprise strike by atomic weapons could be decisive against an adversary who had not taken proper counter-measures before-

---

19 A large part of this discussion was conducted in the pages of *Military Thought*. I was unable to get the original articles, since the circulation of the review is "Restricted". I was also missing several numbers of *Red Star*. I have been obliged, therefore, to make use of quotations fror these articles in Western publications and mainly in the book by H.S. Dinnerstein, *War and the Soviet Union,* which appeared in a revised edition published by the Rand Corporation in 1962, and the article by N. Galai in the *Bulletin of the Institute for the Study of the USSR,* Vol. III, No. 6, 1956.

20 Besides being the editor of the review, *Military Thought,* at the time of the publication of the article in question, Major-General A. Talensky was editor of *Red Star* as well. He published numerous articles on problems of military theory, was Professor in the Voroshilov Academy of the General Staff and a member of the History Section of the General Staff.

hand. Therewith Talensky elevated surprise from its lowly status as a transitory factor of passing importance to something that could in certain conditions decide the fate of the warring parties.

Talensky's espousal of the idea of a general, unique, basic law of war amounted to a frontal attack on the accepted axiom that the USSR as a socialist State was governed by laws of warfare different from those binding on capitalist States. He contended that armed conflict is subject to its own laws and not to different social laws in different countries. Despite the care he took in formulating his views not to explicitly contradict the sacrosanct principles wholesale, he was clearly questioning the strategy of attrition as a sure military means for the defence of the USSR and undermining confidence in those famous "permanently operating factors" which supposedly of themselves give the USSR a clear advantage by providing time to mobilise large forces."

## The Debate

The article by Talensky in *Military Thought* had wide repercussions. The debate in the military literature went on until early 1955. I do not propose to analyse or even survey the whole process of this development of Soviet military thinking after Stalin's death. I shall indicate its decisive stages without treating every reaction and response, referring only to the articles that marked the break-up of the ice and that illustrated the wide scope of the debate and the main differences of opinion disclosed.

It can be assumed that at the start of the discussion, the Party leadership did not back any specific position. The important thing was that it allowed the debate itself to be carried on. There is no doubt that those who took part had the feeling that the reins were loosened and that they could now express differing opinions without feeling the threat of repression hanging over them.

The first critical reactions to Talensky's views by a number of senior commanders, mostly Colonels, appeared two months later in articles in the November issue of *Military Thought*. Col. Shvarov treated Talensky's search for a basic law of war as something sophisticate and artificial; in his view, the most important thing for theoreticians and professional soldiers alike was to settle what the factors are that determine final victory in war. The thesis of "permanently operating factors" provided a full and satisfactory answer to the problem. Major Balshov also saw no point in seeking a basic law of war in military science; in his view there could be no such thing as a law of armed conflict, since the one and only basic law is the general law of evolution that governs the development of society.

One of the highest-ranking commanders to join Talensky's critics was Deputy Minister of Defence Marshal A.M. Vasilevsky. *Red Star* published two articles by him, the first on Army and Navy Day, 23 February 1954, in which he affirmed that Soviet military science, based on the "permanently operating factors" that decide the outcome of war, unlike bourgeois military science gave no undue weight to transitory factors such as surprise. In his second article, published on the anniversary of the victory over Germany, on 7 May 1954, Vasilevsky reaffirmed this approach, quoting Stalin's dictum: "The outcome of a war is decided by the permanent factors."

During the debate, a score or more of articles appeared in *Military Thought* and *Red Star*, the great majority sharply critical of Talensky's positions. Basing oneself on a basic law of armed conflict was condemned as non-Marxist and unscientific. Typical of this conservative rearguard action was an article that appeared in a Ministry of Defence publication, *Soviet Military Science*, written by Colonel V. Petrov and entitled, not very surprisingly, "The permanently operating factors." Col. Petrov argued that scrutiny of the role played by these factors in the Great Patriotic War proved the wisdom and powerful prophetic genius of the Communist Party, which had understood the laws governing warfare in our time long before the war broke out. Petrov averred that the only *correct and certain path*[20a] towards a further strengthening of

[20a] My stress: Y. A.

the defence capability of the peoples of the USSR and of the peoples' democracies was through the "permanently operating factors".

As already explained, the main issue debated was whether a general law of war exists governing States with different social systems, and it was Talensky's stand on this issue that aroused the strongest opposition. Most of the articles dealt with theory and hence with the tenets of a deep-rooted faith: After indoctrination that had lasted so many years, it was difficult to take leave of dogma at one stroke. The army conservatives clung to dogma, fearing that to yield an inch would undermine the very foundation of Leninist-Marxist doctrine and shatter their faith in Lenin's disciple, Stalin. Petrov's phraseology about "the only correct path" — transposed from the language of Party indoctrination to the debate on military doctrine — perfectly characterises this clinging to tradition.

Articles did however appear in 1954 giving Talensky's position a large measure of support. (There was, for example, the article by A. Chilik in *Military Thought* of September 1954.) Both sides to the debate of course contended that their views were based on the teachings of Marx and Lenin. These articles and the fact of their appearance in a variety of journals (mainly publications of the Ministry of Defence) show that while Talensky's views did not express the official line, they were the fruit of the freedom to hold the debate itself, and as we have already noted, the granting of this freedom was a very bold step by the heads of the Army and the Defence Ministry, given its timing — more than two years before the XX Congress. It should not be overlooked that the *Red Star*, which also published discussions questioning sacrosanct precepts of military doctrine, was a widely circulated daily paper, read by soldiers doing their compulsory service, not a few of them Komsomol members.

At the beginning of 1955 the debate took a definite turn towards revision of the rigid tenets of Soviet military doctrine. In February 1955, *Military Thought* published an article by Marshal P. Rotmistrov,[21] entitled, "The Role of Surprise in War in Our Time". The writer affirmed that on the basis of wartime experience it was possible to lay down that surprise, if successful, not only influences the fighting and the course of the campaigns but in certain conditions may even significantly affect the course of the whole war and its outcome. He was clear and definite in stating his opinion that surprise is one of the determinant conditions for successful use of atomic and hydrogen arms, not only in battles and campaigns but in the whole war. These conclusions of Rotmistrov's, formulated without hesitancy or circumlocution, not only reversed the evaluation of surprise as something transitory but called for preparations to prevent surprise use of atomic weapons by the enemy. Publication of this article had been held up — it had reached the review a good deal earlier than February 1955. The date is significant. The article was in the hands of the editors before the deposition of Malenkov, but it was not published until Bulganin replaced Malenkov at the head of the Government and Zhukov was appointed Minister of Defence. Moreover, in the March 1955 issue *Military Thought* published news of a meeting of Bulganin and Zhukov with Armed Forces senior echelons, which apparently took place late in February. Both Bulganin and Zhukov were stated to have advised undertaking a thorough study of modern military technology and advanced military theory. The editors of the monthly apologised for the delay in publishing Marshal Rotmistrov's article and hastened to castigate military theoretical publications, including their own, for not doing enough to develop Soviet military science. Military scientific work had fallen behind, they said, and the science corps had for long been content to serve up well-known truisms while neglecting urgent problems. In the post-war period not a single important work had been published in the field of the theory of military science or of military ideology, while scholasticism and niggling fault-finding still prevailed in the military academies. According to the editors, the main cause for this state of

21 Rotmistrov was an officer in the USSR First Army of Armoured Troops and Head of the Stalin Academy for Armoured Warfare. He wrote numerous books and articles.

affairs was the fear of saying something new or something different from what had been said by some authority or other. The whole field had become a matter of endless repetition and quotation of things said in the past until they had hardened into dogma. Writers found it easiest to copy existing dictums of an authority such as Stalin, thus dispensing with the need to think out serious problems. Creative thought was inhibited and military science suffered in consequence.

This was the first direct, official blow dealt at Stalin, an open invitation to shake off the fear still cast by the shadow of his name. It cannot be over-emphasised that the date of this condemnation — a year before Khrushchev's speech and the XX Congress Resolutions — testifies to an independent, non-conformist stand *vis-à-vis* the Party. The only possible inference is that the article was inspired by Zhukov himself, and what is of the highest interest is the phenomenon of the Defence Ministry's theoretical organ's criticising the non-appearance of works on military ideology.

Shortly before the appearance of this critical article, *Izvestia* published an article on the occasion of the 37th anniversary of the creation of the Red Army by the Chief of General Staff Marshal Sokolovsky, entitled: "The Ever-Victorious Strength of the Armed Forces of the Soviet State". The Marshal twice dealt with the matter of surprise. Firstly:

> As a result of the treacherous surprise attack on the USSR by Fascist Germany, and as a result of the disadvantageous relation of forces thereby created, the Soviet Army was forced to retreat in difficult conditions, temporarily leaving vital regions of the fatherland in enemy hands.

And again

> In present conditions, with the appearance of arms of tremendous destructive power, and as a result of the unprecedented development of Air Force and jet techniques, the importance of the factor of surprise has increased. In these conditions, preparation and power to answer blow with coun-

ter-blow is not in itself enough; the aggressor must be deprived of the surprise factor — he must not be allowed to catch us unawares. ... It is necessary to do bold, original research in order to work out the most important current problems of military science, and mainly the problems connected with conducting military action under the new conditions. The corps of commanders must apply itself to thorough-going, fundamental study of the theory and the experience of past wars and the latest achievements in the military sphere, not only in our country, but also abroad.[22]

Although Sokolovsky here does not attack the "sole" permanently operating factors and even refers to Stalin as the follower of Lenin, the change of emphasis regarding the supposed transitory factor of surprise is perfectly clear all the same. His calling on commanders to study the latest foreign achievements in the military field is something of an innovation. The whole article in fact amounted to a demand for a revision of Soviet military science to adjust it to changing conditions.

This article by Chief of General Staff Sokolovsky, published in the daily mass-circulation paper some weeks after Malenkov's deposition and Bulganin's and Zhukov's promotions, was the first public indication that the authorities were inclining towards accepting Talensky's views. Henceforth, it could be understood, the military leadership would allow not only discussion but also criticism of sacrosanct military doctrines and would itself propose the changes called for by new conditions.

Following on this relatively brief critical reference to the subject in the Sokolovsky article, only a month later, on 24 March 1955, an article by Marshal Rotmistrov appeared in *Red Star*, entitled, "In Favour of a Fruitful Examination of the Problems of Soviet Military Science" — a title which itself marks the permission or even backing granted from the highest levels after Sokolovsky's article. Rotmistrov took issue with V. Petrov[22a] and M. Tarenchuk

---

22 *Izvestia*, 23 February, 1955.
22a See p. 81 above.

over their being satisfied to rely on the "permanently operating factors", and he attacked the argument that since only Soviet military science understands these factors, the USSR is therefore ensured a permanent advantage that will bear fruit in every war. He contended that there were no military leaders anywhere and never had been who did not take into consideration the stability of the rear, the number of Divisions and their quality, the arming of the armies and the organisational qualifications of the commanders and of the higher echelons at staff level; these factors were not a monopoly of the USSR and did not determine any basic difference between Soviet and bourgeois military science. He did not completely write off the "permanently operating factors" but did not consider them principles that only Soviet science could understand; hence sole reliance should not be placed on them. Rotmistrov called on the military to study Western military science and its views on military theory and practice. He questioned the view that the West had no serious military science. He begged to differ from those who contended that the "permanently operating factors" settled the outcome of war. As against Petrov, he reaffirmed what he had said about the factor of surprise in his article in *Military Thought*: in certain cases a surprise attack could be of decisive significance. He rejected the views of Stalin and his supporters that it is always possible to exploit depth of terrain to entice the enemy into the interior of the country in order to defeat him there. He saw the importance of depth of terrain in the possibility it offers of dispersing population, industrial centres and other resources, especially in the age of the atom and hydrogen bomb.

Here Rotmistrov went even further than Sokolovsky in attaching the greatest possible importance to the surprise factor, and even more than Sokolovsky emphasised the need to study bourgeois military science and to develop new military thinking. Rotmistrov's conclusions actually amounted to a flat denial of the originality of Soviet military theory, rejection of rigid dogmas and sheer iconoclasm.

The Fight over Military Doctrine

## *The Summing-Up*

A fortnight after the publication of Rotmistrov's article in *Red Star*, the April issue of *Military Thought* summed up the debate that had been opened in the review 19 months earlier by Talensky, when he was still its editor. An official and authoritative article under the title, "The Results of the Discussion on the Nature of the Laws of Military Science", summed things up in the name of the editorial board. *Military Thought* rejected the views of those who saw no need to seek a basic law of military science because they believed that the famous "factors" settled the outcome of war. There was here, wrote the editors, at the best an evasion of the problem and in the worst case a voluntary or involuntary abandonment of true Marxist dialectical materialism. Military science did call for a basic law. Understanding of the objective laws of armed conflict would assist the institutions of the leadership of Soviet society to mobilise the forces of the people for the solution of the basic problems on which in the last resort depend the course of war and its outcome.

The lengthy debate between the conservatives and the innovators, both sides claiming to speak for Marxism-Leninism, thus ended with the victory of those who sought to cast off the shackles of dogma and to strip Stalin's "factors" of their grandeur as the fundamental law of Soviet military science. The invention of atomic arms, the critical importance of the first atomic strike and the weight of the factor of surprise had combined to impose a re-examination of military doctrine; this could only take place, however, after those concerned had rejected Stalin's "principles" and emerged from the paralysis imposed by them. The official, agreed summing-up on Stalin's military theory necessarily damaged Stalin's status as a military genius and indirectly as a genius in general. The men behind the decision were certainly Zhukov, Minister of Defence, and Bulganin, Head of Government. In all probability they acted with Khrushchev's consent or at least with his knowledge, but it is not clear whether the matter was ever brought before the Party Presidium. Military theory was historically a prerogative of the Party leadership and the initiative for any such debate should have come from them. At this point in time, however, there was no single ruler nor was there a united Party leadership, which meant that the close and powerful bonds of thinking that had previously held firm between the political leadership and the Armed Forces heads were necessarily dissolved. The great certainties about "the only correct path" were no longer self-evident.

The old attitudes did not vanish completely, all the same, at the behest of *Military Thought*. An eminent "last-ditcher" and after all a Marshal of the Soviet Union, Koniev, had his say when he delivered an address on 8 May 1955 at the formal tenth anniversary celebration of the great victory over the Fascist enemy. He was not ready to join in criticism of the past. Unlike Sokolovsky in the *Izvestia* article two months previously,[22c] Koniev did not explicitly refer to the enemy's conquest of important stretches of territory and the threat to vital centres due to surprise; instead he stressed the resistance put up by the Soviet forces even in the first stage of the war, at Brest, Smolensk and on the Dnieper, and the counter-attacks in the face of advancing tanks. According to Koniev, Soviet military science, based on Marxist-Leninist theory, was capable of discovering the laws governing modern warfare and to teach ways to win the war. Soviet military planning was indeed original,[22d] in his view. It is of interest to note that the text of this address was published first in the Party daily, *Pravda,* on 9 May and only the next day in the Government daily, *Izvestia.*

Another Marshal of the Soviet Union, who had been conspicuously conservative throughout 1954, now performed an about-turn. Marshal Vasilevsky, First Deputy Minister of Defence, "toed the line" that had been newly authorised. On the same day that Koniev addressed the official gathering celebrating the tenth anniversary of victory over Germany, *Izvestia* published Vasilevsky's article written for the occasion. The striking thing about this article was the importance Vasilevsky attached to the factor of surprise in 1941:

[22c] See pp. 84–5 above.
[22d] That is to say, authentically Marxist, Soviet, etc., and not "general".

## The Fight over Military Doctrine

> The surprise Hitlerite attack on our country gave the enemy a particularly important advantage, which left a deep impress on the fighting in the first period of the war. In executing its treacherous and unexpected attack on the USSR, the German-Fascist Army secured a serious success at the beginning of the war. It compelled our armies to retreat, it seized considerable USSR territory and got very near to important and vital centres of the country — Moscow, Leningrad, Rostov — and later it even reached the Volga and the great Caucasus Mountains. ... A terrible danger hung over the fatherland. It was a question of life and death for the Soviet State, a question of the freedom and independence of the peoples of the USSR.[23]

There could hardly be a clearer example of the complete *volte-face* that had been executed in one single year.[24] What of the merely

---

23 *Ibid.*, 8 May 1955.
24 Some years later, Col. Korotkov wrote an instructive summing-up of this period in the development of military thinking.

> The second period in the history of Soviet theoretical military thought, from the beginning of 1954 on [Korotkov saw the second period as lasting from 1954 to the mid-'60's — see footnote No. 11 above] is characterised by fundamental changes in theoretical military views, as a result of the combination of atomic-missile armament and its introduction in the Soviet Armed Forces. The year 1954 is an important signpost in the development of Soviet military thought. From that year on began the working out of the wide complex of problems connected with the conduct of warfare in conditions of the use of atomic weapons. ... As with all periods of change, the theory of these years too is characterised by the idea of exploiting atomic arms within the framework of the previous administrative methods of the campaigns and the war. One of the reasons for this is that the ideas and views were born and adopted in a struggle against the old views and met with obstacles blocking their way. Under the influence of Stalin's well-known statement, some military theoreticians were still of the opinion that atomic arms could not change the basic principles of the conduct of war, but many commanders already saw — if not with sufficient clarity — the great effect that the use of atomic

passing effect of "transitory factors" — with surprise among them — on the course of the war? And where was Stalin in all this? The article did indeed refer to him as head of the Central Committee and the Party — but without the traditional, "Lenin's follower".

The later evolution of Soviet military doctrine after this point is not our affair here, but it can be stated that the years 1953 to 1957 were exceptional in the history of the Soviet Armed Forces as regards the possibility offered the senior command of openly discussing and debating problems of the highest concern in the world of military theory. This after Stalin's dictates had for so long deprived the military of the possibility of thinking, disputing and discussing, and attempting to persuade each other on such sensitive issues as the danger that the option of a war of attrition might be pre-empted by a sudden nuclear attack right at the opening phase of a war. The debate only became possible when the political leadership was weak and was involved in a struggle for power within the Party and the opposing groups stood in need of aid from the Army chiefs. The leadership's weakness was also reflected in its relations with the world Communist movement, and here too Army backing was a valuable trump card.

Once this need of the leadership for assistance was past, when the political leadership recovered stability and the senior officers had again been brought under closer Party control, the debate on military theory was practically blocked and its place was taken by the historiography of the campaigns of the Fatherland War and by the commanders' memoirs.

My reading of the material of this whole period — in so far as

> arms would have. They thought that in conditions of atomic warfare, the factor of surprise could have decisive weight not only in a battle or campaign but also on the whole war. ... The years 1954 to '55 are of interest in the history of Soviet military thought, since it was then that our theoretical military views began to change. In 1957 there begin to be clear signs of an independent stage in the history of Soviet military thought, connected with research into the new possibilities of the use of missiles in war and in its campaigns. Korotkov *Op. cit.*, pp. 43–45.

## The Fight over Military Doctrine

I have had access to it — is that the fight of the senior officers, or at least of the majority, to free themselves from rigid military doctrines was also a fight to escape the grip of the Party leadership. They wanted to be free to think and express themselves on military subjects in their own way, free to sum up and reach conclusions for themselves. The formula gradually accepted in the course of the fight was, "Liberation of military theory from the effects and consequences of the cult of personality of Stalin", but in reality it was a fight for the right of the military simply to think, to sum up evaluations of the situation independently and to present the conclusions that followed therefrom. The Armed Forces protagonists did have a considerable measure of success — at least up to the end of 1957 — in weakening the post-Stalin Party leadership's grip on the military theoreticians and Commanding Officers and in challenging its sole right to dictate the line of approach to discussion of theoretical military issues.

## CHAPTER IV

## THE FIGHT FOR GREATER AUTONOMY

A high level of professionalism in the Army — mainly in the officer corps brought with it the aspiration and even the claim to professional and institutional autonomy. Professionalism in the Soviet officer corps was intensified by accelerated technological development in the Armed Forces, which lent the profession of arms a marked accrual of strength. This process was speeded up still more with the appearance of atomic arms.

Under the Stalinist autocracy, the problem of autonomy for the military institutional system was ineluctably swallowed up in the general repression. In the post-war years and especially in the last five years before his death, Stalin's line was clear — to impose and maintain Party domination over the Army and Navy. The commanders went in fear of the KGB: though they were the most highly qualified group in the Forces, they were nevertheless unable to stand up for their rights. The rigidity of the regime and the efficiency of its terror machine ensured their complete subservience.

Stalin's death set off a protracted series of contests between the main foci of power in the USSR.* Many of the issues had long been dormant under the surface; they now emerged, still unclear and undefined, to be fought over by protagonists who were themselves in a state of no little confusion. As we have already shown,* the prestige of the military command was enhanced when members of the leadership turned to it for assistance in their struggles against each other. Army heads gradually began to feel more self-confident and were led to try and free themselves from the close Party con-

---

* See Chapter 2 above, p. 48.

trol. In their relations with the political workers in the Army they wanted to act as commanders in fact. This was not and should not be adjudged disloyalty to the Party — it was simply the desire to be rid of unnecessary interference. The political workers did not lightly give way and relinquish their special status. The struggle was a long and silent one, where a considerable part was played by the character of the individual commander concerned and also by his standing and connections in the High Command.

Apprehension over the consequences of the military Command's working for greater independence and the need to prevent this process from developing further meant that decisions had to be taken on far clearer and more detailed arrangements than in the past in order to regulate the respective powers and responsibilities of the channels of control in the Army and the relations between these channels.

Only four months after Stalin's death, in July 1953 — the month when the Party heads took the unprecedented step of calling on the Army to publicly express its support for the arrest of Beria — the Central Committee Plenary was convened to ratify the arrests. In the course of this Plenary session, several Resolutions were passed which in my view represented the first evident sign of the confrontation between the two instruments of control in the Army, the Party apparatus and the military command. On the one hand, Marshal Zhukov was promoted from alternate to full member of the Central Committee and a number of other generals were also advanced in rank; but at the same session a Resolution was passed that called for "restoring the principles of Party leadership of the Armed Forces and putting the Armed Forces under the direct supervision of the Party and the Central Committee."[1] The wording of this text is something of a give-away. If it was necessary to *restore* the principles of Party leadership, then clearly these principles were not presently being upheld.

"Direct supervision" by the Party in all decisions on national

---

1 Y.P. Petrov, *The Party Organisation and Development in the Soviet Army and Navy*, Voyenizdat, Moscow, 1964, p. 454 (Russian).

defence and on allocation of resources to ensure State security could not of itself solve the problem of the officer corps' aspiration for greater autonomy on the plane of every-day life in the Army. Professional autonomy meant, among other things, less distracting interference on the part of the political institutions and the political workers; it meant being freed to some small extent at least from the shackles of close political supervision.

The tug-of-war between Head of Government Malenkov and his opponents in the Party leadership went on till February 1955, when it ended with the victory of the latter, a victory which, as we have related, was not secured without effective support from the Army heads. The victors appointed the Defence Minister, Marshal Bulganin, as Head of Government and his Deputy Defence Minister, Marshal Zhukov, as Defence Minister. It is a reasonable supposition that at this stage of the internal struggle, the end of only one phase, had they had a choice in the matter the winners would much have preferred to put someone less combative, less self-assured — and less popular — than Marshal Zhukov at the head of the important focus of power of the Ministry of Defence, but they hardly had any choice. Zhukov's appointment at the head of the Armed Forces was a summons to action for the MPA and the Central Committee Secretariat. They would have to alert the political institutions to mount guard in case it should become necessary to halt the process that was developing towards greater independence in the Army and Navy.

As early as March 1955 — a month, no more, after Zhukov took up his post — the Central Committee instructed the political institutions to see to making proper arrangements in the future for directing the Party machinery in the Army and Navy.[2] This amounted to a clear enough criticism of the actions of the political institutions in the past. Strict instructions went out to put the machine in working order.

In Zhukov's first six months as Minister of Defence, his influence could be felt immediately in the professional struggle. The

2 *Ibid.*, p. 454.

## The Fight for Greater Autonomy

status of the Political Administration inside the Ministry of Defence was progressively weakened. Protected by Zhukov, the Ministry felt itself freed from dependence on daily MPA guidance in the matters of Army morale and discipline and perhaps even in planning educational programmes. By the end of the summer of 1955, the MPA began to feel gnawing, secret apprehension that Zhukov intended to subordinate it to the Ministry. The process of reducing the influence of the political institutions in the forces was uninterrupted, and the MPA and the Central Committee were not going to acquiesce in this development.

### *The Role of the Main Political Administration*

The confrontation between the MPA and the Ministry of Defence was discussed by the Central Committee in September 1955. Apparently the deliberations were held in the Secretariat and not in the Plenary. Their outcome was that the mission, the tasks and the content of MPA activity were re-defined by the Central Committee as follows:

> The MPA is the leading institution of the Party in the matter of Party-political action in the forces. Acting by virtue of its authority as a section of the Central Committee, the MPA reports to the Central Committee on its work, on the basis of decisions of the Central Committee and of orders of the Minister of Defence. It is incumbent on the MPA to conduct all the day to day Party-political and educational activity and to direct the work of the political institutions <u>for the purpose of improving the battle-readiness</u> of the troops, strengthening military discipline and raising the political-morale level of the men serving in the Armed Forces. Administration of military publications and of cultural and educational institutions also constitutes a very important part of MPA activities, together with the working out and ratification of study programmes for political instruction and education for serving soldiers.

This "many-sided definition" of the role of the MPA certainly "contributed", comments the military writer Petrov,[3] to "raising its standing" in the conduct of Party-political action in the forces.

The central and important point of these instructions was that the MPA had to report to the Central Committee *alone* and not to the Defence Minister, in spite of its supposedly acting on the basis of his orders as well as those of the C.C. This is certainly a very odd arrangement in a military set-up and bears the mark of the struggle that was being waged between the two channels of control.[4] The wording of the decision indicates the effort made to reach a compromise between the claims of the two channels without the Party's making any significant concession.

It will be remembered that in June 1950[4a] the powers and composition of the Military Councils had been extended and they had been made responsible for the state of battle preparedness and the training and education of the troops. The post had also been reintroduced of the political worker as the "comrade" on the Military Council.[5] Now, five years later, Zhukov — as afterwards charged against him — was trying to reverse the process and "restrict the tasks of the Military Councils".[6] It is evident that Zhukov did

3 *Ibid.*, pp. 454–55.
4 Kolkovicz, *op. cit.*, p. 123, actually considers these Central Committee decision a clear victory for Zhukov and a restriction on the activities of the MPA. I do not see them in this light. The C.C. explicitly said that the MPA was to "conduct day to day activity" to improve the troops' battle-readiness and strengthen military discipline. The accusation was later levelled against Zhukov that he had treated the MPA with contempt, forbidding it to report direct to the Central Committee on the situation in the Army and on its own activities, as enjoined in the Central Committee decision of September 1955 (*Party-Political Activity in the Armed Forces of the Soviet Union*, Voyenizdat, Moscow, 1960, p. 38 (Russian). It is therefore hard to construe the decision as a victory for Zhukov.
4a See pp. 41–42 above.
5 *Party-Political Activity in the Armed Forces of the Soviet Union*, Voyenizdat, Moscow, 1974, p. 283 (Russian).
6 Decision of the Party Central Committee Plenary, October 1957. *Pravda*, 3 November 1957.

## The Fight for Greater Autonomy

not manage to get a decision through the Central Committee to alter the Military Councils' official status, but it is true that their powers were reduced in fact in certain cases. The matter largely depended on the relative personal standing of the Military District Commander, the permanent "comrade" on the Military Council and the Secretary of the highest-ranking Party instance in the Military District. This attempt at re-adjustment was castigated by the Central Committee Plenary when it came to remove Zhukov from his posts in the Army and in the Party leadership.

### Day to Day Activity

Let us take a look at the friction between men of the two control channels on the lower levels of military organisation. We shall cite opinions and instances that illustrate the relations between commanders and the political institutions or between the Commanding Officer and his *Zampolit*.

Col. N.O., Commanding Officer, Independent Signals Battalion:

> The great majority of the political workers were very unpopular indeed in the units. Both officers and men generally regarded them as free-loaners — they put up with them but did not respect them. The politicals rushed about and made a great fuss but wriggled out of responsibility. So the commanders were glad to cut down their influence, but they did not give up easily.

Artillery Colonel B.P.:

> The political workers used to get out of war games and technical lectures. Their professional-military level was much lower than that of officers of equal rank, so that they had to have special exercises arranged for them on a lower level, and this contributed to the commanders' contempt for them.

The other side of the picture is given by Col. B.A., who served all

97

his Army career as a political worker:

> From my experience in the Army, relations between commanders and political workers were not good. The commanders didn't like us. Some of them called us "loafers" and "windbags" — but only among themselves, and not so loud either. They use to say accusingly that we were generally to be found in the rear and not with the unit when it attacked. Relations between us got even worse after the war. There were commanders who did as they pleased without any consideration for their *Zampolits* and interferred with them in doing their jobs. My commander, who was a Colonel like me, also did as he pleased and took every chance he got to reprimand me. Like lots of them, he thought that our job added up to nothing but talk and that he was the only one authorised to give orders and instructions. The C.O.s wanted to take all the credit for their units' achievements and ignored the political workers, who also wanted a share of the credit for their contribution to the unit's battle-readiness. I think that the information[6a] work we did was of considerable value and helped the unit to be better trained and to be better fusiliers. What's more, we, the political workers, were also partly responsible for battle-readiness and in some cases we were even held to blame for a lower level of achievement because of not enough information and we turned out to be the scapegoats.

*Postings and Promotions.* One of the most powerful levers in the hands of the Party-political organisation in the Armed Forces was its practically decisive influence over officer appointments, promotions and postings to different regions of the country. At every stage in all discussions on promotions in rank and on transfers from one post to another, there had to be an official recommendation by the ranking Party-political element. Every recommendation by a commander to his superiors was paralleled by the report of the appropriate political officer (whether *Zampolit*, Head of Political Section or head of the Political Administration), who transmitted his opinion on the man concerned direct to his own superior in the political grades. He was not obliged to tell the commander his opinion on the latter's recommendation. In general, the military rank authorised to recommend promotions refrained from taking a decision running counter to the opinion of the political representative participating in the deliberations. The senior officers' corps was used to this arrangement and had learnt to "live with it". In the period dealt with in this Chapter, however, and especially in its later half. Zhukov and a number of other high-ranking officers attempted to get through their own candidates for promotion even against the views of the political representatives. News of this filtered through in Moscow in 1957. To some extent, the struggle on this issue went all the way down to the lower ranks as well.

*Weekly Reports.* A permanent weapon at the *Zampolit's* disposal available for use against officers in his unit was the Weekly (*Polit-Donyesenye*), which had to go to his next superior Political Section. In this document, the *Zampolit* had to report on the general situation in his unit or formation and especially on the political situation there. The *Zampolit* would not show the Report to the military C.O. or inform him of its contents. Mostly the commander would only get to know what was in the Report in the event of his being summoned to the Political Section of the next highest formation to give an explanation concerning the criticism in the Report. Artillery Col. B.P.:

> One of the main professions the political workers were experts at was informing. They demanded that the officers tell them what they knew about the situation in the unit, about things that were said and done by their (the officers) comrades and by the men, explaining that it was their duty to know the state of mind of the masses. Descriptions such as, "neglects his job", "not interested in his job", "boot-licker", recurred frequently in the secret Weekly Report, applied to officers who were not on good terms with their *Zampolits.*

*Bad Marks*: Another instrument at the disposal of the Party-political apparatus was the grading of officers according to their active participation in the Marxist-Leninist training extension courses that lasted two or three days every month. The officers had to prepare lectures or take an active part in seminar-type discussions on ideological themes. Some importance attached to these grades in the considerations affecting an officer's promotion and this gave the political workers another weapon against the officers. Moreover, the political workers exploited the discussions in the Party *'aktiv'* meeting in the unit or formation in order to criticise some of the officers' actions, relying on the hallowed principles of "criticism and self-criticism". In the period covered in this Chapter, the commanders fought harder than they had previously against this kind of interference.

Col. B.A., who was, as we have noted, a *Politruk*, thought that the political workers wrote unfavourable comments on their commanders and criticised them only when the latter did not give their views any consideration, despised them and made them the butt of their jokes.

Col. N.A., Commander of the Signals Battalion, told a story that throws additional light on the struggle over the authority vested in the commander of the Political Section in a formation:

> Once I demoted a Sergeant in my unit as a punishment for being drunk while on manoeuvres. The Political Section of the next highest echelon to my unit demanded that I remit the punishment, since the man was a Party member and demoting him would undermine the good name of the Party in the unit. I refused to accept this demand. I argued that as commander of an Independent Battalion I had authority equal to that of a Brigade Commander. The sentence was enforced, but because of my refusal and because of my critical comments on the Military District Chief of Staff at a Party meeting, they got their own back on me for a long time, in fact until I was pensioned.

Col. Y.N., Commander in the Armoured Corps, related a whole series of instructive incidents in relations between the military and

## The Fight for Greater Autonomy

the politicals in the two Military Districts where he served:

a. The political workers in the various units in the MD held a small competition among themselves as to who would succeed in pressuring the officers in his unit for the largest "voluntary" contribution to the State Loan. They pressured the officers into raising their participation in the Loan, and naturally this did not make them more popular.

b. A Brigade Commander in a mechanised formation, Col. P., who was famous in the Sub-Carpathian MD, enjoyed a very strong position as a member of the MD Party Commission and could generally stand up for himself in the matter of promoting his officers. His wily *Zampolit* did not make any special difficulties on this ground, but even this Commander, for all his self-confidence, used to try and fix up his proposals on manpower matters and education together with his *Zampolit* before travelling to formation Staff, so as to prevent the *Zampolit* from interfering on the political level of the formation.

c. In another Brigade in the same MD, there was a great deal of friction between the Commander and his *Zampolit*. It was only thanks to the great "pull" of the Brigade Commander, whose brother-in-law was Chief Artillery Officer in the Soviet Army, that his *Zampolit* was transferred somewhere else.

d. When I was serving as second-in-command on Sakhalin Island, my Brigade Commander, Col. Y.T., had a great deal to put up with from his *Zampolit*. The man wrote perfectly disgusting things about him in his Weekly Reports to his political superior in the formation, such as that he did not manage to stop talk among the officers not in line with the Party spirit — an accusation that was considered very serious indeed. Behind the *Zampolit's* back, the Commander called him his "talky-talky deputy", but he told me, his second-in-command, that there was nothing he could do to put an end to the *Zampolit's* "dirty tricks". In desperation, the Commander finally asked to be transferred to another post, only on account of this *Zampolit* who was making his life a misery. His superiors — among them a Commander of an Army — had a favourable opinion of him, but the *Zampolit* was supported by the Party representative on the MD Military Council — the "comrade" — and as a result Y.T. was transferred to a higher post in another formation.

During my service in the Army with General Kreizer, I was present with a number of other officers at a clash between the General and the Head of the Political Administration in his Army. The latter opposed the General in a manner very unusual in the Army and Kreizer did not dare to put his political deputy in his proper place. This instance too concerns a famous General, who was later appointed Commander of the Far East MD.[6b]

All the ex-officers interviewed were agreed that in the event of serious friction between the commander and the political workers, the only solution was to transfer one of them to another unit or formation. In most cases, it was the commander who was transferred. The matter largely depended on the support that each of them could call on in the higher echelons and mainly in the ranks of the Party.

*Political Instruction.* One of the issues in the officers' fight for greater professional autonomy was the use of time in military training. The commanders wanted to lighten the load of political studies and political "information" which weighed on troop training. The four testimonies I have gleaned on this subject for the period 1955 to '57 show that at that time no final decision was reached on reducing the number of hours devoted to political instruction. In the Independent Signals Battalion attached to the MD Command, hours of political studies were reduced from six a week to four; the num-

[6b] The Far East MD is one of 11 frontier Mds, command of which is always entrusted to very high-ranking officers and which have assigned to them large tables of establishment and equipment.

ber of hours was also reduced in units of the Internal Security Army, while there was no change in the Gunnery High School; in the Motorised Formation political studies took up four hours a week. This may not sound like an excessive number of hours, but the snag was that under Defence Ministry standing orders political instruction was not only absolutely compulsory but had to take place in the *first two hours* of the training day. The commander had no authority to free any soldier from attendance, not even for maintenance work in the camp or kitchen duty; he could free soldiers for this purpose during the hours of military training but not in the hours of political instruction. The reader should know that the programme of political studies came to the units from the MPA worked out in every detail, parallel with the military training programme.

### *"Unity of Command"*

Another point at issue was the existence of the post of *Zampolit* at company level, a post re-introduced in 1950.[6e] Advantage was taken of the considerable reduction in Armed Forces effectives after the Geneva summit meeting in 1955 to reduce the number of links in the chain of command of political workers in the Army; the post of *Zampolit* in the company was abolished in August of that year (1955). The post of Regiment Secretary for Party Organisation was also abolished: it had been a full-time post, but now one of the officers filled the post instead, besides performing his usual military duties. (The officers were elected to these posts at Party branch meetings.)

In this way the number of links in the chain of the Party apparatus in the Regiment was reduced as part of the reorganisation of the political machinery in the forces. For the military command, this was a real achievement: the junior commanders could breathe freer and could take action without the *Zampolit*'s treading on their toes. It is reasonable to infer that this was Zhukov's doing. He was

[6e] See p. 41 above.

digging in as Minister of Defence and he demanded that the reduction of effectives should not spare the political apparatus. Some of our ex-officers were of the opinion, however, that Zhukov's appointment as Defence Minister did not lead to any marked change in the relations between the C.O.s and the political institutions in Army units. There may have been a change at the top, they said, due to the internal struggles in the leadership, but it was not specially felt in the units. Others who were interviewed contradicted this and stressed that in Zhukov's time the commander's status was strengthened as against the *Zampolit* in the units and formations. This was insisted on precisely by the Colonel who was himself a political worker. I consider his testimony important, coming as it does from someone who was on the inside of the Party-political machine.

What was going on at this period was a silent test of strength over the interpretation of "unity of command": a struggle over the commander's power to command his unit or formation independently, without interference on the part of the political machine and the Party organisations, which put Party control before all other considerations. The commanders certainly received encouragement in this struggle from Defence Minister Zhukov, who more than once made his views on the matter public. We shall cite, for example, his appearance at the Party conference of the Moscow MD in January 1956, when he said:

> Certain efforts have been made in the MD to bring official acts of the commanders under criticism in Party meetings. Such efforts have to be condemned. In supporting strict officers and generals, the mission we are undertaking is to strengthen the commanders' entire authority.[7]

*Discipline.* All the ex-officers interviewed were agreed that discipline was very much tightened up when Zhukov headed the Armed Forces. The change was a drastic one: heavy sentences were dealt

---

7 *Krasnaya Zvezda*, 25 January, 1956. *Apud* Merle Fainsod, *How Russia is Ruled*, Harvard University Press, Cambridge, Mass., 1963, pp. 483-84.

## The Fight for Greater Autonomy

out even to higher ranks who did not maintain proper discipline. More and more, the commander's order was something to be obeyed without question. Clear and binding instructions to this effect were issued by the High Command. Under Zhukov, the *Zampolit* could not discuss the commander's orders. All the men interviewed emphasised that this was a changed atmosphere.

The military writer, U.P. Petrov, accuses Zhukov of issuing instructions that were opposed to the Party line:

> Zhukov took to ignoring the permanent regulations instructing the Party organisations in the Army and Navy to permeate all aspects of battle preparedness. The Communists were forbidden to discuss problems connected with Army training or to uncover shortcomings in battled preparedness and Army discipline at meetings and conferences. Because of their criticisms of shortcomings in training and Army service, they were made strictly responsible and were even discharged from the Armed Forces.[8]

Even Y.V., who said that the units were not aware of any change in the relations between the C.O.s and the political workers, agreed that "unity of command" took on real significance in Zhukov's time and that there was a noticeable decline in the standing of the *Zampolit*. Many instances had occurred in the early 1950's where Brigade *Zampolits* were promoted to the rank of Colonel, chiefly to give them a rank equal to that of their commanders. Zhukov said very simply, there is only one head of Brigade — and promotion of *Zampolits* stopped. This reform too helped raise the status of the commanders.

Other accusations levelled at Zhukov after his deposition late in 1957 included the following:

> From 1954 on, the Marxist-Leninist instruction-groups in officers' training were unjustifiably suppressed. Senior commanders would appear only infrequently for lectures and

---

8 Petrov, *op. cit.*, p. 463.

talks to the officers on Marxist-Leninist theoretical problems. The ideological education activity of the *Zampolit* often became purely administrative instead.[9]

This accusation against Zhukov was certainly exaggerated. The Marxist-Leninist instruction groups were not suppressed in all the military schools or in all the units. Many commanders apparently refrained from touching this hallowed activity, and I have more than one testimony on this. In the mechanised formation on Sakhalin there was no change: under Zhukov as well Marxist-Leninist instruction was still being given to groups of senior officers at formation level and to junior officers at regimental level. Neither was there any change in Marxist-Leninist instruction in the period in question in the Signals Regiment attached to the MD Command.

*The Resolutions of the XX Congress* of the Communist Party of the Soviet Union in February 1965 condemning the Stalin personality cult had the effect of strengthening the military commanders' position in their test of strength with the political workers and institutions. The texts of Khrushchev's secret speech and of the Congress Resolutions were read out at Party meetings in the Army in circulars from the Central Committee even before they were made public. These circulars showed in detail how the personality cult had led to transformations against the Leninist norms of the Party. They also laid stress on the commanders' share in the victory over the Fascist enemy, and in our officers' view this gave the commanders new courage: till then the credit for winning the war had always gone to the Party and its leaders alone. The fact that these circulars were read out and the shock thereby administered to faithful Party members heartened the commanders and strengthened their position. Col. Y. V., who was very active in the Party

---

9 *The Communist Party of the Soviet Union and the Development of the Soviet Armed Forces, 1917–1964*, Voyenizdat, Moscow, 1965, p. 419 (Russian).

and had been a member of the Party Bureau of his Division, recounts his feelings at the time:

> The shock to the faithful — and to me personally as one of them — was so great that I did something absolutely unheard-of: at the meeting of the Party *"aktiv"* in the Division where the circular from the Central Committee was read out, I got up to speak — even though it had not been settled ahead of time that I should be one of those to take part in the discussion. The usual arrangement was for the representative of the Political Section to fix who was going to speak, that is to say, who would support the Resolution he would put to the meeting. More than this, I spoke against the line signalled in the Central Committee circular — I said it was simply not possible that Stalin should have led the Party and the State for so many years and now suddenly everything was reversed and everything was so very bad. After this extraordinary showing of mine, I was under supervision for three months and kept under control: they laid off me only when Khrushchev said in a Chinese newspaper that Stalin had also done some good things. From then on I stopped believing in what the leadership said and I came to see that the driving force was their personal fight for power.

Publication of Khrushchev's "secret" speech and the XX Congress Resolutions led to an erosion of Party influence in the Armed Forces. In order to counteract this, the Party was called on to strengthen its regular activity in the Party branches in the Army.

*The "Instruction".* The Central Committee had once made it a practice to put out an important basic document known as the "Instruction", which was sent to all Party organisations in the Army and Navy, and which laid down practical guide-lines for specific action in the Armed Forces. These standing orders of the Party in the Army had not been changed since 1934: There had several times been thoughts of refurbishing this by now out-dated document, which did not reflect the many changes that had occurred since its issue in the structure of the Armed Forces and the conditions of Party activity in the forces. Under Stalin, however, it was possible to get along without changing the "Instruction", and the idea of doing something about it was dropped. Now that a real effort was called for to reinforce the tasks and powers of the Party organisations in the Army, after Stalin's death and after the revelations of the XX Congress, the absence of up-to-date guidelines was a problem. The Central Committee therefore decided to issue a new version of the "Instruction", intended to "strengthen the Party's leading role in the Armed Forces and to raise the level of Party activity in the Army and Navy."[10]

The new document was authorised by the Central Committee in April 1957. The full text was not made public but it is clear from sections quoted in *Red Star* of 12 May 1957 that the new "Instruction" stressed the supreme rule of the Party and the Secretariat. It laid down that the MPA acted in the Army as a Section of the Central Committee with independent status. At the same time, however, it also laid down that the Commanding Officer was responsible for both military and political training and that no criticism of his orders and instructions would be permitted at Party meetings. This concession to the professional soldier must have had Zhukov's blessing. Even in the process of buttressing MPA authority, Khrushchev's difficult situation inside the leadership early in 1957 obliged him to make concessions to the senior officer corps.[11]

It is the view of some of our ex-officers that many commanders had their faith shaken not so much in Stalin as in his successors and in the sacrosanct character of the Party these men were the leaders of. This loss of faith was to be seen in their indifference to Party activity and their efforts to get out of branch meetings and even meetings of the *"aktiv"*. "We'd simply had enough of this game — before that we'd been very active in the Party," claims Col. Y. V.

10  Petrov, *op. cit.*, p. 456.
11  Fainsod, *op. cit.*, p. 484, quotes *Kransnaya Zvezda* of 12 May 1957.

## Historiography of the Great Patriotic War

A focal issue in the senior officers' fight was the question, "How did the USSR win the war?" or more exactly "Who in the USSR won the war?"[11a] The commanders wanted to regain the badge of courage and the laurels of victory that they felt were their due.

Stalin's propaganda machine had seen to it that the military achievements and the glorious victory of the Armed Forces should all be credited to the head of the Party, the great leader of the Soviet Union, and to him alone. Set formulas were created for this purpose. The original and main source of these formulas, according to a student of the Soviet historiography of the war, was the speech Stalin delivered in his election "constituency" in Moscow on 9 February 1946. The speech was a sort of manifesto of the re-birth of the Party at the centre of Soviet life. Stalin declared that the war had been "the test of the Soviet system". Victory had been won "not by the courage of the troops or the sacrifices of the population, but principally thanks to the political wisdom of the Party and thanks to the strength of the system that this wise policy had created."[12]

With unfailing persistence, all mention of the senior commanders' share in the victory had been progressively reduced until it was completely forgotten. The most outstanding Commanders had been removed from key positions and sent away to remote outposts far from the public eye. Now, with the tyrant gone, these men began to take thought and to work to change the picture of their part in the war. Commanders, theoreticians and military historians started on the tremendous task of research into the tremendous war, analysis of its strategy, its operational planning, the operative decisions taken and the conduct of the campaign. In Stalin's time, there was no way of writing a history of the war based on research and

---

[11a] It is difficult to discern any particular change on this issue by the end of 1957, so we shall not limit ourselves here to the specific period of this Chapter.

[12] Matthew P. Callagher. *The Soviet History of World War II*, London, Frederick A. Praeger, p. 39.

critical analysis, since one was not permitted to criticise decisions of the High Command and in particular of the Supreme Commander, nor could one analyse the considerations that led to the decisions' being reached. It was of course also forbidden to treat the preparations — or lack of them — on the eve of the war and the conduct of the first phase. Everything that was published referred only to campaigns that were successful, except for two campaigns of 1942 that did not succeed — the one in the Dimiansk region and the one in the Kertch Peninsula. Stalin contended that in both instances the commanders did not carry out the instructions of the High Command.

Marshal Malinovsky, when Minister of Defence, in an address to the Frunze Military Academy in November 1958, referred to the historical publications on the war in Stalin's day more in sorrow than in anger: "It is unfortunate that many of our military historians — and officers too who handle the pen with a greater or lesser degree of mastery — were not accustomed to analysing events critically. Thus there came into being colourless, one-sided, inflated theories that do not provide adequate enlightenment."[13]

The historiography of the war developed into a very large body of writings, chiefly after the XX Congress. The Head of the Military History Section of the General Staff, A. Grilev, told a Party conference ("consultation") of military historians who met in March 1965 to discuss the methodology of military-historical research that in the twenty years since the war ended no less than 4,500 items of military history had been published — essays, pamphlets, articles and 400 large research monographs.[14] At this conference A. Samsonov said that up to the XX Congress, Soviet military-historical science had been in a bad way but that since then the situation had changed for the better.[15]

Years had to pass after Stalin's death for it to become possible

---

13 Marshal Malinovsky, Review of Military History, No. 2, 1959, p. 25.
14 Col. A. Grilev, *Some Methodological Research Problems*, Journal of Military History, No. 7, 1965, p. 6.
15 A. Samsonov, Journal of Military History, No. 7, 1965, p. 101.

to do serious research on the war, despite the large number of military historians who occupied themselves with the subject. At this 1965 conference, Air Force Major General Kopitin stated that over two hundred people were working in the military publishers library alone, 108 of them with doctorates or higher degrees, 80 of them commanders and political workers.[16]

Many Commanders took advantage of the freer atmosphere and began publishing their personal reminiscences and articles on the campaign that they had conducted. According to Kopitin, 80 such memoirs appeared in the years from 1959 to 1965. Although the writers hardly displayed an excess of objectivity, these publications embraced vastly interesting material for a better understanding of the scale of the Soviet High Command effort in the war, the use it made of the experience garnered and its professional military level. In the pages of the military history review, the historians addressed themselves to a many-faceted evaluation of the roles and actions of the commanders in the war and also of their characteristic personal traits. Garilev stressed in the above-mentioned address[17] that one of the most important problems of military-historical research was to reveal the role of the higher ranking commander: "In the Army, far more than in any other public sphere, what is effective is the will-power and the action, the character and qualities of the single commander."[17a]

In the writings assessing the commanders and their share in the victory, the influence is evident of the relations between the Party leadership and the Army heads and of the silent struggle between them which we have so often referred to and which sometimes "went public" at various stages in the post-Stalin period. In fact, the history writing was constantly brought into line with the leaders' current needs in this struggle of theirs. The assessments of the share

---

16 Major-General in the Air Force A. Kopitin, Journal of Military History, No. 7, 1965, p. 101.
17 Grilev, *loc. cit.*, p. 12.
17a By "the single commander" he does not mean the individual commander. He is referring to the famous "unity of command", when the commander gives orders that have to be obeyed.

of leaders and commanders in strategic and operational planning were unhesitatingly altered from time to time according to the needs of the moment. Nor had the writers any qualms over criticising or altering the earlier assessments or in applying stereotyped, uncomplimentary epithets to men who had been pushed out or whom the leaders no longer delighted to honour.

The outstanding example of this process is the narration of the great campaign on the Volga — the Battle of Stalingrad — without question among the decisive campaigns in the whole of World War II. Immediately after the war, the military historians wrote with the absolute certainty typical of the period that the planning of the Red Army counter-attack on the Volga was worked out by Stalin himself personally. Later on, after his death, this constatation was amended. In treating this subject, the editors of the official History of the Great Patriotic War cut down Stalin's share in planning the campaign and not only his share but also that of the High Command and the whole General Staff, so as to create the impression that the main role in the counter-attack was played by the Command of the Stalingrad Front. Moreover, the editors gave the Stalingrad Front Military Council the credit for "introducing a series of proposals and considerations which were among the most important in the strategic planning of the campaign on the three fronts that took part in the counter-attack."[18] It comes as no surprise to discover that Khrushchev was a member of the Stalingrad Front Military Council. He clearly felt the need to have his name glorified and his part in the victory in the war for the fatherland magnified, and in particular to diminish the share of Supreme Headquarters and of Zhukov. In these efforts of his to spotlight the importance of the Command of the Front and the importance of his own personal share in planning the campaign, thereby putting in the shade the share of Stalin and of Stalin's Headquarters Command and the General Staff, Khrushchev was supported by senior officers who commanded on the Stalingrad front, such as Yeremen-

18 *History of the Great Patriotic War of the Soviet Union, 1941–1945,* Voyenizdat, Moscow, 1961, Vol. 3, pp. 17–19 (Russian).

ko, Chuikov, Malinovsky[19] and others (sometimes referred to in the West as "the Stalingrad group"). Over against them, Zhukov, Vasilevsky and others affirmed the opposite. Zhukov wrote:[20]

> The basic and decisive share in the overall planning and in ensuring the execution of the counter-attack at Stalingrad belongs with absolute certainty to the High Command Headquarters and to the General Staff.

And Vasilevsky wrote:[21]

> Headquarters and the General Staff went through the whole campaign with great ability, holding firm to their purpose. The precisely worked-out plan of campaign displayed originality of conception and profound operational-strategic content. ... The fact that Stalin was in command of Headquarters gave the plan of campaign added weight and value.

Only a year after Khrushchev had been deposed and the last volume had been published of the History of the Great Patriotic War, a new work appeared with the same title as its predecessor, but somewhat shortened, which treated the subject of the Stalingrad counter-attack as follows:

> The Headquarters of the Supreme Commander, while bringing together the forces and the means for the projected counter-attack, simultaneously worked out the planning that was to put into effect. By Mid-September the High Command delegated its representatives, General Zhukov and Vasilevsky,

---

19 Malinovsky later changed his stand and in an article of 2 January 1963 he stressed the role of HQ in planning the campaign and even Zhukov's participation, without any excessive emphasis on the role of Khrushchev. This can perhaps be seen as the beginning of Malinovsky's disenchantment with Khrushchev and of the split between them.
20 G. K. Zhukov, *Memories and Reflections*, Novosty Press, Moscow, 1971, p. 400 (Russian).
21 A. Vasilevsky, *My Entire Life's Work*, Politizdat, Moscow, 1973, p. 268 (Russian).

to the Volga battle zone. They were to study the exact situation at the front, examine the troops preparadeness to pass over from the defensive to the counter-attack and decide on the additional means needed for this purpose. At the end of September, Headquarters discussed the results of their journey and drew up the plan for the projected counter-attack in very general outline. The continuation of the planning work was conducted by the General Staff. ... The Commanders of the Armies were also called in to cooperate, and later on the Military Councils and Staffs of the Fronts in the region as well; the comments of these last complemented, completed and concretised the HQ directives. Thus the strategic plan was the outcome of a great creative effort of the collective Command.[22]

One thing that is clear in this version is the need of those who deposed Khrushchev to diminish his stature and to strip him of the cloak of the great strategist that he had tried to put on.

The swing of the pendulum in the assessments of the share of the different senior commanders in the planning of the campaign was also influenced, interestingly enough, by something not specifically Soviet — the ancient rivalry between field commanders and General Staff — *Staebler und Truppiere* — in German military historiography. The special Soviet contribution was of course the Party: besides the military, the Party people appeared on both sides of the barricades, often exploiting the rivalry in order to further their own personal careers and boost themselves at a time of struggle within the leadership.

A severe critic of these procedures wrote in 1965:

> Exaggeration of Stalin's role at one moment and exaggeration later of the role of the Stalingrad Front Command in plan-

---

22 *History of the Great Patriotic War of the Soviet Union, 1941–1945. Abridged,* Institute of Marxism-Leninism, attached to the Party Central Committee, Voyenizdat, Moscow, 1965, pp. 209–10 (Russian).

ning the counter-attack stemmed from considerations connected with the state of affairs at the moment of writing.[23]

The same critic goes on to give an additional example of suppression of the facts in Volume 3 of the big *History of the Great Patriotic War*, in the account given there of actions planned for the Soviet forces in mid-1943 in the Kursk region. He contends that matters were discussed not only with Khrushchev, Ponomarenko and Rokosovsky but with Zhukov as well, who proposed a well-thought-out plan on how to commit the forces.

The one-sided presentation of the planning of the Volga and Kursk campaigns earned criticism on other occasions in 1965, after Khrushchev's deposition. The critics for their part used terms such as "subjectivism" and "voluntarism", terms of disapproval that had been applied to Khrushchev's style of leadership, in order to cast still further opprobrium on Khrushchev, while they reinstated Zhukov as strategist.

In summing up, it must again be stressed that the senior officers' fight to secure a great degree of professional autonomy should not be regarded as a repudiation of the Party as guide and leader in the vanguard of the State, the Army and the people. The contest was basically one between differing perceptions on the part of the military commanders on the one hand and of the Party on the other as to the powers and the authority that should be accorded to each of them, both in professional military decisions at the highest levels and in day to day Army life in the units and the formations.

The commander's perception stemmed from his training, which was meant to fit him to prepare the military unit entrusted to his command to carry out combat missions or other war tasks, enable him to lead it successfully in war and qualify him to be responsible for its actions. In the natural way of things, a military commander does not doubt that he is in sole command of the

---

23 A. Korotkov, *Party Considerations in Military Historical Science*, Journal of Military History, No. 10, 1965, p. 6.

military unit — be it Regiment, Division or Army — which he is appointed to train, prepare and lead into battle. Accordingly he will fight for his right to act independently, to give orders that will not be 'discussed' in the Party *'aktiv'*, the Political Section or Political Administration, something he regards as harmful to discipline and 'unity of command'. This last indeed exists mainly in theory and is seriously eroded by constant interference from the Party-political channel. The commander is embittered at being robbed of too many training hours in the day to the detriment of battle readiness and he tries to cut down the loss. He wants the promotions to go through of the officers he recommends, since as commander, he can judge their qualifications better than the political apparatus; he knows too that this issue largely decides his standing in the eyes of his subordinates.

Over against this view of things, the Party holds that for the sake of ensuring the loyalty of the Armed Forces to leadership by the Party, it must utilise its supervisory organisations and apparatus to prevent any possibility that a position might be created where commanders would have unlimited control of the units entrusted to their command.

These contradictory perceptions come into conflict in daily life, and the clash between them produces the unavoidable friction between the Party organs and the Army commanders that we have delineated in this Chapter.

## CHAPTER V

## THE RISE OF MARSHAL ZHUKOV

The status of the Armed Forces among the political power-centres in the years 1953 to '57 was closely bound up with the personality of Marshal Zhukov, because of the leading part taken by him in the fight of the officer corps for a greater degree of professional autonomy. The rise of this great soldier, the hero of so many famous Soviet victories, to the very top level of the military and political leadership is a matter of the greatest interest, and his personality and career deserve a chapter to themselves.

His childhood and youth left their mark on the man and the path he took. The early stages of his military and political development helped fix his ideological stance and his military thinking and set his course as a future commander.

### Childhood and Youth

Georgi Konstantinovich was born in 1896 to a family of poor peasants in Strelkovo village in the Kaluga District. He recounts in his memoirs[1] that his father was the village shoemaker and also worked as an agricultural labourer. His mother was obliged to hire herself out for hard, menial work. The small piece of land they owned was not very productive and when their old house collapsed they had to sell their cow to pay for building a new one. Georgi began to help with the harvest at the age of seven, but all the same he was sent to the church school in the nearby village. The family was

---

1  Georgi Konstantinovich Zhukov, *Memories and Reflections*, Novosty Press, Moscow, 1971 (Russian). It should be kept in mind that Zhukov's memoirs, like all similar material in the USSR, went through censorship and painstaking editing before publication.

so poor that they could not even buy a school-bag for the new pupil. His father was a hard man and did not spare the rod. The child took the punishments meted out to him in silence and would not ask to be forgiven, even when the blows dealt him were redoubled. Here were the first signs of the obstinacy, pride and willpower that were to be permanent traits of Zhukov's character.

The boy loved to go hunting and fishing but he also kept on learning. He finished school at the age of ten with an excellent report. In honour of the occasion, his father made him a pair of high boots and his mother a new shirt. This completed the schooling provided by his parents. Having learnt to read and write, the boy must now learn a trade. So he was sent to Moscow at the age of eleven to be apprentice and servant to a well-to-do uncle, who owned workshops and did business in the fur trade. The apprentice worked long hours and suffered many a beating, but he was industrious and made good progress. At the same time he attended evening classes in general subjects at the elementary school level and passed the examinations at the age of fourteen. His ability to retain what he learnt and his perseverance in pursuit of the goals he set himself were already clear.

Zhukov became a craftsman earning relatively good pay. He carried out the jobs entrusted to him and secured his employers' confidence. News of political agitation among the workers did not interest him. In what he writes about his life on the eve of the first World War and in its opening stages, he shows no sign of rebellion or resentment over his position as an artisan: "In those years my orientation on political questions was weak; but it was clear to me that *Izvestia* and *Pravda* expressed the interests of the workers and peasants."[2]

*In the Army*

*Called up, 1915.* When war broke out, Zhukov was not seized by patriotic fervour and did not volunteer for the army. He went on

2  *Ibid.*, p. 27.

working as a furrier until he was called up to the Cavalry in August 1915. The hard life in the Cavalry suited him, and the old saying, "Cossack, put up with things and you'll get to be Hetman", seemed to fit his temperament and his future. At the close of his training, in the spring of 1916, Zhukov was chosen as one of the thirty best men in the battalion and was sent on a course for NCOs — "I'm sure you'll make a good NCO," his platoon commander told him.

*1916, Wounded, Decorated.* In his memoirs, Zhukov pays tribute to the care with which NCO candidates were chosen and the excellent training they received. It was not until September 1916 that he took part in active fighting. In October he was wounded on patrol when his horse stepped on a mine. He received his first two decorations — the George Cross, twice — for his wound and for capturing a German officer. This ended his actual combat experience in the first World War.

*1918, Joins the Red Army.* We come now to the revolution of February 1917. In his book, Zhukov reiterates that he took no particular line at that time, that he did not know where he stood on political problems, but for all that he thought that only the Bolsheviks could give the people peace, land and freedom. Though he was elected head of the Soldiers' Committee by the men in his company and was elected by his platoon to represent it on the Battalion Council (which turned Bolshevik), he says nothing of any political activity on his part in all this stormy period. The Battalion Committee gave the soldiers their discharge and Zhukov was back in his village before the end of the year. He fell ill and it was only in August 1918 that he volunteered for the Red Army.

*1919, Joins the Bolshevik Party.* In March 1919, Zhukov was accepted as a member of the Bolshevik Party. He writes: "From then on I tried to subordinate all my thoughts, aspirations and actions to my duties as a member of the Party, and when it came to confronting our country's enemies, then I reminded myself that the Party demanded of me that I be a model Communist in the service of my people."³ For all its stilted wording, this declaration has the ring of sincerity.

*The Civil War.* For the greater part of the civil war, Zhukov fought as an NCO in Timoshenko's regiment. He was wounded and returned to active service. At the beginning of 1920 he was sent on a cavalry commanders' course, but remained on active combat duty while on the course. In August of that year he was made platoon commander and not long after company commander. His slow promotion in this period is all the more surprising when it is compared with the advancement of other commanders, his contemporaries, and particularly so since he had joined up in 1918 and his background was a model one — worker and soldier, decorated for combat action, excellent NCO. Moreover, Zhukov volunteered for the Army in the month when Trotsky announced that all NCOs would be made platoon commanders and would be given every opportunity to get to the top as professional soldiers. If we compare Zhukov's career at this point with that of other commanders, we find, for example, that Chiukov, who like Zhukov was of peasant stock and joined the Red Army in 1918 and the Party in '19, was already second-in-command of a regiment; he became regimental commander while Zhukov was still an NCO and by 1925 had already graduated from the Frunze Academy. Malinovsky, a townsman who entered the Red Army not in the crucial year of 1918 like Zhukov but in 1919, was already in command of a battalion and then of a regiment during the Civil War while Zhukov had not yet got any higher than company commander. Rokosovsky's story was similar to Malinovsky's — true, Rokosovsky was the son of a railway-worker. Timoshenko's career was meteoric: only a year older than Zhukov, like him of peasant stock, with even less formal schooling, he emerged from the partisan groups that formed the Red Guard to become Divisional Commander during the civil war and Corps Commander as early as 1925, when Zhukov was still only regimental commander.

3   *Ibid.*, p. 51.

No explanation is forthcoming for Zhukov's remaining in relative obscurity in spite of his combination of peasant background, some education, combat experience and specific training during the civil war itself. In the civil war period about 400,000 men, some of them NCOs and some new recruits with no previous military experience at all, were put through short courses for postings at officer level, while Zhukov was not given command of a platoon until two years after he volunteered for the Army. It was only in 1923 that he was made second-in-command of a cavalry regiment and shortly thereafter commander.

His being given command of a regiment affected him deeply. He believed that he was not sufficiently schooled or trained for so responsible a post: he considered the regiment as the basic combat unit that combines all the types of land forces, and he thought of command of a regiment as a most important step towards acquiring mastery of the art of war. He tackled his task with all his formidable energy, will-power and persistence, showing exceptional organising ability in bringing his regular army unit up to the level of battle readiness. He went without sleep, extending his military instruction, reading especially in the field of tactics, in the belief that he lacked theoretical formation to meet the demands a regimental commander is faced with. His revered model was Bluecher, distinguished Bolshevik, gifted commander, marvellous comrade.

*Regimental Commander.* The seven years as Regimental Commander during which Zhukov took two long, basic courses for cavalry commanders very largely afforded him the background and training he felt he needed for his future actions. On the first of these courses, he still found difficulty in preparing a lecture on "The basic factors influencing the theory of the art of war" — according to him he did not know how to tackle the subject and had to ask his comrades for help. Marshal Bagramyan, who was in one of these courses along with Zhukov, said that he was considered one of the most gifted in the group. He said that Zhukov was not only endowed with strong will-power but with a capacity for original thinking as well. More than once he surprised his comrades with a new idea in the field of tactics and was able to defend his ideas with logical arguments.[4] Bagramyan had no inducement to flatter Zhukov when he came to publish his memoirs forty years later and the description throws light on Zhukov's formation as a commander.

Zhukov continued to be conscious of his weakness in Marxist-Leninist theory, but nevertheless he was given "united (or "sole") command" of his regiment in 1926. This meant that he was to be responsible for Party tasks in his unit as well as military ones. Perhaps those who recommended him were not seeking over-much expertise in questions of ideology or he may not have proved an easy partner in double harness. "Unity of command" had been introduced in 1924, and Zhukov's views on the matter remained constant throughout his career:

> The most important thing in the 1924 military reform was the institution in practice of unity of command in the Armed Forces. This meant increased responsibility for the commander *vis-à-vis* the Party for both the political and the military aspects of Army life, and along with this it strengthened the discipline and the combat readiness of the Armed Forces.[5]

Zhukov's regiment became known for excellent performance, thanks to his untiring exertions, his exacting discipline and his meticulous attention to detail, and it was chosen as one of the first two experimental armoured regiments in the Soviet Army. It was said that Stalin himself chose Zhukov and Pavlov for this purpose.[6] It is not clear exactly when these regiments began their trial manoeuvres, which were carried out in the Byelorussian District — Zhukov does not refer to it in his memoirs at all. The outstanding author-

---

4 A. Bagramyan, *How the War Began*, Voyenizdat, Moscow, 1971, p. 14 (Russian).
5 Zhukov, *op. cit.*, pp. 87–88.
6 P. Ruslanov, *Marshal Zhukov*, Socialist Announcer, New York, April 1955, p. 37 (Russian).

ity in this field, John Erickson, states that the first light tanks (the T-18) reached the Soviet Army in 1927.[7]

In these years, Zhukov distinguished himself as regimental commander, taking part in Division and District manoeuvres, which obliged him, as he says, to go into operational problems. In 1939 he took part in an extension course for senior officers in the Frunze Military Academy, applying himself to the study of works on military theory by senior commanders like Shaposhnikov, Tukhachevsky and Traiandaphilov. The way was thus opened to his appointment to higher posts. For about a year in the 1930's, Zhukov was regimental commander in Rokosovsky's Division. Rokosovsky gave him high praise, recommended his promotion, and remained a friend of his from then on. For some two years, Zhukov was Second-in-Command of Cavalry and devoted himself to developing the conception and practice of the use of armoured Divisions. He then returned to the Byelorussian MD as Divisional Commander for three or four years. The story goes that he was chief Soviet observer in Spain in 1936,[8] but he makes no reference to this in his book. In 1937 he was very active in deliberations on the role of the armour in combat; together with Shaposhnikov, he favoured the concept of forming armour concentrations and giving the armoured formations an independent role alongside motorised infantry, as against the opposite concept of distributing the tanks among the different units as support for the infantry.

*Corps Commander.* In 1938, after a year and a half as Corps Commander, Zuhkov was appointed Second-in-Command, Byelorussian MD. He is thought to have spent a period as adviser to the Chinese Army but he gives no hint of this either.

Zhukov has this to say of his time as Corps Commander: "I devoted myself to studying questions of operational strategy, since I was of the opinion that my attainments in this sphere were limited.

---

7 John Erickson, *The Soviet High Command, 1918–1941.* The Macmillan Company, London, 1962, p. 184

8 Otto Preston Chaney, *Zhukov,* University of Oklahoma Press, Oklahoma, 1971, p. 27.

I recognised that I needed to study Party-political questions, and I spent nights reading the Marxist-Leninist classics. I found this study very difficult indeed, particularly Marx's *Das Kapital* and Lenin's philosophy, but my sense of responsibility constrained me to make the effort to master this material."[9]

The treason trials and the execution of practically the entire senior command in 1937 was to haunt Zhukov all his days, and a score of years later when he thought the power was in his grasp he tried to redress some of the wrong done to the commanders he admired. At the time, however, he was among those whose path to swifter promotion was now cleared. He was given opportunities to prove his military gifts and to display his virtues as a commander, and these brought him up the very top echelons. In the great patriotic war against Germany he was to rise to the rank of First Deputy to the Supreme Commander, Stalin.

*1939, the Khalkin-Gol Campaign*: Zhukov's first operational test as commander in the field was against the Japanese Army on the borders of Outer Mongolia in July and August 1939. At the beginning of July, a limited Japanese initiative was met with a speedy and smashing counter-blow by all the available Soviet forces. This victorious if limited engagement was followed up in August by a campaign planned by Zhukov in its every detail. He wanted to make sure: he asked for considerable reinforcements of elite forces and he got them within weeks — relatively little delay, given the remoteness of the region and the communication difficulties. Every logistic resources was strained to effect this re-equipment and reinforcement, an effort of organisation of a type not exactly common in the Soviet Army at that date. Zhukov brought all his exceptional ability into play in exploiting the features of the terrain and elements of deception and camouflage. He made use for the first time in the Soviet Forces of the specific qualities of armour acting in combination and coordination with other land forces and the air force.

My belief is that Zhukov was always more of a field commander

---

9   Zhukov, *op. cit.*, p. 143.

than a Sstaff officer. One trait of his, however, was probably more a matter of his personal history and character than of his military formation — his indifference to the rate of casualties; for him the cost in casualties was not an important element when weighed against the aim to be achieved. He changed commanders twice over at Khalkin-Gol in order to have another attack made, when the Division had suffered very heavy losses and the two previous commanders had not been able to get the Division to attack again.[10]

*"Hero of the Soviet Union"* — *1940, General of Army*: On his return to Moscow after the victorious Khalkin-Gol campaign, Zhukov was decorated "Hero of the Soviet Union" and had the privilege of being congratulated by Stalin himself. He was made Second-in-Command of the Kiev Special MD and later commander. In June 1940 and before the customary interval had elapsed for a promotion in rank, the Council of Commissars of the Soviet Union appointed him to the rank of General of an Army.

His successive advances embued Zhukov with a measure of self-confidence that he had lacked before.[11] He spoke out boldly, attacking the system of Political Commissars and demanding "unity of command". Clearly he could only do this because of the general recognition of his capacities.[12] Bagramyan was appointed Head of Operations, Kiev MD, shortly before Zhukov completed his

---

10 Ruslanov, *op. cit.*, p. 70.
11 On Zhukov's service as Commander of the Kiev MD, Lauterbach, author of *These are the Russians*, cited by Chaney (*op. cit.*, p. 65), states that this was the first time that Zhukov appeared not only as a military commander but also as a political leader. He says that Zhukov directed matters with the fullest self-confidence in the knowledge that his superiors had given him *carte blanche* — the Ukrainian Party leaders looked to him for leadership and that was what he gave them. This seems to me much exaggerated. Without some solid proof, it is difficult to accept that in the regime that prevailed in the USSR in 1940, Stalin would have allowed the Party leaders of a Republic as "sensitive" as the Ukraine — the second largest in the USSR — to look for leadership to the MD Commander and not to the real leader. First Secretary Stalin in person.
12 Chaney, *op. cit.*, p. 66.

term as Commander there, and he writes: "Zhukov's successes did not surprise me. He not only possessed outstanding military gifts and high intelligence but was also endowed with a will of iron. When he had a goal in view, he marched towards it, never turning aside."[13] When Zhukov left the MD, says Bagramyan, it was clear to everyone that the Army people, the Party and the State representatives in Kiev had all the deepest esteem for him.[14]

*January 1941, Chief of General Staff*: Zhukov was appointed Chief of General Staff in January 1941 and a month later was elected an alternate member of the Central Committee of the Communist Party. As soon as he took up his post as Chief of General Staff, he at once pressed on with his sustained fight for "unity of command", for strengthening the authority of the military Commanding Officer as against the political officer. Zhukov wrote a key article in *Pravda* on 23 February 1941 in honour of the 23rd anniversary of the Red Army, in which he pointed to the measure taken in August 1940 to restore "unity of command" and stressed the necessity of doing away with constant interference from the Political Commissars. He called for wider rights and authority for the commanders and for stricter military discipline.

### 1941 — The German Invasion

"Unity of command" was abolished and the system of Military Commissars re-introduced on 16 July 1941, less than a month after the German attack. In view of Zhukov's consistent stand on the issue, it is of interest to note that he did not offer any opposition or even criticism. In his memoirs he reports the abolition of "unity of command" without comment, in transparently Party style: "In July, in order to strengthen Party-political action and reinforce Party influence in the Armed Forces, the institutions for political propaganda in the Army were organised anew and the institution

---

13   Bagramyan, *op. cit.,* p. 15.
14   *Ibid.*

of Military Commissars re-activated."[15] The reason for his acquiescence must be sought in the tremendous shock of the surprise invasion, the prevailing panic and lowered morale, and the early, bitter defeats — it is hardly probable that he approved. He could only have been angered by a step of Stalin's that he saw as proof of lack of faith in the Army commanders.[16]

The severe defeats suffered by the Red Army in the summer of 1942 and the lessons learnt from them finally produced a series of changes, and outstanding among them precisely renewal of "unity of command."[17] Erickson also lists new Field Service and Combat Regulations, revision of tactical doctrines, improvement of Staff procedures. These changes, in Erickson's view, were accepted because the influence of the younger generals was now beginning to tell. Though circumstances did not seem favourable, the commanders, and mainly the younger ones, waged a struggle to "give the officer back his proper place."

They were aroused and angered by the rigidity of the Supreme Command, concentrating the whole conduct of the war in its hands intervening in tactical and operational questions. They complained of the Military Councils' constant interference and the double-headed system of command — the (Political) Military Commissars. They aimed mainly at restoring unity of command,[18] and though the political workers were of course obstinately opposed they had to give way at last. Stalin was now paying more heed to his Generals than he had done previously.[19]

"Unity of command" was restored, as we have said, and the

---

15 Zhukov, *op. cit.*, p. 270.
16 Chaney, *op. cit.*, pp. 91–93.
17 See Chapter 4.
18 Erickson refers to a specific letter addressed to the Central Committee by Colonel Voronov from the Stalingrad Front, in which he urges a return to the previous state of affairs: "There is only one path to take — unity of command." Erickson points out that this was certainly not an isolated instance. *The Road to Stalingrad,* Harper and Row Publishers, London, 1975, pp. 371-72.
19 *Ibid.*

post of Military Commissar abolished in October 1942. The system was now called, "complete unity of command." It would be no surprise if Zhukov's hand were seen here — he was, after all, one of the two Marshals closest to Stalin at the time. A Soviet historian says that the change reinforced the commanders' authority and made it possible to strengthen order and discipline in the Armed Forces.[20]

*The Campaigns.* Zhukov's eminence in the hierarchy of command, second only to Stalin, and his part in the final victory cannot be adequately presented in this work. We can do no more than recall the main points of reference in the sequence of his postings: his role in the defence of Leningrad in 1941; the blow he dealt the German Army in its advance on Moscow in the winter of 1941 to '42; his key role in the operational-strategic planning on the eve of the great Battle of Stalingrad and in the gigantic campaign that followed in 1942; the Kursk campaign in 1943; the massive offensive in Byelorussia in 1944; and the onslaught on Berlin in 1945.

A very considerable literature has been written both in the USSR and in the West on this great and terrible war, and in these accounts the giant figure of Zhukov stands out very plain. He will go down in history as the strategist who influenced all the decisive campaigns in the hard and protracted fighting on the Eastern Front, a Commander who never lost a battle, one of the greatest soldiers of them all.

The victories won under Zhukov's command earned him an appreciation from the Soviet officer corps that was unique, an almost boundless admiration. Much was said in the Army of his rare gifts as a leader and strategist and even more of his inflexible will-power, the uncompromising discipline he demanded of his

---

20  *The Ideological Action of the Party at the Front, 1941–1945,* Voyenızdat, Moscow, 1961, p. 15 (Russian).  *Apud* Roman Kolkovicz, *The Soviet Military and the Communist Party,* Princeton University Press, 1967, p. 67.

subordinates, his unflinching execution of every mission entrusted to him with a ruthless disregard for difficulties or losses. He became a national hero in the eyes of the Army and the whole people, a symbol of victory, his popularity surpassed only by that of Stalin himself.

## 1946, End of the Chapter

*February — Elected to Supreme Soviet.* In the first elections to the Supreme Soviet after the war, 10 February 1946, every important electoral district included Zhukov in its list of candidates, with the emphasis of course on his services in the war. *Red Star* published the speeches made about Zhukov at "election" meetings, with their well-drilled formulas of praise:

> The Soviet people is well acquainted with the renowned leader, Georgi Konstantinovich Zhukov, whose name is linked with the many great victories of the Red Army. It is natural that we should choose to elect a man so close to us as a most desirable representative of the Soviet people.[21]

Zhukov was elected (along with other commanders) to represent the "Special Electoral District", the Party organisations in the Army.[22] He continued to serve as Commander of the Soviet Occupying Forces in Germany and USSR representative on the Allied Control Council until April 1946. Then he was brought back to Moscow and appointed Commander of the Land Forces. On the 1st of May he stood beside the other leaders and military commanders on the Lenin Mausoleum for the review of the military parade in the Red Square.

*July — Transferred to Odessa MD.* And now in July 1946, only a few short months after Zhukov's appointment at the peak of his fame to be Commander of the Land Forces, *Pravda* published the

---

21 *Krasnaya Zvezda*, 5 January 1946, *apud* Chaney, *op. cit.*, p. 346.
22 Chaney, *op. cit.*, p. 347.

announcement of his transfer to the Odessa MD and his replacement by Marshal Koniev. Why was Zhukov removed from his important military posts and then from the Party Central Committee as well? Of all the conjectures that have been put forward, I incline to accept the simplest and most obvious — that Stalin was jealous of Zhukov, jealous of his popularity as the symbol of victory in the war, confirmed by his election to the Supreme Soviet. As Khrushchev said in his "secret" speech to the XX Congress, Stalin was not prepared to have achievements at the front attributed to anyone but himself.[23] With his pathologically suspicious nature, Stalin was bound to want to remove the conquering hero from public view, to "cut him down to size". Let other senior officers who had also had a share in the victory take note. By demoting the man who had done more than any other to hold the Soviet Army together in the worst years of the war, Stalin showed his chief military advisers that any slightest inclination they might have to turn the Armed Forces into an independent political force would be crushed ruthlessly. It was even said that Stalin ordered Zhukov's portraits removed from all military bases. The Army leadership was to be intimidated and reduced to absolute compliance.[24]

*1949 — Transferred to Urals MD.* In 1949 Marshal Zhukov was transferred to a still more remote post as Commander of the Urals MD. He was now a man wounded to the depths of his being not only by these transfers but even more so by his removal from the Party Central Committee. Years later he at long last voiced his anger over this, when the 1957 Central Committee Plenary session decided to exclude him from the Presidium and for the second time from the Party Central Committee. He thanked his colleagues for pointing out to him the error of his ways, but he bitterly re-

---

23  *Khrushchev Remembers,* translated and edited by Strobe Talbot, Bantam Books, London, New York, Toronto, 1971 (by arrangement with Little, Brown and Company, Boston), p. 648.
24  Malcolmn Mackintoch, *Juggernaut,* Secker and Warburg, London, 1967, p. 267.

jected the contention that he had not learnt the lesson of his previous exclusion:

> In meting out punishment, some comrades have said that I was already excluded from the Central Committee once before, in Stalin's lifetime, and that I did not at that time understand the need to correct those mistakes of mine on account of which I was excluded. Comrades! At that time I did not — I could not — acknowledge that my exclusion from the Central Committee was a proper measure: I did not accept that the charges made against me were well-founded.
> Today it is different. I admit my errors; I have presented the Plenary with a thorough-going acknowledgement of these errors, and I hereby give my word to the Central Committee of the Communist Party that I shall remedy all my shortcomings.[25]

If what Zhukov said here was true — that in 1949 he did not admit any blame and did not acknowledge the propriety of the measures taken against him — then his conduct was indeed exceptional for Stalin's time and is an additional, striking testimony to his courage.

*1952 — Deputy Minister of Defence.* In mid-1952 Stalin took a number of measures to strengthen and give encouragement to the Armed Forces, presumably under the impact of the Korean War and increases in the US Army. A number of senior Soviet officers who had distinguished themselves in World War II were returned to key posts, among them Sokolovsky as Chief of Staff and Zhukov as Deputy Minister of Defence and Inspector-General of the Army. Zhukov's appointment was not published in the press, but his election as an alternate member of the Central Committee in October 1952 showed that Stalin's decision to raise him up from the dust

---

25 *Pravda*, 3 November 1957. I have been unable to find any other material on Zhukov's reactions to his deposition by Stalin.

also held good for the Party hierarchy, and it was this that brought Zhukov's return to the notice of the public.

## Death of Stalin

*Beria Arrested.* On 6 March 1953, on the morrow of Stalin's death, Marshal Bulganin was appointed Minister of Defence, and Marshals Vasilevsky and Zhukov were appointed his First Deputies.[26] Zhukov became once again the dominant figure in the Armed Forces, thanks to his special and renewed prestige in the eyes of the Army and the people. It followed that when the Party Presidium decided three months later to move against their colleague Beria, they were backed by Zhukov and the Army. Zhukov was one of the Generals who arrested Beria — according to Khrushchev, it was he who ordered Beria to raise his hands. Zhukov may well have hated Beria very particularly. One source put this down to "information" against Zhukov that Beria's people supposedly transmitted to Stalin, thus contributing to his downfall.[27] In my view, there is no need to trace Stalin's action to this "information" alone — it would merely have served to spur on his jealousy and suspiciousness.

Preparations for the arrest of Beria had to be made in secret, mainly by concentrating forces loyal to the Army Command so as to neutralise the forces headed by three Interior Ministry Generals, Artemiev, Spiridonov and Smilov, the garrison forces in the Moscow MD, in the city and in the Kremlin.[28] As against this, the Moscow AA defences were commanded by General Moskalenko, an adversary of Beria's, who took part in arresting him. Reports vary concerning which forces were brought in to neutralise Beria's army support in the capital and ensure the success of the opera-

---

26 *Izvestia*, 7 March 1953.
27 Chaney, *op. cit.*, p. 354, gives Colonel Rastvorov as authority for this statement.
28 Mackintosh, *op. cit.*, p. 287.

tion.²⁹ The most reliable account would seem to be that of N.O.²⁹ᵃ on how the Kantomirov Armoured Division, which was stationed only 20 kilometres from Moscow, was brought up and deployed in the environs of the Kremlin. According to N.O., this troops movement was carried out at Zhukov's direct orders to the Divisional Commander over the head of the Moscow MD Commander, and Zhukov followed up this derogation of all ordinary channels of command by directing the Kantomirov Divisional Commander to take orders from then on from him, Zhukov, personally and no-one else. It is very doubtful whether any Divisional Commander in the Armed Forces would have obeyed orders from any other Marshal without first trying to confirm the orders through his own channels of command. As a rule — and most certainly in 1953 — it was customary not to take responsibility on your own shoulders alone but to seek double and redoubled insurance, to secure "cover" and extra backing for yourself in every instance. No-one else but Zhukov could have secured obedience to this most irregular direct command. The matter was perhaps facilitated by the wartime stories in the Command about Zhukov's giving the Divisions direct orders over the heads of their appointed Commanders in the hour of need. Probably the decisive reason for the Divisional Commander's obeying Zhukov's order was that he of course knew that the Moscow MD was commanded by an Interior Ministry General.

*1955 — Zhukov Minister of Defence.* Zhukov's success in executing the manoeuvre that got rid of Beria, which was due in large measure to his personal authority in the Army, marked him as a valuable ally in the contests within the political leadership. His en-

29 Chaney, *op. cit.,* p. 354, says that two Guard Divisions were brought from the Urals MD, where Zhukov had recently been in command. This last fact may give some colour to Chaney's account, but it nevertheless seems highly unlikely that such considerable forces could have been moved unobserved over so great a disttnce, given the presence of MVD representatives in all formations.
29ᵃ The Soviet ex-officer cited in Chapter 2 above.

hanced prestige was signalised by his election as a full member of the Party Central Committee. An important landmark was his appointment as Minister of Defence in February 1955 to succeed Marshal Bulganin, who was put at the head of the Government when Malenkov was ousted. Malenkov's adversaries in the leadership had needed the support of the central personalities among the heads of the Armed Forces — Bulganin and Zhukov. The support had been forthcoming and those who gave it were duly rewarded.

Even before this date, the Army had begun to break out of the state of petrifaction and the obscurity in which it had been confined by Stalin. Atomic arms were being developed and the means for delivering them to their targets. A long overdue debate was initiated on theoretical military doctrine, which went on until the spring of 1955. The internal contest inside the leadership during this period afforded the Army heads a measure of freedom to raise their status and to refurbish the Army's glorious reputation, which had become somewhat tarnished towards the end of Stalin's autocracy. Zhukov played a characteristically bold and energetic role in this shake-up, one that enhanced his standing in the officer corps. He is credited with responsibility for the new stress on modern strategic doctrine on nuclear warfare, the series of articles on changes of doctrine that appeared in military publications after he became Defence Minister were the long-delayed reaction to the "new look" in the USA of 1953 and '54.[30]

Zhukov re-emerged as a political figure too. He gave an interview to a group of American journalists, headed by Reston and Konigsberg, only a few days before his appointment as Minister of Defence, and the interview was published in full a week later in *Pravda*. Marshal Zhukov told the Americans: "A bad peace is preferable to a good quarrel. The time has come to do away with military rivalry. ... It is not worthwhile exchanging

---

30 *Ibid.*, p. 358, n. 49. For this evaluation of Zhukov's standing at this stage, Chaney refers to G. D. Embree, *The Soviet Union between the 19th and 20th Party Congress, 1952–1956*, pp. 192–93, and R. Garthoff, *op. cit.*

military missions — we must first establish relations and reach mutual understanding on political, economic and cultural questions."[31] There can hardly be any doubt that this interview of Zhukov's at this time and what he said had been settled in consultation with the political leadership, if not dictated by them, in spite of the *élan* and assurance with which he spoke. Bringing the popular Zhukov forward and into the limelight as a political figure would help Khrushchev and Bulganin to consolidate their hold on power after Malenkov's removal.

The new Soviet leadership began to put out feelers with the West. In Vienna on 15 May 1955 a political agreement was signed with Austria, by which the USSR and the Western Powers would evacuate their forces from Austrian soil, while Austria for her part undertook to be neutral. This was the first step towards a dialogue between the former wartime allies. The parties now agreed to convene a "summit" meeting of heads of the three Western Powers and the Soviet Union.

*Geneva "Summit" Meeting.* Zhukov was a member of the Soviet delegation to the meeting in Geneva in July 1955, together with Bulganin, Khrushchev, Molotov and Gromyko. Before the composition of the Soviet delegation was made public, President Eisenhower was supposed to have said that if Zhukov were to be present, he would welcome the opportunity to renew his acquaintance with him.[32] Bulganin said, "If he (Zhukov) decides to meet Eisenhower privately during the talks, it's his personal affair — the Soviet Government is not accustomed to directing its people's personal connections."[33]

Zhukov and Eisenhower did meet a number of times in the course of the "summit". The heads of the Soviet delegation were clearly interested that these meetings should take place and en-

---

31 *Pravda,* 13 February 1955.
32 *New York Times,* 15 June 1955, pp. 1–2, *apud* Chaney, *op. cit.,* p. 365.
33 Chaney, *ibid.*

couraged them, obviously hoping that the friendly personal relations that grew up between Zhukov and Eisenhower in 1945 would help now in creating greater confidence in the sincerity of USSR intentions. The U.S. Ambassador to Moscow, Charles Bohlen, took part in the "summit" and acted as interpreter at the meetings between Zhukov and Eisenhower. His opinion was that the Russians brought Zhukov with them as a gesture of friendship to Eisenhower.[34] Eisenhower in his book, *Mandate for Change*, goes so far as to say that the Americans were not sure whether Zhukov might not have been made Minister of Defence and "groomed" for Geneva precisely because of his anticipated influence in putting the Soviet case to him, Eisenhower.[35] He describes the "heavy-handed hints" and tactical moves of the Russian delegation to get him and Zhukov together: a few minutes after the Russians' arrival at a dinner in his (Eisenhower's) honour, he found himself left alone with Zhukov, while the others stayed at a discreet distance.[36] Eisenhower gives his impressions of the changes he saw in Zhukov after the ten years since they met in Germany and Moscow in 1945:

> The first part of our meeting was given over to pleasant reminiscences about the war and immediate post-war events. Once we began to talk about the serious subjects engaging the attention of the conference, however, it became crystal clear that Zhukov was no longer the same man he had been in 1945. In our wartime association he had been an independent, self-confident man who, while obviously embracing Communist doctrine, was always ready to meet cheerfully with me on any operational problem and to cooperate in finding a reasonable solution. This he did on his own; on one occasion he had even abruptly dismissed his political adviser, Andrei Vishinsky, telling him to leave the room so that the two of

---

34 Charles E. Bohlen, *Witness to History, 1929–1969*, Norton and Company, N.C., New York, 1973, p. 385.
35 Dwight D. Eisenhower, *Mandate for Change, 1953–1956*, Doubleday and Company, Inc., New York, 1963, p. 524.
36 *Ibid.*, p. 523.

us might talk confidentially. In many ways it was evident then that Zhukov was just what he appeared to be — a highly important man in the Soviet government, perhaps second only to Stalin himself. During my visit to Moscow in 1945 this evaluation of his position and influence was many times reaffirmed. Now in Geneva, ten years later, he was a subdued and worried man. In a low monotone he repeated to me the same arguments that had been presented to the conference by the chairman of the Soviet delegation. This was not ordinary talk; he spoke as if he was repeating a lesson that had been drilled into him until he was letter-perfect. He was devoid of animation, and he never smiled or joked as he used to do. My old friend was carrying out orders of his superiors. I obtained nothing from this private chat other than a feeling of sadness.[37]

Eisenhower's impression of Zhukov as "a subdued and worried man" may after all have been mistaken — it is certainly not in accord with Zhukov's real position in the highest Soviet leadership at this time. The explanation for his manner during this talk may well be that the conference deliberations on global policy concerned a sphere where Zhukov had no experience, and in order not to make mistakes in face-to-face confrontation with Eisenhower, the experienced statesman, he had indeed learnt his "lessons" by heart and repeated the arguments of the head of his delegation word for word. His experience, self-confidence and leadership were all in military matters, and these were no less in the forefront than they had been in 1945. In political matters Zhukov acquired self-confidence fairly speedily and began to see himself as part of the top-level political leadership of the Soviet Union.

*1956 — Alternate Member, Supreme Soviet Presidium,* Zhukov's high standing in both spheres, the political as well as the military, would seem to be borne out by his addresses on military policy and

[37] *Ibid.,* p. 525.

on the history of World War II, by his place in *Pravda* photographs and at official receptions. His eminence was secure even before the XX Congress in February 1956 and before he was elected first alternate member of the Presidium, in defiance of the accepted rule of alphabetic placing for the alternate members. It was the first time that a professional soldier had risen so high in the political apparatus. His personal preponderance in the new "collective leadership" may have been even greater than indicated by his political title. We must realise, however, that his great qualities as a soldier and all his achievements would not by themselves necessarily have brought him to this eminence. It was made possible by a combination of circumstances: the absence of a popular figure of any stature among Stalin's successors; the importance of the Soviet Armed Forces globally in this period of "peaceful co-existence", and the dependence of Khrushchev and his colleagues on the Army when they had Pokrebyshev and Beria executed. At the XX Congress, Zhukov was one of the few speakers who did not praise Khrushchev — or his report.[38] Whatever the exact weight of the different circumstances we have listed, there is no question but that in 1956 and '57 Zhukov appeared as one of the strongest personalities in the leadership.

Whether or not the public image of Zhukov was a disproportionate and exaggerated reflection of his real influence and power, it was certainly a source of concern to Khrushchev and the Central Committee's Main Political Administration in the Armed Forces. These people feared that Zhukov's popularity and his increasingly firm hold on the Armed Forces might reach the point of endangering Party control over the Forces and even threaten the position of the First Secretary as head of the political leadership.

---

38 These considerations were put forward by Bertram D. Wolfe, *Khrushchev and Stalin's Ghost*, Frederick A. Praeger, New York, 1957, pp. 39–40. It should not be overlooked that Wolfe's book was published before the deposition, when Zhukov was still on his way up. Accordingly Wolfe's judgment as regards Zhukov's importance in the collective political leadership must be treated with a certain caution.

## The Rise of Marshal Zhukov

*Sixtieth Birthday Decorations and Celebrations.* After the crises in Poland and Hungary in 1956, which had been "solved" with Zhukov's active participation, the Presidium of the Supreme Soviet awarded him the Order of Lenin and — for the fourth time — the Order of the Golden Star on the occasion of his sixtieth birthday. These honours were given very unusual prominence, announced in large letters on the front page of *Pravda* with a big picture of the decorated Marshal, accompanied by greetings and paeans of praise from the Central Committee and the Council of Ministers:

> We greet you, great commander, renowned servant of the Communist Party and the Soviet State, in appreciation of your achievements in the upbuilding of the Army in dark days for our country. You led the Armed Forces of the Soviet Union with great ability in decisive battles for the freedom and independence of the fatherland.[39]

These praises were showered on Zhukov not as in 1946 by the usual run of speakers at an election meeting, but by the Central Committee of the Communist Party of the Soviet Union and the Council of Ministers of the Government, all given unprecedented high relief in *Pravda*. It would seem that there were no honours left to bestow on him. True, it was the custom to award decorations to the heads of the government on their reaching sixty, but this time the praises and the enthusiasm knew no bounds, something extraordinary under the Soviet regime, where honours are accorded in exact proportion to services rendered or anticipated.[40]

---

39  *Pravda*, 2 December 1956.
40  Two years later, Defence Minister Malinovsky reached the age of sixty. He too was decorated with the Golden Star (for the second time), and it was decided to erect a bust of him in his home town; but the notice appeared only in the name of the Supreme Soviet, it was only five lines long, there was no photograph of him, and the news was in a corner of the front page and not in the middle.

## Zhukov as Others Saw Him

In November 1966, the Soviet monthly *Journal of Military History* published a ten-page article on Zhukov when he reached the age of 70, when the writers no longer needed fear Stalin's wrath nor the jealousy of Zhukov's rivals. The survey of Zhukov's whole military career expatiated particularly on his "highly valued" achievements as wartime commander "in the service of the people and the Party". In the Great Patriotic War, "his military gifts and his art of command came to full flower, his many personal qualities playing their part: his lively intelligence, his excellent memory that enabled him to keep in mind the smallest details of the operational-strategic situation, his ability to win collective support for his decisions and actions and listen to good advice, and at the same time to spur on his subordinates, exploiting their strengths and capacities to the utmost. ... Zhukov displayed a marked capacity for sizing up a complicated strategic situation and reaching an accurate prognosis of the development of events. ... His outstanding character traits were iron will-power, coolness and presence of mind in the most critical circumstances, and inflexible determination in carrying out decisions once reached — traits that he displayed best in the most difficult hours on the field of battle. And with it all, the commander Zhukov, product of Soviet military schooling, never lost sight of the primary importance of maintaining the soldiers' morale for winning a battle, a campaign, the war as a whole."[41]

All the same, the writer of the article, Col. Svetlishin, did not hide his opinion that Zhukov, then Chief of General Staff, personally bore part of the responsibility for the eve of war shortcomings in the deployment of the forces and their battle readiness.

Two matters connected with this article may or may not afford the reader some wry amusement, depending on his point of view. Svetlishin quoted the following sentence from Bagramyan's memoirs, which were then, he said, ready for the press: "Of all the

---

41 Colonel Svetlishin, "From Simple Soldier to Marshal," *Journal of Military History*, November 1966, pp. 31–39.

commanders who sprang up with lightning speed in the years before the war, Zhukov was without question the most brilliantly gifted personality of all."[42] Of the whole paragraph quoted by Svetlishin, this was the only sentence that did *not* appear in Bagramyan's book! The manuscript which Svetlishin said was ready for the press in November 1966 was not brought out until 1971 — the sentence about Zhukov was presumably not the only thing suppressed. This is one of the things to be remarked on — that it took five years for Bagramyan's memoirs to pass through all the stages of Soviet control of publications. The other is the question why the censorship objected to high praise of Zhukov at so late a date, when it could no longer do any harm. Perhaps it was a matter of taste, the praise seemed a shade too lavish. Perhaps someone was still jealous.

In the same November 1966 issue of the *Journal of Military History* there was an article by Marshal Rokosovsky on the fighting at Volokolamsk in October 1941, when he was Commander of an Army and Zhukov was Commander of the Western Front. He says of Zhukov: "In my eyes Zhukov always remains the man of firm, resolute will-power. He was immensely gifted, even brilliant, strict and meticulous; he stood up for himself and pressed straight towards his goal. Certainly every great commander has to have these qualities and Zhukov was endowed with them all." For all that, there is a qualification. "But", writes Rokosovsky, "his unswerving determination at times went beyond the permissible bounds. I have to record that in the heat of the battle for Moscow, the Commander of the Front in my view permitted himself unjustified harshness."[43]

Indeed, Zhukov's inflexibility in performing the tasks entrusted to him, his harshness and rough ways were legendary. Colonel Y. N. recounts a personal experience of his:

> In 1943 I was second-in-command of a tank brigade in the First Corps of the Guard, commanded by General P. P. Pa-

---

42 *Ibid.*, p. 34.
43 Marshal K. Rokosovsky, "Towards Volokolamsk," *loc. cit.*, p. 47.

nov. The Corps, which was part of the Supreme Command reserve, saw action on the Byelorussian front and took part in the liberation of Gomel and environs. Before us were well-entrenched German forces. A patrol of Corps Command reported that our tanks could get through the nearby forest and reach the German rear. This was primeval, virgin forest — and it was muddy. Maybe if there had been more order, we could have got through somehow or other. But every unit commander was in a hurry to advance and in no time at all there was a complete jam — we simply sank in the mud and there we were, stuck in the forest. The commanders' throats were sore from shouting as they tried to get their units out. I didn't see General Panov anywhere — he was stuck somewhere else, apparently. The situation was that it was impossible to move either forwards or backwards, with the whole Corps there in the forest.

Suddenly there was a noise, everyone rushing about shouting, "Zhukov, Zhukov!" The commanders started clearing out, either deeper into the forest or inside the tanks. From my vehicle I saw Zhukov, cane in hand, striking the tank turrets. When the tank commander put his head out, Zhukov shouted at him, "Why aren't you moving?" The officer answers, "There's a jam — I'm stuck." In response Zhukov hits him over the head and shouts, "Move! Forward, forward!" And here I see a Colonel running. Zhukov stops him and shouts, "Where are you running to?" He answers, "I'm running forward," and Zhukov's reaction — a blow over the head of the Colonel. He almost hit me too, but I managed to duck aside. And then something happened that one's mind simply boggles at — inside thirty minutes the whole Corps was out of the forest and advancing on its target. Zhukov was there representing the Supreme Command, I think.

Later, when Zhukov was in command of the Byelorussian First Front and the Corps was attached to his Front, I was present at large-scale meetings that he called for consultation: everything Zhukov said testified to his extraordinary intelligence, but every other word was a juicy curse. He was famous as a "born curser", absolutely the opposite of Marshal Rokosovsky, known for his courteous and cultured way of speaking.

Y. N. said that the officers considered Zhukov a gifted soldier but knew him to be harsh, cruel, even tyrannical. "We knew that he was the only one who dared to contradict Stalin. We appreciated his military genius, and many admired him. He was greatly praised — but was not loved. We were afraid of him."[44]

## 1957 — Full Member, Central Committee Presidium

Zhukov reached his highest point in the Party hierarchy in mid-1957. His support helped to decide the outcome of the serious crisis that broke out at the end of June. Zhukov backed Khrushchev and his supporters in the fight for power inside the leadership, and as one of the victors he was made a full member of the Presidium of the Central Committee of the Communist Party. This rise of a professional soldier was unprecedented. It was the highest and the last in the long series of offices he held.

### Summing-Up

Zhukov's military career falls into separate stages, each characterised by a different kind of development.

In the first stage, as NCO, platoon commander, company commander, even as regimental commander, he still lacks self-confidence. His advancement lags behind that of contemporaries who began more or less on a level with him.

In the next stage, the later 1920's, Zhukov establishes himself as commander; he diligently absorbs the doctrines and methodology acquired on courses, where his natural ability and instinctive grasp of things military mark him out. He brings his regiment up to a

---

44 Recorded testimony of Lieutenant-Colonel Y.N.

very high standard and catches the eye of top-level commanders, even perhaps of Stalin himself. His advancement is still slow and he serves six whole years as Brigade Commander, but for the first time he feels himself a commander among his peers.

In the third stage, from the beginning of the 1930's till 1937 with its wholesale executions of senior officers, Zhukov's advancement is speedier, but he has not yet caught up with his fellows. He comes to the fore for the first time with his concept of the structure and utilisation of forces in the discussions over the role of the armour in combat.

In the fourth stage, from 1937 on, the decimation of the senior command opens up opportunities which he seizes upon energetically. He grows more self-confident and shows himself a commander of superior ability. His personality traits are manifested — iron will, resoluteness, fearlessness and unflinching determination in pursuit of goals set.

The fifth stage of Zhukov's career — at the head of the Soviet Armed Forces in World War II — was of course of unprecedented brilliance and distinction. The great campaign that he commanded or planned and directed revealed him as perhaps the greatest of all the military commanders in the war.

I feel that an observation is called for, finally, with respect to Zhukov's political career. He was never a politician, to my mind. His character unsuited him for the contest that circumstances forced him into in the Party-political arena, and that is why his star waned as fast as it did.

## PART III

## PARTY CONTROL RE-IMPOSED

## CHAPTER VI

## THE DEPOSITION OF MARSHAL ZHUKOV

### Background and Reasons

We shall now examine the causes that led Khrushchev and the Party leadership to remove Marshal Zhukov from all his posts in October 1957. Zhukov was at that time a member of the innermost political circle. For over four years he had served the new leadership loyally wherever it needed his help — in getting rid of Beria, in ousting Head of Government Malenkov and finally in defeating the "anti-Party group" — and he had been among the decisive elements in the victory of Khrushchev and his supporters. In foreign affairs too the leadership had had recourse to his services in its attempts to reduce international tension and convince the Western Powers at the Geneva Summit Conference of the sincerity of its intentions regarding "co-existence". His popularity was also made use of in extending Soviet influence in neutral countries: his lengthy visit to India was given the widest publicity in the USSR, in India itself and in the rest of the world.

There is no doubt that the new leadership needed Zhukov while they were in the process of getting firmly settled in the saddle after the death of Stalin. They depended in no small measure on the very great popularity that he enjoyed and that they themselves lacked. His support had been of value at the XX Congress in maintaining the Stalinist line in favour of heavy industry.[1] Why then did Zhukov's fellow-members on the Presidium decide on his deposition only four months after he had helped them overcome their adversaries

---

1   Bertram D. Wolfe, *Khrushchev and Stalin's Ghost*, Frederick A. Praeger, New York, 1957, p. 40.

and been elected a full member of the Presidium? The irony of it is, of course, that it was Zhukov's help in making the leadership secure that enabled it to go ahead without him. Briefly, the Party machine would not for long tolerate a forceful, popular military leader in a strong bargaining position to secure a variety of advantages for the Armed Forces and even to divide the Forces from the Party.[2]

Zhukhov's swift rise in the political sphere was, as we have said, the result mainly of his stand as Army head during the internal struggle for power and his exceptional popularity in the Forces and in the nation at large as the soldier who won the war. This was precisely what aroused the leaders' fears and suspicions, fears that apparently began to form as early as 1953 and that developed as he affirmed his hold on the Armed Forces and decreased his dependence on the political machine.

As military commander, Zhukov worked steadily to increase efficiency, strengthen discipline and real "unity of command", and to promote the troops' combat readiness and their equipment with modern arms. He pressed for recognition of the independent worth of the commander as such and for a significant reduction of the Party-political interference that caused confusion at all levels of command. It was he who headed the struggle for greater professional and institutional autonomy for the Army, interpreting "unity of command" in straightforward military fashion. He put military effectiveness well above Party control and indoctrination and said so emphatically over and over again both to commanders and political workers. This was not a fight for its own sake against the political machine but was dictated by purely military considerations. Zhukov had always demanded exact and full execution of every command and of every instruction; his entire emphasis and all the changes he instituted were the fruit of his views as a professional soldier — he had set himself the task of improving Army functioning and performance. All the same, whether it was deliberately and

---

2   R. Kolkovicz. *The Soviet Military and the Communist Party,* Princeton University Press, 1967, p. 131.

from the outset or not, Zhukov's actions contributed to a marked weakening of Party influence and standing in the Army. The resolutions of the October 1957 Plenary (which we shall treat more fully later) accused Zhukov of having deliberately restricted the sphere of action of the Military Councils in the MDs [Military Districts], in the Armies, in the Fleets and flotillas, seeking to turn them into purely advisory institutions alongside the commanders; he had wanted the post of political member ("comrade") in the Military Councils to be abolished, and the Military Councils' personnel to be appointed by the Ministry of Defence and not the Party Central Committee, and this in disregard of the fact that Central Committee members — Party Secretaries of the Republics, Party Committee Secretaries of Districts and Regions — also served on the Military Councils, alongside the military commanders and workers of the Party-political machine in the Army; he had in every possible way eliminated the role of the Military Council members and had held "consultations"[2a] without them, in spite of their presence being obligatory.[3]

It must be recalled that the Secretary of the Party in the various Republics of the Union enjoyed a very high status as the senior Party personality in each Republic. His membership of the MD Military Council, which was authorised to deal with and decide on all major questions of Army life and activity,[4] ensured the Party Secretary considerable influence in Army affairs, including promotions and postings. We cite the testimony of Lieut.-Col. N. O. concerning a Party conference of the Byelorussian MD: those present included the Minister of Defence, Marshal Malinovsky; the MD Commander, Marshal Timoshenko; and the Party Secretary of the Byelorussian Republic, Mosherov. Mosherov spoke first, before Malinovsky and all the other representatives present (of whom N. O. was one), and there was no question as to who was the most im-

---

[2a] This was the technical term for Military Council meetings.
[3] Y. P. Petrov, *Party-Political Activity in the Soviet Army and Navy*, (Russian), Moscow, 1964, pp. 462–63.
[4] See Chapter 5 above.

portant person there. According to N. O., in some military matters the status and importance of the Byelorussian Party Secretary was greater than that of the MD Commander and at times his opinion even outweighed that of the Minister of Defence. In case of friction between the Party Secretary of the Republic and the MD Commander, the former could easily telephone to the First Secretary of the Party himself and ask him to use his influence in support of his views, while the MD Commander could not. The Party Secretary of the Republic had still another weapon at hand — informing: N. O. states that it was sufficient if the Party Secretary in question told the First Secretary over the telephone or at a meeting, "It looks to me as if that Marshal of mine has not acted recently in the Party spirit," and there would be a black mark against the Marshal.[5] This view is supported by other testimony, but it seems that it is mainly the larger Republics that are concerned.[6] The Party leadership and the MPA[6a] were very apprehensive lest this important channel of supervision and influence in the Army — MPA representation on the Military Councils — should be weakened or even lost. They saw and feared a threat to the very basis of the relations between the Party and the Army — in the last analysis, absolute domination by the Party.

The period 1955 to '57 when Zhukov was reinforcing his control of the Armed Forces in matters of strategy, armament and organisation, and when the part of the High Command in the great victory and his role in particular were being given more and more prominence, was also the period when Khrushchev was fighting his way to the top. Khrushchev's path was not strewn with roses and myrtle all the way. It was not a straight ascent, as witnessed by the events at the end of 1956 and the beginning of '57, and he too needed to have attention directed to the great and important part he had played in winning the war and especially in the Stalingrad

---

5 Recorded interview with Lt.-Col. N. O.
6 Interview with Prof. Michael Agursky, in Israel, July 1975.
6a Main Political Administration, the Party political arm in the Armed Forces. See Chapter 4 above.

campaign, during which he was Party representative on the Stalingrad Front Command. In order to glorify his role in initiating and planning the Stalingrad campaign and in its successful execution, it was necessary to downgrade the share of the High Command representatives in the campaign — Zhukov and Vasilevsky. These two were Khrushchev's rival contenders for the crown as the main initiators and planners of the campaign and they indeed had the right to it, according to the vast amount of material published on the subject.[7] One way of countering their claims was to get them out of their high positions in the Army and put an end to their influence in the military journals and in publications about the war. Vasilevsky was already removed from his post as Deputy Minister of Security in 1956. When the Central Committee appointed the editorial board to bring out the official history of World War II, Zhukov was not included, but he was not yet removed from his posts because he was still needed. The conflict over Stalingrad was mainly between Khrushchev and the two Marshals, but in the overall picture the political leadership was seeking to have the credit for the victories accorded to the Party itself and not to one or other of the military commanders.

Zhukov's rivals in the Army took Khrushchev's side in this struggle and naturally so did the MPA. The scales began to turn in favour of the Party in mid-1957 and this conflict was decided — along with much else — when Zhukov was deposed in the autumn of that year.

### June 1957, Full Member of Central Committee Presidium

When Zhukov was made a full member of the Presidium after his part in the events of June 1957, he was increasingly sure of himself as one of the inner leadership, and it was at this point that the other members of the political leadership began to sense the double danger from Zhukov's downgrading Party supervision and indoctrina-

---

7 See comprehensive interview with Vasilevsky on the subject of this campaign in the *Journal of Military History* (*Red Star* publishers), No. 10, October 1963, pp. 13–25.

tion in the Army, on the one hand, and on the other from Zhukov's own performance. They feared that he would apply his conception of "unity of command" to relations between the Ministry of Defence and the MPA as regards the powers of the Supreme Military Council and the extent of Central Committee interventions in military affairs. This specific accusation is brought out in the official explanations of the October '57 Plenary resolutions:

> Zhukov sought by every means to have the Central Committee withdrawn from solving the major questions in the life of the Army and Navy. ... Actions calling for collective discussion and consideration were carried out by Zhukov personally, without decision or endorsement by the Central Committee. In seeking to weaken leadership and supervision over the Armed Forces by the Party, its Central Committee and the Government, Zhukov insisted that it was necessary to set aside the Supreme Military Council, which constitutes the collective institution whose members include candidate members of the Presidium, members of the Central Committee and military and political leaders of the Army and Navy.[8]

The structure of relations between the Army on one side and the Party and its organs on the other that Zhukov tried to organise was seen, rightly or wrongly, by the political leadership and even by some senior commanders as intended to withdraw the Army from Party supervision. The October '57 Plenary resolutions stated this perfectly clearly:

> The Central Committee Plenary notes that former Minister of Defence, Comrade G. K. Zhukov, has recently violated the Leninist Party principles of leadership of the Armed Forces inasmuch as he adopted a line intended to set aside leadership and control over the Armed Forces on the part of the Party, its Central Committee and the Government.[9]

8 Petrov, *op. cit.*, p. 462.
9 *The Communist Party of the USSR Concerning the Armed Forces of the USSR* (Russian), Moscow, 1958, p. 407.

The Deposition of Marshal Zhukov

The official account goes on to state that Zhukov displayed a disregard for the MPA, forbidding it to report to the Central Committee on the condition of the enlisted men and their actions.[10] No clear factual proof exists of this official statement that Zhukov "adopted a line intended to set aside etc. etc. ..." or that he actually forbade the MPA to report to the Central Committee, and one may legitimately have doubts on the matter. What is important is that this is how Khrushchev and his colleagues in the leadership presented Zhukov's intentions and actions.[11] They were of the opinion that he was acting against the principle itself of Party leadership of the Armed Forces and against the main instruments by means of which this leadership and control was effected. Zhukov's behaviour was represented as endangering the Party's rule over the Army.

*July 1957, Speeches and Celebrations*

Zhukov's appearances and pronouncements after the June '57 Plenary session gave sufficiently striking evidence of how sure he now was of himself. On 2 July, two days before the decisions of the June Plenary were made public, the Party military *"aktiv"* was convened: Army people from the Ministry of Defence and from the military academies, commanders and political workers from the various Armies as well as the Secretaries of the main Party organisations in the Army, some 900 persons in all. Zhukov addressed the *"aktiv"*, attacking the "anti-Party group" and stressing that

10 Petrov, *op. cit.,* p. 463. It should be noted that the head of the MPA was appointed by the Central Committee and reported to it; his status was that of a Section Head on the Central Committee.
11 This supposed order of Zhukov's has also been reported as a concession demanded by him after his election as full member of the Presidium. R. Garthoff, *Soviet Strategy in the Nuclear Age* (Frederick and Praeger, New York, 1962), pp. 30–31, basing himself on reports by Harrison Salisbury and Sydney Gruson in the *New York Times* of 9 July and 3 November 1957, says that this supposed demand was "leaked" to the newspaper by "Soviet sources" in Moscow.

no-one had supported it in the Plenary. After detailing the harmful actions of the persons concerned in their opposition to all the reforms that had been proposed — improved economic organisation, increased rights for the constituent Republics of the Soviet Union, and relaxation of international tension — Zhukov affirmed, "The Army is always ready at the first call of our fatherland-Party and Government to fight courageously in defence of the interests of our Government."[12]

On 13 July, at the ceremony in Leningrad to celebrate Soviet Navy Day and in the presence of all the local leaders, Zhukov declared:

> The successes in the political sphere and in the practical field prove the correctness of the general line of our Party, supported by our whole nation. Every single individual in the nation does his duty. Nevertheless, as the saying goes, "There's a black sheep in every family", and as you all know there were some black sheep in the Presidium in the forms of Malenkov, Kaganovich, Molotov and Shepilov. This group tried to take over the leadership of the Party with the aim of getting our Party to deviate from the Leninist orientations adopted at the XX Congress and to lead it along a path not in line with the vitally important interests of the fatherland and the Socialist camp.[13]

On 14 July 1957, Soviet Navy Day, Zhukov made a speech aboard the battle-cruiser *Ordzhonokidze* in the name of and as emissary of the Government and the Central Committee, along the same orthodox lines:

> The peoples of the Soviet Union and the fighting men of the Army and the Navy put complete and unqualified trust in their Communist Party. ... While discussions were proceeding in the Plenary, the people of Leningrad showed that the Party

12 *Red Star* 5.7.57, *apud* Chaney, *Zhukov*, University of Oklahoma Press, Oklahoma 1971, pp. 399–400.
13 *Pravda*, 14.7.57.

and the people are of one piece, and that no-one will ever succeed in making a breach in this monolithic unity. Under the experienced leadership of our Party, Soviet men and women march forward with bold assurance towards the victory of Communism in our country. ... All praise and glory to the Communist Party of the Soviet Union that inspires us with its spirit and organises all our victories.[14]

The speech that generated more controversy and interpretations than all the previous ones was delivered the next day, 15 July 1957, at the *Bolshevik* factory in Leningrad. Speaking in the name of the Party Presidium and of the Armed Forces, Zhukov declared, *inter alia*:

> Those who took part in the [sc. "anti-Party"] group came out particularly against the slogan put forward by the Central Committee on the initiative of Nikita Khrushchev — catch up with the United States in the near future in the production of meat, milk and butter [sc. per head of the population]. They had no consideration for the fact that this slogan was wholeheartedly endorsed by the entire Soviet people. ... They lagged behind the development and growth [sc. of the Soviet Union]. They forfeited their right to lead the Party and even to be considered as full, worthy members of our great Communist Party. ... The anti-Party group obstinately opposed the measures adopted by the Party to put an end to the results of the cult of personality and chiefly to expose those who bore most of the blame, those who at the time made possible the violations of constitutionality and to bring them to account for the deeds they were responsible for. Now that the un-Party acts of the group have been uncovered, it has become clear why they were against exposing the un-Party acts that had been committed. ... Dear comrades, let me assure you in the name of the Armed Forces — and by your intermediary all you sons of Leningrad — that the Army and the

14 *Pravda*, 15.7.57.

Navy stand firm and sure, guarding the interests of our great land, and always ready to carry out the will of the people, whom they have served faithfully for close on forty years. Three cheers for the men of Leningrad, worthy sons of the brave Soviet nation! Long live our Communist fatherland-Party! [15]

*Pravda's* treatment of this speech is of the highest interest. It quoted the speech in the direct voice, but paragraphed it before the end, summarising thus: "In his speech, Zhukov gave facts concerning the violations of constitutionality by those who took part in the anti-Party group." It then gave the rest in direct speech, as before. It refrained from detailing what the facts were that Zhukov gave, and the conclusion seems inescapable that the speech referred to matters involving leaders outside the "anti-Party group.[16] Some sources believe that the leadership had reached a consensus not to carry criticism of Stalin and attacks on the "anti-Party group" to the point where there would have to be undesirably thorough investigation into past crimes of the regime; they see these speeches of Zhukov's as intentionally or unintentionally threatening the consensus[17] and in so doing "playing with political dynamite".

Along this line of thought, the German researcher Boris Meisner affirms that the demand to have Malenkov, Molotov and Kaganovich brought to trial could not fail to "rouse the most serious apprehensions on the part of the new leadership. It threatened a chain

15 *Pravda,* 16.7.57.
16 There has been a certain confusion among Western researchers and commentators over the two speeches in Leningrad on two consecutive days. Chaney reads a provocation to the Party leadership into a speech of Zhukov's, based on the assumption that it was delivered to the audience on the *Orzhonikidze,* which it was not. Apart from this confusion, Chaney's comments on Zhukov's self-glorification in these speeches at the expense of the Party are not borne out by the text of the speeches. *Op. cit.,* pp. 401–2.
17 Carl Linden, *Khrushchev and the Soviet Leadership, 1957–1964,* Johns Hopkins Press, Baltimore, 1966, p. 48, Linden also confuses the two speeches of the 15th and 16th July (see footnote 16 above).

reaction that could lead to unforeseable and uncontrollable results. As it was, Khrushchev's famous speech about Stalin at the XX Congress had done the Party no little harm, both at home and abroad. By contrast, the image of the Army, which had also been grievously blemished by the crimes of the past, would now be much improved, and the ground would be prepared for the rise of a modern Bonaparte — a role for which, from the viewpoint of the masses, Zhukov seemed to have all the qualities needed.[18] It was not the attack on the "anti-Party group" that was such a serious matter. Zhukov was not the only one and not the first to make these accusation, but the consequences that he drew — that Malenkov, Molotov and Kaganovich should be excluded from the Party and put on trial — went beyond what had been decided at the Plenary and what was acceptable to most of the other leaders.[19] It is my opinion that Meisner is right, and that the real sting was indeed in Zhukov's call to expose those chiefly responsible for illegalities, without saying that he was referring to the "anti-Party group" alone. It was known that he was mainly concerned to see Tukhachevsky rehabilitated. A trial of even the four alone could have led to a chain reaction with unpredictable results. Nor should it be forgotten that the purges were not officially condemned until October 1961. The censored paragraph in *Pravda* must have carried an even bigger charge of political dynamite than what was printed — why otherwise would it be censored?

Khrushchev is said to have told Tito in August 1957 that Zhukov also asked the Presidium to have the Armed Forces represented on the KGB administration, and that he wanted the Army itself to

---

18  Boris Meisner, *Russland unter Chrushtschew,* P. Oldenburg Verlag, Muenchen, 1960, pp. 60–61.
19  Zhukov's part in defeating the plans to unseat Khrushchev may have been decisive in the June crisis, but neither this in itself nor the sum total of Zhukov's services to Khrushchev really turned Zhukov into an immediate threat to the regime, as argued by Timothy Colton, "The Zhukov Affair Reconsidered," *Soviet Studies,* University of Glasgow, Vol. XXIX, No. 2, April 1977, pp. 188–89, and Linden, *op. cit.,* p. 43.

take responsibility for the Internal Security Army[19a] and for security in the Frontier Force.[20] The Yugoslav Ambassador at the time, Veljko Mićunović, who was on exceptionally friendly terms with Khrushchev, relates in his book, *Moscow Diary*, that on the 26th of October at a reception given by the Iranian Ambassador, Khrushchev informed him that in the afternoon the Presidium had been discussing "the conduct of Marshal Zhukov following the June plenum." He mentioned the following example of Zhukov's antiparty behaviour: "At the time of the events in June connected with the Molotov-Kaganovich-Malenkov group Marshal Zhukov told certain people that he, Zhukov, would call out the Army and the people and settle accounts with M-K-M if it should be necessary..." Khrushchev told Mićunovic, "The party could never permit a person who had such an opinion of himself as Marshal Zhukov, who considered that it depended on him alone when the Army should be called on to intervene in domestic affairs, to be minister of the armed forces of the Soviet Union. If in June he threatened to call out the Army and 'restore order', that meant that he was capable of using the troops against Molotov and Malenkov today and of using the same troops against someone else tomorrow."[21] So we see that Khrushchev and his colleagues in the political leadership had grounds for fearing that Zhukov's increasing hold on the Army and his belief in himself might endanger their own standing, if crisis conditions were to recur. To put it somewhat differently, if circumstances were propitious, Zhukov might take upon himself the role of leader or of head of the leadership.

It should be remembered that at this stage the atomic armament of the USSR was proceeding apace, and in the leadership's view

---

[19a] A force created by Beria, independent of the Ministry of Defence.
[20] Garthoff, *op. cit.*, pp. 30–31. I have not found any confirmation of the demand regarding representation in the KGB. If it was made, a certain weight would attach to it.
[21] Veljko Mićunović, *Moscow Diary*, Doubleday and Company, Inc., New York, 1980, pp. 305, 308.

this made it vitally necessary to strengthen Party control of the Armed Forces.

## How It Was Done

As early as 1955, when Zhukov was appointed Minister of Defence and his influence was growing steadily, Khrushchev and his colleagues already began to take steps to prevent him from securing too complete a hold. The list of Marshals and Generals who were promoted in 1955 and '56 and appointed to important posts included some of Zhukov's rivals, mostly men close to Khrushchev who had served with him during the war and at Stalingrad or had been otherwise connected with him. They owed him their present promotion and could naturally be expected to support him in his fight for power at the centre. The key appointment was that of Marshal Malinovsky as Commander of the Land Forces, since he was a "founding member" of what Western commentators have called Khrushchev's "Stalingrad commanders' group". Apparently the only person who did not sense the significance of this appointment was Zhukov himself. Khrushchev already foresaw that a confrontation with Zhukov would one day be unavoidable and he set about isolating him by every possible means.[22]

Zhukov had proved himself a brilliant commander and a strategist of genius, but in these internal manoeuvres he was a veritable tiro, unable to compete in political manipulations with the cunning and experience of Khrushchev and the other Party leaders.

It is not clear exactly when and by whom the decision was taken to start with practical preparations for removing Zhukov from his position at the head of the Armed Forces and in the Party leadership. It looks as if steps were taken as early as July 1957 to check Zhukov's offensive against the Party elements in the Army — and to prepare the ground for further steps. The decision was taken, it is reasonable to assume, during the month of September within

22 Malcolm Mackintosh, *Juggernaut*, Secker and Warburg, London 1967, pp. 291–92.

a restricted circle of part of the members of the Presidium. It may even have been at the beginning of September, since the decision to have Zhukov go on a mission to Yugoslavia (to take place early in October) was of course connected with the decision to depose him, and the date must have been fixed in consultation with Belgrade in September.

The defeat of the "anti-Party group" in the June 1957 crisis and the entrenchment of Khrushchev and his supporters in the leadership was itself what made it possible to take means to strengthen the Party front in the Army and weaken Zhukov's hold. The need to do so was the more urgent because of the very fact that Zhukov was now a member of the Central Committee Presidium and could, it was feared, utilise his new standing in order to restrict MPA authority in the Army and Navy still further. In *Red Star* of 19 July an article appeared that included the following sentence: "It is necessary to completely root out the harmful influence of the cult of personality in Army affairs." This can be seen as the opening shot fired at Zhukov, without naming him by name: three months later he was openly accused of fostering a cult of his personality.

*Re-writing history.* As the leadership regained stability after the June crisis, it felt the need to glorify the Party's role in the great victory and Khrushchev at its head felt the need to glorify his personal role in winning the war.[22a] It was therefore necessary to rewrite the history of the war, and the natural tendency and desire of senior commanders to bring out their share and that of the Army would have to be ignored to a greater degree than previously. In July, the leadership purged the editorial board of the important *Journal of Military History* (*Voprosi Historii*), because of the line it had taken on the role of the Army and its commanders in winning the war as against the restricted role it allotted the Party and its representatives. In September, the Central Committee appointed an editorial board of twenty-eight historians and Party and Army people to produce the official *History of the Great Patriotic War* (which finally appeared in five volumes in 1961). The Resolution

[22a] See Chapter 4 above.

appointing the board laid down a detailed instruction to stress the role of the Party as the organiser in the fighting against the enemy.[23] Zhukov was not made a member of the board. This was probably the signal that his fate was now settled.[24] Practical preparations for his removal may have begun even earlier, at the end of August and the beginning of September, when he was on holiday in the Crimea.[25]

*Attacking Zhukov's views.* As we have already shown, it was in July that articles began to appear attacking the view that commanders' orders must not be open to criticism by their subordinates. Articles by senior MPA officers, including one by General A. G. Ritov and another by Lieut.-Gen. M. H. Klashnik, appeared in *Red Star* and other army papers, dealing explicitly with the new instructions laid down that year for the MPA,[25a] and stressing that the commander and his subordinates were equally in duty bound to accept the principle of "criticism and self-criticism" in Party meetings in the forces. Klashnik wrote that attempts were being made in some units to distinguish between "Communists — whom it is permitted to criticicise — and others whom it is forbidden to criticise." This was a fundamentally wrong way of presenting the problem, he said.[26] These shafts aimed at Zhukov without naming him and others like them came mainly from the MPA heads.

In August and September articles appeared in the press on neglect of Party activity in Army and Navy units. It was reported that criticism was voiced at meetings in Army units over the weakening of Party-political activity. A long article appeared in *Pravda* on 24 September, signed "V. Sverdlov, M.Sc.", entitled: "The Communist Party — leader and organiser of the popular masses in their struggle for the October victory [sc. the 1917 Bolshevik Revo-

---

23 Panel M. Cocks, "The Purge of Marshal Zhukov," *Slavic Review*, Washington, 1963, Vol. 22, p. 485.
24 *Ibid.*, p. 497.
25 Meisner, *op. cit.*, p. 61.
25a See Chapter 4 above.
26 *Red Star*, 31.7.57.

lution]" — one of those programmatic headlines, a word of warning to all concerned. An article in *Red Star* two days later affirmed: "It is the Party that inspires and organises all the victories of the Armed Forces." These publications do not appear to have caused Zhukov concern.

Zhukov's demand for rehabilitation of Stalin's 1937 victims[27] was not getting any support from his Party colleagues, and it must be assumed that he had not consulted them on this issue before his speeches of mid-July. On 10 August, *Red Star* published a biographical article on Marshal Bluecher, which could be regarded as some sort of rehabilitation of the Civil War hero, and it is almost certain that it was written at Zhukov's prompting.

*Showering honours.* At this time Zhukov was occupied more particularly with organising the Army's new missiles system. He was also preparing for his forthcoming visit to Yugoslavia, apparently without sensing the beginning of the campaign set going against him by Party elements. His failure to perceive what was happening may also have been due in part at least to the honours that were being showered on him: his being invited to go abroad on an important mission; his taking part in discussions with foreign representatives visiting Moscow; having his name and picture in all the papers. It is not out of the question that his fellows in the leadership arranged all this deliberately and with malice aforethought, in order to lull him into a sense of security.[28]

Zhukov left for Yugoslavia on 4 October, accompanied to the airfield by his first Deputy Minister, Marshal Koniev, a bevy of Generals, Deputy Foreign Ministers, pressmen and others. On his journey, Zhukov stopped over for a ceremonial visit to the Fleet at Sevastopol. The port was filled with a cheering crowd as he left for

---

27 *Pravda,* 24.9.57.
28 I remember Zhukov's appearance at many public receptions at this time, sure of himself, pleased with his fresh eminence. In conversation with heads of diplomatic missions, he pronounced on political questions with great assurance, and we all seized every opportunity to exchange a few words with him, as he was considered a rising star.

Yugoslavia by sea aboard the *Kuibyshev* at the head of a naval flotilla.

*A welcome distraction.* On 4 October, the first man-made satellite, the Sputnik, was launched from the Soviet Union. The achievement was wildly cheered in the media. *Pravda's* headlines on 6 and 7 October read: "The earth's first artificial Sputnik created in the land of the Soviets — Victory for Soviet science and technique — Honour and glory to Soviet science and technique — The peak of science — 'The Russians have Won the Race' — the world marvels at the grandiose victory of Soviet science and technique." What was particularly stressed was joy and pride over the Soviet Union's overtaking the West, which had been ahead in this sensitive area. For over a week the public was kept busy with a flood of news about the Sputnik in space and the world-wide repercussions. Zhukov's mission was given nothing like the showing he had had for his visit to India: there were only short news items in the inside pages. The speeches he made were either not mentioned at all or had everything political in them simply cut out.

With the approach of the 40th anniversary of the October Revolution, the usual extensive propaganda build-up began in the media. There was the traditional setting of slogans and the summings-up of achievements of the regime. It was sought to create an atmosphere of excitement and celebration, even of exaltation. On 17 October, the newspapers reported the return of the flotilla to Sevastopol and the news that Zhukov had extended his mission with a visit to Albania, which meant that his voyage was taking longer than had been planned. It lasted until 26 October.

*Warning signal.* On 18 October, the Navy paper, *Sovietski Flot*, published a leading article under the headline, "The Unity of Party and People is unshakeable." Again a headline of the kind employed by the Soviet leadership to signal to a public experienced in deciphering these messages that an event of some importance is in the offing. Formulas like this one indicate that a political struggle of some kind has been taking place at the top and that additional amplification will certainly be forthcoming. These signals mostly appear when the struggle is already decided but on occasion while it is still taking place.[29]

*19 October Meeting of Party General Committee Presidium.* The operation to depose Zhukov received its final decisive impetus at the session of the Central Committee Presidium on 19 October 1957, convened in the absence of Zhukov, far from Moscow. The historian Petrov states simply: "On 19 October 1957 the Presidium of the Central Committee heard the report of the MPA head, A. S. Zheltov, and passed a Resolution on Party-political action in the Soviet Army and Navy." He then goes on to give this account of what followed. "The Central Committee[29a] sharply censured the small measure of appreciation[29b] accorded Party-political action in the Soviet Army and Navy. In the light of the gravity of the defects[29b] revealed in Party action, the Central Committee decided to bring the problem to meetings of the [Party] *"aktivs"* in the MDs and the Navy. Members and alternate members of the Central Committee Presidium took part in the discussions in the *"aktivs"* concerning the Central Committee decisions. In these Party *"aktivs"*, new facts came to light on Zhukov's ignoring the Party line on leadership of the Armed Forces as well as serious deviations in the

---

29 For example, at the end of the struggle over the ousting of Malenkov from his position at the head of the Government, on 8.2.1955, the day before the news was published that he had been replaced by Bulganin, *Pravda* carried a leading article entitled, "The people is the basis of the power of the Soviet State." Before the end of the article comes the signal: "The Soviet people, bound together in force around the beloved Communist Party, directing all its exertions towards further development. . . ." When the struggle was over, *Pravda* had another leader, under the title, "Under the wise leadership of the Communist Party", ending with the following: "The great unity of the Communist Party, the Government and the people — this is the source of the power of the Soviet State and the source of all its victories."

29a Not necessarily the Presidium, it should be noted. The reference may even be to the Central Committee Secretariat.

29b The "small measure of appreciation" and the "defects" in question were presumably "revealed" in the MPA report — there was no love lost between Zhukov and Zheltov.

functioning of the Ministry of Defence. Taking all this into consideration, it was decided[29c] to transmit the problem of improving Party-political action in the Army and Navy to a session of the Central Committee Plenary, to which would be invited a wide circle of Party and Army activist personnel."[30]

This brief, almost cryptic narrative in fact provides a most instructive picture of Soviet technique in these matters. Khrushchev and those of his colleagues who were in the secret of the plans to oust Zhukov must have feared possible dissatisfaction and even opposition among some of the Army senior command or on the part of Zhukov himself or his close friends in the Army, and they took their precautions accordingly. There is practically no doubt that it was decided at the 19 October session to remove Marshal Rokosovsky from his post of Deputy Minister of Defence and send him off to be Commander of the Trans-Caucasian MD; it was a matter of forestalling possible difficulties in the Defence Ministry or in discussions in the Party *"aktiv"* in the Ministry. The announcement of Rokosovsky's new post was published in very unusual fashion in P*ravda* in the following terms: "The newspaper *Zarya Vostoka* of 23 October reports that Marshal of the Soviet Union K. Rokosovsky has been appointed Commander of the Forces in the Trans-Caucasian MD" — as if *Pravda* had no Moscow source for this piece of news and had to take it from a local paper. This was obviously done to minimise the importance of the transfer, which nevertheless had to be made public to bring it to the attention of the senior command concerned.

We can now briefly resume some of the main steps taken up to this point: the intensive propaganda campaign of the summer months, already described; getting Zhukov out of Moscow on the mission to Yugoslavia; removing his friend Marshal Rokosovsky from the arena; Zhukov's place taken during his absence by his

---

[29c] The decision may have been part of the 19 October Resolution, but is conveniently presented as the result of the "discussions" in the *"aktivs"* We discuss these "discussions" further on.

[30] Petrov, *op. cit.,* p. 467.

First Deputy, Marshal Koniev, a fierce adversary of his from as long ago as the Berlin offensive; Khrushchev's closest friend, Marshal Malinovsky (who will show himself Zhukov's severest critic) in Command of the Land Forces. Into this battle array, in accordance with the Central Committee instructions, senior commanders, and political officers — all of them Zhukov's subordinates — are sent in to sit in "consultation" with MD and Navy commanders and to put it to them, with the assistance of Central Committee Presidium members and alternate members, that "defects" have been uncovered in the Supreme Commander's application of the Party line on leadership of the Army as well as "deviations" in the functioning of the Ministry of Defence.

The presence of Presidium members at the *"aktiv"* meetings would make it quite clear to the Army and Navy commanders that there was no room for differing opinions or appreciations and that they had to toe the line, follow suit and go along with the accusations. It is doubtful whether any officers at all, even the highest-ranking, dared express support for Zhukov at these meetings. Khrushchev himself is said to have sat with the senior command of the Moscow MD, presumably to discuss Zhukov, on 25 October.[31]

*26 October, Zhukov returns, ousted as Minister of Defence.* Before Zhukov's return to Moscow, the decision on his deposition from the post of Minister of Defence was taken by the Presidium of the Supreme Soviet, but it was not announced until after he returned on 26 October. Zhukov's reception at Vnukovo airfield was very unlike the ceremony at his departure. He was met by Marshal Malinovsky and a few officials. His colleagues of the Party Presidium and the Government were conspicuous by their absence. He was driven direct from the airfield to a session of the Party Central Committee Presidium, in the course of which a proposal was made — and rejected by Zhukov — for his promotion to Deputy Prime Minister.

---

31 Chaney, *op. cit.*, p. 409.

## The Deposition of Marshal Zhukov

Six hours after Zhukov's arrival in Moscow, Tass published an announcement on the changes at the head of the Defence Ministry; an hour later it was broadcast over the radio in the evening news programme as the fifteenth item in order of importance. On the morrow, 27 October, *Pravda* printed two brief official announcements, one after the other:

> The Presidium of the Supreme Soviet of the USSR has appointed Marshal of the Soviet Union Radion Yakovlevich Malinovsky as Minister of Defence of the USSR.
> The Presidium of the Supreme Soviet of the USSR has released Marshal of the Soviet Union Grigori Konstantinovich Zhukov from his post as Minister of Defence of the USSR.

This closed the official, technical side of the first stage of the deposition. It constituted the principal measure taken in order to withdraw the Armed Forces from Zhukov's control and remove them from his sphere of influence.

*Deposed from Party leadership.* The next stage was to be his deposition from his post in the Party leadership. This would be done at the session of the Central Committee Plenary already decided on. It was a complicated matter, which had to serve a number of purposes at the same time:
1. The contentions advanced to support the deposition from the Party leadership must include justification for his deposition from the post of Minister of Defence.
2. It must be convincingly conveyed by the composition of the Plenary that the double deposition was being carried out with the accord and support of the most eminent senior commanders.
3. The Resolutions to be passed — their title, their content and their wording — must serve as overture and lever for a large-scale, protracted campaign to destore closer control of the Armed Forces by the Party and its organs.

*29 October Plenary Resolutions.* The full title of the Resolutions passed on 29 October, generally referred to as The Resolutions of the October '57 Plenary, was: "Resolutions of the Central Committee Plenary as regards improving Party-political action in the Soviet Army and Navy." If the public was to be convinced of the correctness of the decisions to depose Zhukov and "improve Party-political action" and if all the aims listed above were to be attained, it was not enough to rest content with merely publishing the Resolutions; it was necessary to prepare leading articles in the Press criticising Zhukov and reports on meetings of Party *"aktivs"* in Moscow and in the main cities of the Republics and the Regions, all unanimously and wholeheartedly endorsing the decisions and singing the praises of the leadership. Publication of the Plenary Resolutions was accordingly postponed for a number of days until the whole spectacle had been properly prepared and staged, and only then did the curtain rise, with the publication of the Plenary Resolutions in *Pravda* on 3 November. In order to prove that the deposition was supported by senior commanders, the published text of the Resolutions included the statement that the deposition was passed unanimously by all the members of the Central Committee, the alternate members and the members of the Control Commission, and was supported by all Army personnel and Party and Government workers present at the Plenary session.

The Plenary Resolutions gave the following grounds as justification for relieving Zhukov of his post as Minister of Defence:

> Former Minister of Defence Zhukov has recently violated the Leninist principles of leadership of the Armed Forces and followed a line of eliminating the leadership and supervision of the Army and Navy by the Party, its Central Committee and the Government. The Plenary affirmed that a personality cult began to be implanted in the Army with the participation of Zhukov himself. ...
>
> By his conduct Zhukov failed to justify the trust placed in him by the Party: he showed himself to be a public servant who did not fulfil his obligations from the political viewpoint and who inclined to adventurism both as regards understanding of the major problems of the foreign policy of the USSR

and as regards his manner of directing the Ministry of Defence.[32]

The charge of "not fulfilling obligations from the political viewpoint" meant simply that Zhukov was accused of not accepting the basic axiom that the Party is master of the house. The notion of "Bonapartism" does not appear in this text, though the sentence about a personality cult is a hint in this direction. The "adventurism" which allegedly marked him as unfit for his office added up to acting on his own initiative without always waiting to discuss and discern the Party line.

Marshal Koniev was harnessed to the task of de-throning Zhukov from his pre-eminence as the ever-victorious commander. In a long, blatantly tendentious article in the same 3 November issue of *Pravda*, he not only accused Zhukov of violating Lenin's principles and of arrogantly implanting a cult of his own personality, but also enumerated his shortcomings as Chief of General Staff and his mistakes in the conduct of the war. Koniev contended that Zhukov as Chief of General Staff had been responsible for the state of unpreparedness on the frontiers which made possible the surprise at the beginning of the war. He went on to assert that the plan that led to victory at Stalingrad was not Zhukov's but the fruit of the labours of the Front Command and the Defence Ministry. Koniev contended further that Zhukov erred in the Damiansk campaign in the winter of 1942 to '43 and on the Ukrainian front near Lvov; he even accused him of mistakes in the battle for Berlin.

On the same day, 3 of November, important additional details concerning the "unanimous, wholehearted" support for the deposition appeared in *Pravda* and *Izvestia* leading articles stressing the eminent military personalities who had taken part in the Plenary discussions: Marshals Koniev, Rokosovsky, Sokolovsky, Yeremenko, Timoshenko and Biryuzov; Admiral Gorshkov, Generals of the Army Batov, Zakharov, Kazakov and others. Many of them, the leading articles stated, had known Comrade Zhukov for de-

32  *Pravda*, 3.11.57.

cades and worked together with him. They pointed to his serious shortcomings and severely criticised his errors and "deviations". They "unanimously" condemned his incorrect and un-Party conduct as Minister of Defence of the Soviet Union. To complete the picture, the same issue published what Zhukov himself had said in the course of the Plenary sitting to the effect that he thoroughly understood his mistakes, confessed the error of his ways and gave his word to the Central Committee that he would correct all his shortcomings.

The operation itself, meticulously planned and prepared, was soon over, completed without a hitch according to the set timetable. The explanations and justifications smoothed the way for the Party leadership to tackle its main objective — re-asserting and tightening its control over the Army.

### *Was There a Real Danger of Zhukov's Making a Bid for Personal Power* ?

There are two questions here. Did Zhukov really seek to take power, to become a new Bonaparte? And how did the Party leadership evaluate the situation that came into being in mid-1957? Did they in fact believe that there was a real danger of an attempt at a Bonapartist *coup* on the part of Zhukov?

In order to answer the first question, it will assist if we briefly recapitulate Zhukov's actions and the tendencies he displayed.

1. He began introducing arrangements in the Army in line with his conception of "unity of command" — a conception differing in large measure from that accepted in the Party leadership.

2. He reduced the powers of the MPA and its organs and their authority to intervene in "all aspects of Army life"; he reduced the officers' stint of obligatory Leninist-Marxist studies and the nuisance of political indoctrination for the troops in the morning hours.

3. He encouraged writing on the war and its campaigns in order to bring to the fore the part played in the victory by the Armed

Forces commands, at the expense of the share of the Party and its leaders, which had been stressed previously.

4. He wanted to turn the Military Councils into purely advisory bodies and to reduce the authority even of the Supreme Military Council.

5. In matters of postings and promotions he shook off the authority of Party elements, which had always been decisive in practice.

6. As a member of the Central Committee Presidium, he appeared in public, speaking with assurance in the name of the Party and as its emissary, as an equal or even leading partner in the deposition of the "anti-Party group", concerned to purge the leadership of those guilty of past crimes and demanding that all those responsible be brought to trial. He reaped a harvest of admiration as a war hero and basked in the sunshine of public approval.

Does all this taken together indicate an intention or constant aim on Zhukov's part to cut the Army off from the Party and to seize the State power from the leadership? Did he seek to become another Bonaparte? It seems not. His intentions were in fact much more modest and limited. He saw himself as a faithful Communist, devoted to the Party, who for 38 years had tried to subjugate all his thoughts, aspirations and actions to his duties as a member of the Party. He saw the Party as a body caring for the citizens of the State, the only body with the authority to lead the State and capable of doing so. Zhukov's inability to thoroughly master Marxist-Leninist doctrines and his lack of ideological pretentions (as compared with his predecessors Frunze and Tukhachevsky) did not affect his perhaps somewhat simplistic devotion to the Communist idea as a motive force.

Zhukov's involvement in matters of State and Party stemmed largely from his concern for security matters in their broad sweep and from his professional judgement on how to develop and upbuild the Armed Forces, a judgement based on strategic perception and military thinking. Zhukov took part in getting rid of Beria and he supported Khrushchev against Malenkov and the "anti-Party group" mainly because he saw it as in the interest of the security of the Army, which was in duty bound to defend the State under Party guidance. At bottom he was and to the end he remained a soldier in every fibre of his being.[33]

Zhukov was no politician — he had no talent for confronting lions in the den of political manipulations and in this respect was even an innocent. Otherwise it is difficult to grasp his simplistic attitude and his lack of flexibility in dealings with the MPA, not to mention his lack of elementary suspiciousness with regard to the Party leadership. Even more, a review of his behaviour in the period before his removal gives the clear impression that he really had not the slightest idea that the leaders were conspiring together to depose him and condemn his actions. Nothing that he did after the death of Stalin provides support for the contention that Zhukov, the professional soldier, strategist of genius, victorious commander, was consciously in the grip of an ambition to overthrow the leadership and seize power with the support of the Army. And yet, in certain political circumstances, if the internal struggles in the political leadership were to lead towards a collapse, Zhukov might perhaps have decided that it was incumbent on him to take over in order to "fix things up", and it is not inconceivable that he might not have been in any hurry afterwards to surrender the power. But this is pure speculation — the circumstances at this time were not such as to drive him to such lengths.

As to the other question, whether the Party leaders were genuinely convinced that a Bonapartist danger threatened from Zhukov's side, we have already shown that Khrushchev and his colleagues began taking measures to prevent Zhukov's securing an excessive hold on the Army as early on as 1955, when he was just starting on his rise to political eminence. This sort of technique is native and natural to a totalitarian regime. The military command oversees a tremendous organisation of a special kind; it has at its orders a well-oiled machine and forceful means of extraordinary power.

---

33 This is how he impressed me in the brief conversations I had with him at the very period when he was among the top Party leaders, an impression shared by my colleagues.

## The Deposition of Marshal Zhukov

More than any other body in the country, the Army enjoys the confidence and affection of the people. The regime and its leadership must therefore insure themselves and must from time to time resort to various measures in order to ensure that absolute control of this formidable power will not be wrenched from its grasp. All the same, it is necessary to look at the general background in mid-1957. At that time, did the leaders see a real danger of a step in the direction of a take-over by Zhukov and therefore decide to depose him? Among the accusations levelled at Zhukov in the October Plenary resolutions there is no direct mention of Bonapartism, although the sentences about "a cult of his own personality" and "a line of eliminating supervision of the Army by the Party" taken together may hint at far-reaching ambitions, but neither in the *Pravda* editorial of 3 November nor in Koniev's venomous article in the same issue was there any explicit accusation of Bonapartism. The furthest that Koniev went was to say that Zhukov regarded the Army as his own private estate.

The accusation of Bonapartist leanings was not made publicly until February 1959 at the XXI Congress, fifteen months after Zhukov's deposition. It came at the end of the speech of Defence Minister Malinovsky, after he had dwelt on the help afforded by the October '57 Plenary resolutions in "improving Party-political action in the Army and Navy" and strengthening the Armed Forces in the spirit of Leninist principles of Party leadership, he went on to say,

> More than ever before, the Central Committee discerned in time former Defence Minister Marshal Zhukov's aspirations to cut the Army off from the Party and gave this new Bonapartist apparition the knock-out blow.[34]

Malinovsky repeated this accusation at the XXII Congress in October 1961, speaking of "the Bonapartist ambitions of Zhukov to seize power personally."[35]

---

34  *Pravda*, 4.2.59.

Khrushchev himself did not accuse Zhukov of Bonapartism until much later, when he wrote in the second volume of his memoirs:

> In time, however, he [Zhukov] assumed so much power that he began to worry the leadership. One by one, the other members of the Presidium started coming up to me and expressing their concern. They asked me whether I could see, as they could, that Zhukov was striving to seize control, that we were heading for a military *coup d'état*. We received information that Zhukov was indeed voicing Bonapartist aspirations in his conversations with military commanders. We couldn't let Zhukov stage a South American-style military take-over in our country.[36]

This passage in Khrushchev's memoirs deserves consideration, since Khrushchev was the prime mover in the decision to depose Zhukov. From all the foregoing it looks as if Khrushchev had no real grounds to fear an immediate threat for even one in the fairly near future) of a military *coup* led by Zhukov against the Party. It is more reasonable to assume that under the influence of the trauma of the June crisis that ended in Khrushchev's partial victory (with Zhukov's help), he feared Zhukov's rising power and was apprehensive of another leadership crisis when Zhukov might be liable to join with his rivals — and even perhaps put himself at their head. The danger hanging over Khrushchev's head was sufficient for him to draw the resolute conclusion that he must get rid of this potential threat. The explanations and the justifications afforded publicly would of course be different and as harsh as possible. Zhukov's standing and the power already concentrated in his hands called for sophisticated and conspiratorial methods in the preparations, lest it occur to Zhukov to use his power or resist his deposition. Khrushchev's expression, the "Bonapartist ambitions" that Zhukov

---

35 *Stenographic Report of the XX Congress of the CPSU* (Russian), Moscow, 1962, p. 120.

36 *Khrushchev Remembers,* Translated and edited by Strobe Talbot, Little Brown and Company, Boston, 1974, Vol. 2, p. 14.

## The Deposition of Marshal Zhukov

was supposed to have voiced, can be understood as trenchant opinions voiced by Zhukov in his conversations with military commanders concerning the supervision of commanders by the MPA workers. To interpret this as Bonapartism was certainly exaggerated, but did not run counter to the rules of Bolshevik dialectic.

The proof that Khrushchev and his supporters did not really believe that Zhukov was planning a South American-style *coup* to take over power from the Party[37] but rather that they saw him merely as a potential danger is afforded by the fact that Zhukov was not expelled from the Party: there was not even a demand for his expulsion (at least not publicly) — such as had been heard at the time regarding the "anti-Party group". Zhukov was not arrested. He did not lose his rank as Marshal.[38]

He continued serving until March 1958, when he retired with a good pension and was given a comfortable apartment in Moscow.[39] After

---

37 If Zhukov had really intended a South American-style *coup*, he must have had at least some associates at his side or other helpers in the planned conspiracy; but then these associates would have been arrested or deposed and publicly condemned. In fact nothing was heard of arrests or condemnations of Army people at this time.

38 Instances of loss of rank and posting occurred before Zhukov's deposition and after it as well: in 1956 the Chief of AA Defences, Kuznietsov, was demoted, and in 1963 Marshal Vorontozov.

39 Western researchers analysing Zhukov's deposition see the period after the June crisis as the decisive one, when fears and concern were aroused in the hearts of the leadership. In spite of the fact that the accusations in the October '57 Plenary resolutions refer to Zhukov's actions over a longer period, most of these researchers concentrate on Zhukov's Leningrad speeches as a challenge to the leadership. We have no possible way today of knowing for certain whether the leaders really evaluated Zhukov's behaviour in his last period in office and particularly his Leningrad speeches as being preparatory to a seizure of power. My belief, as I say above, is that they had no basis for this, which is why they did not treat Zhukov as someone who had conspired against them. I have however a piece of unofficial evidence, according to which a certain statement was supposed to have been made at the Central Committee; I consider it reliable though I have no additional confirmation. Lt.-Col. Y. V., already

Khrushchev's deposition, his successors saw fit to change the official attitude to Zhukov and to bring him back before the public. He was invited to the dais of honour at the great military parade that marked the 20th anniversary of the victory over Fascist Germany. In May 1965 I was present in Moscow on a week's visit, and I was invited together with our Ambassador to witness the great parade in the Red Square. I recall how surprised we were when we discovered Zhukov standing among the leaders atop the Lenin Mausoleum, dressed in his Marshal's uniform, his breast covered with medals and decorations. My surprise was shared by the diplomats and senior Government officials surrounding us, for Zhukov had disappeared from view eight years before and all they had heard of him since then was denigration.

In his book, *Party Organisation and Development in the Soviet Army and Navy* (published by the official Party publishers), which we have cited freely in these chapters, Petrov terminates his factual account of Zhukov's deposition as follows:

> This is the Party logic and morality that has been formed in the course of many years: anyone who attempts to oppose

cited in these pages, who was a veteran in the Party institutions in the Army, stated that after Zhukov's deposition, a circular letter classified "Secret" was read in the Party Bureau of the Division (the Party control arm), in which it was said, *inter alia*, that Zhukov wished to seize power, and that he had readied a regiment or regiments in the environs of Moscow, some of whose men were specially trained for the Cheka-type operations and spying. Zhukov was to be at the head of the move to seize power. This does not sound convincing to me, introduced like this into a Central Committee circular immediately after Zhukov's deposition. It can be accepted — and it is more likely — that all this was added by the senior political worker from the Political Administration who read out the letter and who took the liberty of adding on a bit in the spirit of the wholesale attacks current on Zhukov. Officers whom I interviewed contended that the whole packet of accusations against Zhukov was not accepted by them as credible and that observations were heard such as, "It's all Khrushchev s plotting ..." It looks as if it was not the credibility of the accusations that determined the issue but well-rooted Party usage.

the Party and to take upon himself roles that belong to the Party is no longer worthy of trust, regardless of his achievements in the past.[40]

When Soviet author Petrov uses customary phraseology and writes, "whoever opposes the Party", he means whoever opposes the inner Party leadership that is in power at the time in question, and not anyone who opposes the rule of the Communist Party in the country and aspires to put an end to that rule. "The Party logic and morality that has been formed in the course of many years" means, in other words, that whoever fights the leadership and loses to his rivals in the fight runs the risk of being declared an opponent of the whole Party. Were not Malenkov, Molotov and Kaganovich called "the anti-Party group"?

In sum, the collective leadership prevailed after the June crisis, but Khrushchev's victory was not yet complete. He had to make some compromises, such as letting some of his opponents stay on the Presidium. He could not be certain that peace and quiet had been fully secured and that a crisis would not occur in the leadership after a time. In this situation, especially troubling significance attached to certain things that Zhukov said during the June crisis and in his Leningrad speeches. The need was becoming pressing to introduce reforms in order to tighten the Party control over the Armed Forces — control which had slackened somewhat. It was clear enough that tightening control would meet with opposition from the Minister of Defence, who was considered the prime mover — or the guilty party — in this slackening.

In the Soviet regime, all these considerations combined to point the way to the characteristic conclusion — that it was preferable not to run the risk of a possible take-over or even of opposition on the Army and its heads. Hence too perhaps the complete consensus in the leadership over deposing Zhukov, unlike the differences of opinion with the "anti-Party group" over reforming the national economic councils, over tractor stations and the like, or

---

40 Petrov, *op. cit.*, p. 464.

even over nominations to important posts. The leadership feared a threat to the very existence of the principle of the Party dictatorship. Without question, this principle united all groups and all those of different views, conservatives and reformists alike, and taught them to do what seemed necessary to forestall this danger.

*CHAPTER VII*

THE OCTOBER 1957 PLENARY RESOLUTIONS

The main purpose of the October 1957 Central Committee Plenary Resolutions on "improving Party-political activity in the Army and Navy" was, as we have explained, to get the Armed Forces back under the lead of the Party and more closely supervised by the Main Political Administration and its organs, so as to forestall any possibility of the Army's detaching itself from the Party and turning into an independent focus of power.

The Plenary decisions were the end of the chapter as regards the deposition of Zhukov, but they were the prelude to a thoroughgoing reform of the relationship between the Party and the Armed Forces. This was evident in the characteristic drafting of the Resolutions, which signalled to whom it concerned that they represented a new "general line". They were cited and relied on for many years as a turning-point of historic importance in the development of the Forces.[1] Yet only a year after the Plenary, Minister of Defence Marshal Malinovsky published an article significantly entitled, "Let us apply the Resolutions of the October Central Committee Plenary, and not hang back"[2] which was in fact in-

---

[1] Marshal Gretchko: "The October Plenary was a decisive event in the life of the Party, the State, and the Soviet Armed Forces ... beginning a significant new stage in the development of the Armed Forces". *A renewed spring forward in party Political Activity in the Soviet Army and Navy,* Voyenizdat, Moscow, 1960, p. 26 (Russian).

[2] Marshal Malinovsky: "We make bold to affirm that the decisions of the October Plenary opened a new phase in the upbuilding and improvement of the Armed Forces, their combat preparedness and their political education. ... The favourable and effective influence of the

tended to undo or at least put a brake on the damage their application was doing. We shall now analyse this paradoxical development.

## *What Was in the Resolutions*

Let us first present some passages from the Plenary Resolutions that speak for themselves. The starting point in the preamble was the arms race in the capitalist States, which made it necessary to promote the combat preparedness of the Forces, strengthen military discipline and educate the troops in devotion to the fatherland and the Party. The Resolutions affirmed:

> The Central Committee Plenary holds that it is of the greatest value for solving these problems that Party-political action in the Army and Navy be improved and be directed to reinforcing the combat power of our Armed Forces and unifying all their personnel around the Communist Party and the Government....
>
> In fact, however, Party-political action still suffers from serious shortcomings and even at times from simple failure to appreciate the value of Party-political action itself. ...
>
> The XX Congress set the Party and the people the task of keeping our defences level with contemporary science and preserving the security of our Socialist State. In solving this problem an important role falls to the Military Councils with the sole Commanders, to the political institutions and the Party organisations in the Army and Navy. All of them must carry out the policy of the Communist Party firmly and consistently. ...
>
> The primary source of strength for our Army and Navy lies in the Communist Party, their organiser, leader and educat-

Plenary Resolutions is reflected in all the later development and improvement of the Soviet Armed Forces." *Red Star*, 1 November 1958. Other passages from this article are quoted later in this Chapter.

ors. ... We must always remember Lenin's teaching: "The policy of the military institution, like that of all the other institutions and Ministries, is carried out strictly on the basis of the general directives laid down by the Party through the Central Committee and under its direct supervision."[3]

*Supplementary Regulations.* On the heels of these weighty but general Resolutions, more detailed decisions were reached and made public regarding the various spheres of action envisaged. While a constant flow of propaganda stressed the general line, supplementary instructions were issued, regulations formulated and interpretations and "explanations" multiplied. The efforts to apply the decisions in practice continued for years, not always with success. Some of the desired changes could be introduced at once, while for others more preparation was needed. The first Instruction was issued within a fortnight after the October Plenary and it directed that more time must be given to political education of members of the forces — "one of the basic forms of educational activity in the Army". The military historian Petrov recounts: "Instead of one hour of study of current political affairs once a week (as ordered by the previous Minister of Defence Zhukov), it was again made law that members of the forces must receive political information in the morning hours, twice a week, 30 minutes each time, and that two evenings a week must be devoted to cultural-educational activities."[4] The not immediately obvious difference between the previous hour once a week and half an hour twice a week was that the political studies now took place obligatorily in the morning hours, and according to the officers we interviewed, even in the first early hours of training, when the men were still fresh and took things in better. What is more, the commanders were forbidden to exempt soldiers from these studies, not even for kitchen duties or similar services. These instructions were

---

3 *The Communist Party of the USSR Concerning the Armed Forces of the USSR,* Moscow, 1958, pp. 406–7.
4 *The Communist Party of the USSR and the Development of the Soviet Armed Forces,* Moscow, 1965, p. 429.

181

strictly implemented, including the two evenings a week dedicated to culture.

The next thing reorganised was political study for the commanders corps. "Study of Leninist-Marxist theory by the officers was made an integral part of officer training. In the 1958 training year, 50 hours of service time were devoted to Marxist-Leninist instruction."[5]

As part of the over-all effort to prevent the Army from detaching itself from "the Party and the people" or, as it was put in the deliberations of the Central Committees of the Republics and Regions, "to strengthen the bonds between the toilers and the fighters,"[6] many attempts were made to bring the men in the units closer to the civilian population in the places where they were stationed. Doubtless, targets were set, and statistics are available. One report stated that in the Carpathian MD in the course of 1959, activists of the Party, Government institutions and economic undertakings who appeared before the soldiers delivered some 3,000 lectures; according to the same source, army personnel in the MD for their part delivered some 10,000 lectures to the toilers of the Ukraine. In spite of it all, according to our evidence these efforts met with absolutely no success at all, for neither side had the least interest in the matter. A political worker in the Army, who used to have to give the local Party organisations a report on Party-political activity in his unit, says that in fact he had nothing to tell, and interest dwindled rapidly. In most places, "Army Day" once a year was sufficient: a meeting of the local Party organisation and visits to the units by schoolchildren. Active participation by Army people in civilian Party institutions also slackened off and finally disappeared.[7]

---

5 *Ibid.*
6 *The People and the Army are One,* Voyenizdat, Moscow, 1959, p. 41, apud *The Communist Party of the USSR and the Development of the Soviet Armed Forces,* p. 430.
7 Testimony of Col. B.A., who served as a political worker.

## Explaining the General Line

"Discussions" on the Plenary Resolution were held at meetings of the Party organisations in the Army, at commanders' "consultations" and at meetings among themselves. A large place was given to the subject of the Resolutions in the daily press and periodicals, both of the Army and the general public.

In February 1958, advantage was taken of the 40th anniversary of the creation of the Red Army to start off a fresh wave of propaganda in the spirit of the October Plenary in all the media and at appearances of important personalities before Army units. The party paper, *Communist,* published an article by Bagramyan, who said that the Plenary Resolutions — "imbued with Leninist idealism" — showed the Party's earnest desire to strengthen the Armed Forces (and not the contrary, of course — no such idea was ever so much as hinted at). Improved Party-political activity was what was really needed to strengthen the Army. The Army, he said, constituted the real school for political education. It was there that the Army's educational problems were solved by the combined and coordinated efforts of the commanders, the political workers and institutions and the Party organisations.[8] The Party's "information" organisation in the Army had its hands full "explaining" that the new general line was really in perfect harmony with the idea of "unity of command". To do this it had to call in question the straightforward, professional meaning that Zhukov had given the term "unity of command" — only one head to the regiment. This meaning, which had only begun to gain currency in Zhukov's time, had to be changed back again. The commanders were understandably attracted to Zhukov's version and it took a great deal of authoritative "explanation" to convince them that they were in need of partners to share the conduct of the regiment's affairs. Here is how it was put in a publication of the Lenin Military-Political Academy:

---

8 A. Bagramyan, "The Army's Glorious Path", *Kommunist,* No. 2, Moscow, 1958, pp. 47–48.

> The Central Committee directed particular attention to Leninist understanding of the meaning of "unity of command" in the Soviet Army. ... This [sc. "Leninist understanding"] teaches us that putting "unity of command" into practice means getting to the stage where all commanders and those in charge not only concern themselves with the military training of the officers and men but also educate them with the constant support of the Party organisations and so develop their high-level political-morale and fighting qualities.⁹

Minister of Defence, Marshal Malinovsky, explained "unity of command" as being on an entirely different basis from command in capitalist armies. "With us, it ["unity of command"] develops and grows stronger on the basis of the Party, and this is precisely what constitutes the specific thing about it. This means, first and foremost, strict implementation of Communis Party policy by every "sole commander". He must possess profound political consciousness and political attainments; he must constantly demand of himself and his subordinates personal responsibility in carrying out service duties, self-effacement [sic] and concern for the soldiers."¹⁰

The new head of the MPA, General P. Golikov, was very good at these "explanations":

> Unity of command, in theory and in practice — and not only according to external form — can only be strengthened on the basis of energetic implementation of the October Plenary Resolutions. Life teaches us that the "sole" commanders' authority is only strong where there is well-organised Party-political activity, where there is systematic action to educate Party members and candidate members [sc. in the ranks] in the spirit of the Communist idea and where the Party organisations act with flaming enthusiasm on a high level of criticism and self-criticism.¹¹

---

9   *The Communist Party of the USSR and the Development,* ... p. 427.
10  R. Malinovsky, *Standing Vigilantly on Guard for Peace,* apud *The Communist Party of the USSR and the Development,* ... p. 424.
11  P. Golikov, "Let us ceaselessly improve Party political activity in the

The October 1957 Plenary Resolutions

The political leadership did not of course confine itself to "explaining" the changed meaning of "unity of command" but also set about introducing organisational reforms to put the change into effect. What the leadership was most concerned over was the attitude of the senior command in the Armed Forces. In Zhukov's day and with his assistance, the Military District Commanders and those of parallel rank had begun to act much more like "sole" commanders, making their own decisions on military affairs in the MD and in the forces under their command. The situation with senior commanders' having fairly wide powers entrusted to them without close Party supervision, in control of tremendous force, sometimes all on their own far from the centre, able to give their subordinates orders on military matters and service matters too — this situation did not fit in at all with the aims of the October Plenary Resolutions. The leadership therefore decided on far-reaching reforms of the powers entrusted to the senior commanders. The preparations for

Soviet Armed Forces", *The October Plenary Resolutions in Application*, Voyenizdat, Moscow, 1959, p. 27 (Russian). Another ceaseless improver, the head of the Political Administration and member of the Military Council of the Northern Fleet, Read Admiral Aberchuk, could do no less for his part than insist that putting Party decisions into practice was what would guarantee stronger "unity of command" and elevate the role of the commanders corps in training and educating those under them. He proceeded to list six things that the October Plenary Resolutions demanded of the "sole" commander: "First, as regards his outlook and activities, the "sole" commander" has to be a devoted Party man, heart and soul. ... Always and in all respects, he must put Party policy and directives into effect. Secondly, he must not only be an expert in military matters but also an educator, a political activist armed with the victorious conceptions of Marxism-Leninism. This necessarily makes him an enthusiastic propagandist for Party views, decisions and directives. Thirdly, the commander will only be able to record achievements if he relies on the Party organisation. ... Sixthly, for there to be an organic link binding the military and political leadership to the education of the soldiers, there has to be unity of action on the part of the commanders, the political workers and the Party organisations. After all, they are all aiming at the same goals." *Ibid.*, pp. 152–54.

introducing these reforms took nearly six months. The instrument chosen as the proper one for ensuring close supervision of the senior commanders and limiting their powers was the Military Council.

## Reform of the Military Councils

In April 1958 the Central Committee decided on some quite fundamental changes in the composition of the Military Council and in the attribution of their powers. Petrov gives the following account of the reform:

> The Central Committee of the Party found it necessary to change the Military Councils ... and enlarge their composition. Taking part in the Military Council of the Military District, Army Group, Navy, Army or Flotilla, would be the Commanding Officer, presiding over the Council, the Military Council "comrade" [sc. political worker], the Secretary of the local Party Committee, the commander's second-in-command, the chief of staff, and other responsible workers.[11a] In the regulations confirmed by the Party C.C., it was stressed that the purpose of the Military Councils was to solve all the most important problems of Army life and activity. The Councils were responsible to the C.C., to the Government and to the Defence Minister for the state of the troops and their combat preparedness. The Council had to pay constant attention to the state of discipline and to see to transmitting Party-political activities to the Army. ... The rights and duties of the "comrade" on the Military Council were considerably extended. ... Decisions in the Council were by majority vote and were binding on all the Council members. They were carried out by order of the commander. In the event that the "comrade" disagreed with the majority decision reached at the Council.

---

[11a] According to Col. N.O., sometimes one of the "responsible workers" was also the KGB representative.

he had the right to transmit his views to the C.C., the Minister of Defence and the Government. ...
The Military Councils now became the real institutions of collective leadership [sc. in the Armed Forces]. ... Their composition had to be confirmed by the Party C.C.[12]

The Central Committee ratified the personal composition of the new Military Councils in August 1958.

Similar decisions had been taken in the past, in July 1950, concerning the composition and powers of the Military Councils.[13] After Stalin's death, however, the practical enforcement of these decisions had weakened under Zhukov's influence, and it was therefore necessary to renew them and make them even stricter. In an article of February 1958, Defence Minister Malinovsky pointed to the need to reinforce the Military Councils: "The Military Councils have a growing role," he wrote. "More and more they have become institutions vested with wide powers, bearing entire responsibility to the Party and the Government for the state of affairs in the Army, maintaining the principle of unity of command to the full and strengthening it."[14] It is more than doubtful whether Malinovsky's predecessor as Defence Minister, Marshal Zhukov, could ever have brought himself to say that the Military Councils were "maintaining the principle of unity of command to the full" and even strengthening it: This called for a greater degree of dialectic skill than Zhukov was blessed with. Malinovsky apparently had had a better Marxist formation to assist him in his career as Defence Minister in this difficult period of "reforms".

One of the most purposely weighted decisions was that taken in April 1958 by which the head of the Political Administration of the Military District and equivalent instances would also serve as the "comrade" on the MD Military Council.[15]

These changes taken together — the new composition and pow-

12  Petrov, *op. cit.*, pp. 468–69.
13  *Ibid.*, p. 453.
14  *Red Star*, 1 February 1958, apud *The October Resolutions* ... p. 8.
15  Petrov, *op. cit.*, p. 472.

ers of the Military Councils and the merging of the two posts of Political Administration head and Military Council "comrade" — meant a reversion to a much earlier stage. The definitions in the Central Committee Resolutions and the regulations issued subsequently left no doubt about the extent of the reduction in the commanders' authority: Zhukov's "sole" commander was now made dependent on the Military Council members, and mainly on the "comrade", even in purely military affairs such as maintaining discipline and combat preparedness. What was involved here was more than intrusive Party supervision, it was direct intervention by the Party representative in "every sphere of Army life and activity", almost as in the period of the creation of the Red Army and the appointment of the first Military Commissars. What had happened was that the Party leadership had simply panicked at the possible prospect of the senior command's cutting itself off from the Party and becoming an independent focus of power.

## The MPA Streamlined

Along with the "reform" of the Military Councils, it was necessary to tighten up direct control from the centre over the activity of the political institution in the Armed Forces, the MPA, was reorganised so as to present a structure at once more centralised and more flexible. Petrov relates:

> In April 1958 the Central Committee found it would be more effective to centralise Party-political activity in the arms of the forces by abolishing the intermediate link in the Land Forces, the Navy and the Air Force. The name "MPA" was now changed to "Main Political Administration of the Soviet Army and Navy".[16]

In the cadre of these changes, in April 1958 the Central Committee issued annexes to the directives of the Party organisations in the Armed Forces, stressing the responsibility of the Party organisations

16 *Ibid.*, p. 469.

for the implementation of Party decisions. The annexes defined the rights of Communist Party organisation representatives regarding "criticism and self-criticism", giving Party cells more extensive rights to discuss personal problems. Other means were also provided for expanding and enhancing the role of Party organisations in the life of the units.[17] These additional rights and powers that were now accorded the Party organisations clearly lowered the status of the Commanders and especially of the Regimental Commanders (and others on the equivalent command level). While in theory it was not permitted to criticise the Commander's orders and instructions, in practice the enlarged powers of the Party organisations and political institutions meant that the Commander was certainly no longer "sole" commander. In cold hard fact, he was largely at the mercy of his sharers in the command — which may very well have been the intention of the Central Committee.

*More Party Members in the Armed Forces.* Defence Minister Malinovsky, after boldly affirming that giving the Military Councils "entire responsibility" meant maintaining the principle of unity of command to the full,[17a] had to try and show how this would happen. "The Regimental Commander," he wrote, "is supported in his work by the Party organisation, but at the same time he himself, as a Party member, orients the activity of the Party organisation towards better implementation of combat affairs, battle preparedness and political programmes, and also for strengthening military discipline".[18] A commander who was not a Party member would be still more at a disadvantage: he could not even accept this piece of advice from the Defence Minister and "orient" the Party organisation to help him, and on the other hand he was very largely dependent on it.

For the sake of strengthening the Party organisation in the units or, as it was worded, "for the sake of ideo-organisational strength-

---

17 *Party Political Activity in the Armed Forces of the USSR,* A Historical Survey, Voyenizdat, Moscow, 1974, p. 317 (Russian).
17a In the article of 1 Lebruary 1958 already cited. See p. 187 above.
18 *Red Star,* 1 February 1958, *loc. cit.,* p. 14.

ening of the organisations", more candidates for Party membership were mobilised than previously, and transfer was speeded up from the status of candidacy to that of full member. In the first half of 1958 alone, the number of new candidates accepted was 20 per cent higher than in the second half of 1957. The proportion of candidates admitted as full members went up by a third. Over 37 per cent of the new candidates were officers.[19] In the four years following the October Plenary, two and a half times as many members were accepted into Party organisations as in the four years before the Plenary. Alongside this, a great effort was made to get the commanders into the political organisations in the Army. It was reported that in 1959 the number of Regimental C.O.s and naval commanders in the Party institutions was fourteen times as many as in 1957.[20]

*The MPA Offensive.* In Zhukov's day, the political workers had felt despised and humiliated, and the political institutions had seen their authority very considerably reduced. Now they had been given the signal to go ahead and they sallied out to do battle and settle accounts with the Commanders — and not exactly on the score of military efficiency or of the Commander's fitness for his post. Attacks by the political workers took various forms. The famous rights of "criticism and self-criticism" were supposed to stop short of the commanders' direct orders and instructions in the purely military sphere, but this was not adhered to. Petrov says this explicitly and gives it a favourable gloss:

> Criticism and self-criticism were not limited now to the sphere of Party activity but expanded into the military sphere as well, helping to disclose failings that hampered progress in the Armies. ... Criticism by the Party helped many Commanders to correct their shortcomings.[21]

This criticism caused the commanders no little annoyance and not

19 *October Plenary Resolutions,* ... p. 30.
20 Petrov, *op. cit.,* pp. 475–56.
21 *Ibid.,* p. 477.

least because the political workers were not for the most part distinguished for their military knowledge and experience. The commanders bore direct responsibility for spheres of action which largely determined the targets their units were supposed to attain, while the "politicals" who criticised and interfered had no such responsibility. The Army commanders' dissatisfaction increased in direct proportion to their critics' growing self-assurance.

Under the influence of and pressure from the political institutions, many commanders were discharged from the Army. Many political officers tried to secure suitable military posts in the place of those discharged, and in many instances they succeeded. Not unnaturally, this process angered the commanders, and not surprisingly these developments in the units and formations — side by side with the renewed restrictions on the powers of the senior commanders — had their effect on military discipline. The political workers were not easily to be deterred from keeping up their assault on the commanders, and protests against their conduct began to be heard as early as February 1958. Writers chose the tactic of stressing given parts of the October Plenary Resolutions and certain clauses of the later documents, doing so at first with marked caution so as not to seem to question the sacred character of the Resolutions themselves, perish the thought.

The first to launch the counter-offensive was Col. Talensky, the military theoretician who had been the first to open the debate on Stalin's military doctrine in the early 50's. He did not question the October Plenary decisions — he simply ignored them. In an article of his that appeared at the end of February 1958 on the occasion of the 40th anniversary of the founding of the Red Army, Talensky reviewed the path taken by the Army and its achievements in the course of its 40 years of existence, without devoting even a single sentence to the "historic decisions" of the Plenary and their contribution to improving the Army.[22] According to the rules of the game in Soviet publications, a deliberate "oversight" of this nature on so "live" an issue and one of such great signi-

22  *Red Star*, 26 February 1958.

ficance in Army life — especially in an over-all survey like this — must call for an explanation. It can be assumed that the fact of ignoring the Resolutions in itself constituted criticism of the exaggerated importance previously accorded them.

A few days after the publication of Talensky's article along with all the other articles in honour of Red Army Day, the Commander of the Far East MD dwelt at length and in detail on the achievements of commanders in his MD in raising the level of combat preparedness of the troops; he described the tactical exercises carried out successfully by his officers and their progress in handling new weapons. Party activities and the Plenary Resolutions got only a brief mention and Zhukov's deposition was not referred to at all.[23]

What is noteworthy here is the change of style in the military press as compared with the previous five months. It was something new to read praise of the commanders without repeated stress on the contribution of the political workers and the political institutions. The wind was veering round.

During March 1958 articles by political workers again attacked the commanders for not sufficiently appreciating criticism in Party meetings and for taking it out on the political workers. An outspoken article of this kind came from the Head of the Political Administration in the Navy:

> We in the Navy love and appreciate the political workers with strict principles who speak out boldly against shortcomings and are not afraid to spoil relations if necessary.[24]

He attacked certain commanders for their hardness in having a political worker discharged because of the way he criticised them. The article was clearly intended to encourage the political workers not to be afraid of the commanders and not to shrink from "spoiling relations" with them, hinting that if they were attacked as a result they would be defended.

23 Major-General B. Penkovsky, *Red Star*, 2 March 1958.
24 Captain (Grade A) A. Biduk, *Red Star*, 18 March 1958.

## The October 1957 Plenary Resolutions

It is clear that in spite of the unfavourable aftermath of the Plenary policy in the units themselves, the Central Committee and the MPA were not prepared to give ground. Proof of this is to be found in the additional decisions, instructions and regulations that continued to be published in the course of 1958. It must nevertheless be assumed that undermining army discipline was not in fact the main intention of the Plenary when it framed the October Resolutions, and the leadership found itself obliged to seek ways to reduce the commanders' opposition to the reforms and lessen the harm done. It was probably in this connection that the MPA head, General Zheltov, was replaced by General P. A. Golikov, who had won fame as a soldier and was likely to be acceptable to commanders in the field.[25]

*"Unity of Command" to the Fore Again.* The political workers' assault on the commanders continued and apparently even increased, and as a result discipline declined still more. The very foundations of the Army were being undermined and some reaction was clearly becoming imperative. One of the accepted techniques for criticising a given state of affairs in the Army or for reacting to a given phenomenon was to start off with an article by a military correspondent in the Army daily paper, *Red Star*. A key article of this kind, entitled, "Unity of command — how to strengthen it constantly", appeared in *Red Star* in August 1958. The article dealt directly with the painful problem of the relations between the political worker and the commander, or more precisely with the political worker's insulting attitude towards the commander and his failure to treat him as "sole" commander. The writer, a Colonel, described his visit to a certain formation:

Discipline was not good in some units of the formation. The

---

25 Golikov was a combat officer. In 1939 he was already in command of the 6th Army and in 1940 he was for a time Chief of General Staff. In the war (in 1941) he commanded the 10th Army. In 1942 he was Commander on the Briansk Front and after that on the Voronezh Front. From August to October 1942 he was second-in-command on the Stalingrad Front. He served as Head of the MPA until 1962.

Political Section decided to discuss this problem at a meeting of the Party *"aktiv"*. And this is how they got ready for the discussion: — the head of the political Section was to address the meeting on the subject; he did not consult the Commander of the formation or the C.O.s of the units at all on how to present the matter. Some of the officers only learnt about the meeting that was planned when they were asked to report on the state of military discipline in their units. Was this perhaps an isolated instance of the politicals' permitting themselves to ignore the commanders? No, unfortunately not. Here is another example: ... an appointment to a post in the Komsomol. ... In this case, all the negotiations over the appointment and then the appointment itself were carried out behind the back of the commander. ... And after all, it is he who bears the responsibility and he should have been consulted. All these things, whether intentionally or not, depreciate the position of the unit commander. ... Lack of friendly coordination between the commander and the head of the Political Section has a bad effect on the state of Partypolitical action. Here is an example: In certain units, complaints against a number of Communists were submitted to the Party organisation on the grounds that these men did not set a personal example in carrying out the commander's instructions in matters regarding their service, but the complaints did not worry the leaders of the Party organisation and the workers of the Political Section. There must be an improvement in educational action so that the soldiers will learn to respect their commanders' orders.

... All the facts cited here prove that the question of strengthening unity of command and supporting the commanders' authority needs to have more attention paid to it.[26]

That an article so openly critical of Party organisations in the Army was allowed to be published in the period of implementation of

---

26 Colonel M. Yerzunov, "Let us constantly strengthen unity of command," *Red Star,* 9 August 1958.

The October 1957 Plenary Resolutions

the October Plenary Resolutions proves that these bodies had gone far beyond the permissible bounds in their assault on the commanders. They had to be reined in, and this was no easy matter. Once the reins had been loosed after the deposition of Zhukov, it was hard to pull them in again even partially.

### A Year Later

In October 1958 it was the turn of the political institutions in the Armed Forces to receive new Central Committee instructions and regulations. These were issued in a lengthy document, replete with the traditional obligatory quotations from Lenin's writings. The document was intended to reinforce the political institutions, but it had probably been in preparation for some time and had already been overtaken by the course of events. In it a recurrent refrain could be heard that must have afforded commanders a moment's grim amusement: "Expanding the tasks of the political institutions and Party organisations and strengthening Party-political activity among the troops to the utmost helps strengthen unity of command."[27]

This affirmation had already been flatly disproved by reality. "Unity of command" had been weakened, not strengthened. Discipline in the Army had gone to pieces and the commanders were having great difficulty in functioning as "sole" commanders."[28]

As part of the moves to get the commanders to cooperate more willingly, an attempt was made to raise the ideological level of Marxist-Leninist instruction for officers, generals and admirals. In October 1958, a regulation was issued jointly by the Defence Minister and the Head of the MPA, which sought (in the words of

27 "The new attitude concerning the political institutions in the Soviet Army and Navy," *October Plenary Resolutions* ..., pp. 42–43.
28 See beginning of this Chapter (7) above. My statements on the decline of discipline in the Armed Forces are based on the opinions of all the former Soviet ex-officers interviewed and on the remarks scattered freely and lavishly in the Soviet publications, mainly in the pages of the monthlies and the Army periodicals, as well as on the articles cited in this Chapter.

a military writer) "to link words and deeds, to link the propaganda with the deeds of building up Communism and with the tasks of the Armed Forces."[29] In the opinion of our ex-officers, the Marxist-Leninist training remained as boring as ever, and those who had to attend did their best to get out of it.

By November 1958 matters were sufficiently serious to call for open official intervention. Defence Minister Marshal Malinovsky himself, in an article in *Red Star* reviewed the changes introduced as a result of the October 1957 Plenary Resolutions, discussed the shortcomings still existing, and then went to openly criticise insufficient discipline in the Forces. "The need for conscious discipline has increased in this age of modern technique," he affirmed. "Hence in the future too our attention must focus on the problem of strengthening military discipline. Many people think little of tidy soldierly appearance, but it is important as the external sign of inner qualities of morale. Educating the soldiers and taking care of them has to go together with uncompromising strictness on the part of the commanders towards those under their command and of the Party towards its members and the Komsomol. Without close unity between these two things — education and strictness — there is no prospect of improving discipline. An important condition for strengthening discipline is strict application of Leninist principles — the principles of unity of command. The task of the political institutions, the Party organisations and the Communists is to strengthen unity of command in the Army and Navy and to maintain the authority of the commanders. They must inculcate a sense of responsibility in all the soldiers about fulfilling the duties of the service and obeying the orders of the commanders and those in charge. For Party work, preference should be given to the Communists among the combat officers.[30]

If one follows up Marshal Malinovsky's many appearances and declarations since his appointment as Defence Minister about a

---

29 Colonel M. Kalashnik, "A renewed spring forward...", *October Plenary Resolutions....*, p. 55.
30 *Red Star*, 1 November 1958. See footnote 2 above.

## The October 1957 Plenary Resolutions

year before the publication of this article, one will plainly see that there has been a change here, a real shift of emphasis. After he replaced the deposed Zhukov, Malinovsky was very active in all the efforts to make the Army recognise that the Party and its organs must take the lead in all aspects of Army life. Though he always spoke of the need for discipline — and of "unity of command" as an important condition for better discipline — he had previously laid the main stress on strengthening Party activity, increasing the responsibility of the Military Councils and so forth. He used to say that the status of the "sole" commander" in the Soviet Armed Forces differed from that of commanders in other armies precisely because it developed and grew stronger on the basis of the Party. True, in the article quoted above too, Malinovsky recalls the need for the commander to rely on the Party and on "criticism and self-criticism" for help in uncovering shortcomings. All the same, so that there should be no mistake about his main intention this time, he returns again and again to the dominant theme that it is absolutely essential that the Pary organisations use all their power to strengthen the commanders' authority and to support their strict demands on those under them.

It is certain that both the political officers and the military commanders were able to see the difference in the tone of this article, indicative of the Minister's new state of mind. They rightly interpreted the broad hint to the political workers that their job was to assist the commanders and not to interfere with them.

Now, a year after Zhukov's deposition and the October Plenary Resolutions, when the damage to the Army from the assault launched by the Party elements was already clearly apparent, even the Political Administration workers themselves were obliged to change their tune in their propaganda. Thus, for example, a Military Council member, head of the Political Administration of the Far East MD, wrote:

> The duty of the commanders of the political institutions and the Party organisations that stems from the October Plenary Resolutions is to strengthen unity of command by all the

197

means at their disposal, to support the commanders who make strict demands and to educate the soldiers in the spirit of absolute obedience to the commanders and those in charge.[31]

In 1959 Minister of Defence Malinovsky reverted to the question of discipline and the political workers' interfering with the work of the commander and warned them not to damage the running of the Army system, saying, "If you harm the work of the commander and go over his head, the result is bad. You get the wrong results and produce disorder, and where there is disorder there are quarrels, struggles and disasters."[32]

Marshal Zakharov, like Malinovsky, waxed wrath over the grave results of poor discipline in the units: "With the swiftly changing conditions of modern warfare, when the soldier no longer wields a sword but new arms of tremendous power and destructive capacity, lack of discipline can lead to catastrophe."[33] Marshal Gretchko also made his contribution about "the growth of the absolute role of the sole commander, who in the new conditions has to have an outstanding capacity for taking decisions and who has to rely on himself and respond speedily to changing situations."[34]

These passages may seem to testify to no more than a change of emphasis. However, since they came from Army chiefs and MPA heads, they provide a clear demonstration of how the Soviet machine changes direction in carrying out decisions. Other passages in these same articles were written along the accepted lines that had been laid down with the introduction of the reforms, but Soviet readers develop a keen sense of direction and of changes in the wind, and would not be misled by the covering jargon.

The "general line" and the aims of the October 1957 Plenary

---

31 Colonel A. Shmelev, "A renewed spring forward..." *October Plenary Resolutions* ..., p. 249.
32 Marshal Malinovsky, "A renewed spring forward ...." *October Plenary Resolutions* ..., p. 16.
33 Marshal Zakharov, *ibid.*, p. 70.
34 Marshal Gretchko, *ibid.*, p. 33.

The October 1957 Plenary Resolutions

had not changed during 1958, but in order to lessen the damage caused by their over-zealous application, the stress was changed in orienting the political elements in the Army. Instead of stressing the right to intervene in all matters within the commanders' sphere of command, the stress was now on assisting the commanders to act effectively as "sole" commanders," supporting their authority and "educating" the men to obey them. Both things — the right to intervene and the duty to assist — had of course been there all along, but by the end of the first year the pressure of reality had brought the second to the fore again. The change of stress did not however affect the respective powers of the senior commanders and their Military Councils. The Military Council remained a "collective institution" and not an advisory body (as it had been previously), and the powers of the "comrade" were not reduced.

## "Quis Custodiet ipsos Custodes?"

In August 1960 a further reform was introduced in the Army and Navy Main Political Administration. The standing of the MPA *vis-à-vis* the Military Councils was defined as follows:

> The Central Committee decided to set up a Bureau of the Administration. ... The method of taking decisions in the Bureau was the same as that in the Military Councils, that is to say, by majority vote of the members, the decisions being implemented by order of the Head of the Administration. A member of the Bureau has the right to report to the Central Committee on his view (if he is in the minority). ... The Central Committee found it necessary to define the task of the Bureau in administering the Military Councils and electing their members. Proposals on the composition of the Military Councils are submitted to the Central Committee jointly by the Ministry of Defence and the MPA, which are also bound to conduct criticism of the practical action of the Councils and report on the results to the Government and the Central Committee. Deputy heads of the MPA at the same

time also hold the post of "comrades" in the Military Councils of the various arms of the Armed Forces.[35]

This reform drew still tighter the noose of Party Supervision over the Commanders of the different arms and the senior commanders in each arm. The presence on the Military Councils in the different arms of Deputy Heads of the MPA, vested with the powers of the "comrade", made for still closer supervision of the highest-ranking officers. Setting up the Bureau of the Administration, and giving it the right to report to the Central Committee on minority opinion, meant in fact supervision over the supervisors themselves.

The fundamental problem remained unsolved: the contest went on between the two channels of control in the Armed Forces and there is no reason to think that it would not keep on going on in the future.

---

35  Petrov, *op. cit.*, p. 470.

## CHAPTER VIII

## EDUCATION AND POLITICAL SUPERVISION

The Soviet Armed Forces network of education and political supervision is the direct offspring of the principle that the army has to be under the lead of the Party. This is the bedrock of Soviet Communist Party theory. The Red Army was accompanied by stringent political supervision from the day it was founded.

The political apparatus is the Party's instrument for training men and officers alike to be loyal to the Party and its ideology and to the Soviet State. The apparatus is there to see to it that the army should not deviate (perish the thought) from the paths of complete obedience to the political leadership.

The foundations of the centralised system of education and supervision were laid as early as March 1919, at the VIII Party Congress. From then on the Party leadership at the head of the Soviet State has consistently invested very considerable resources in building up the defences of the State and the regime. In this great undertaking the political apparatus has had an active role assigned to it by the Party — political indoctrination. The apparatus has undergone numerous organisational and other changes in the course of its existence and we have already remarked some of the ups and downs in its relations with the military command.

The backbone of the political apparatus in the army is constituted by what are called the political institutions. Text-books of the military political colleges define the basic tasks of the political institutions in the Armed Forces as follows:

> The political institutions of the Army and Navy are the institutions of the Communist Party of the Soviet Union for

orientation and guidance within the Armed Forces of the Soviet Union; the political institutions actively carry out the policy of the Party; they educate and organise the Communists and Komsomolists* and all who serve in the Army; they mobilise the fighting masses to perform their combat and study tasks withsuccess. ...

The role and the responsibility of the political institutions are now** even greater than in the past on account of the need to strengthen the defensive power of the State and the combat readiness of the Armies to the utmost.[1]

To this definition of the tasks of the political institutions the handbook, "Party Organisation and Development", adds the following:

Relying on the powers vested in the Party organisations (in the Armed Forces), the political institutions have the task of constantly ensuring the Party's exclusive influence on the entire life and activity of the Armed Forces, strengthening their fighting power and training the fighters in the spirit of Marxism-Leninism for limitless devotion to their people, the Socialist fatherland, the Communist Party and the Soviet Government.[2]

In sum, the political apparatus in the Armed Forces has three main tasks: Party-political education and indoctrination; political supervision — which includes very large powers in the matter of appointments and promotions; and assistance in reinforcing military power.

The political apparatus that was set up to carry out these tasks was a complex, widely ramified affair. The main schematic structure of the apparatus as it appears in the Soviet political handbooks is shown in outline in the annexed diagram. It is in my opinion

---

\* Members of the Communist Youth organisation of the Soviet Union.
\*\* 1974.
1 *Party-political Action in the Soviet Armed Forces,* Voyenizdat, Moscow, 1974, p. 145 (Russian).
2 *Party Organisation and Development,* 3rd Ed., Politizdat, Moscow, 1973, pp. 231–32 (Russian).

correct to consider the Military Councils, including the Supreme Military Council, as part of the political apparatus and within the sphere of political supervision. One would also be justified in including the KGB people, who are referred to as "accredited representatives".

The over-all structure presented in this diagram shows the position at the end of the 1960's. It will be remembered that the Political Administrations in the three separate arms (land, sea, air forces) were abolished in 1958, when the connection between the Main Political Administration and the Political Administrations in the Military Districts and corresponding levels was made a direct one. In 1963 a Political Administration was set up for the Strategic Missiles Command (in effect, a separate arm). In 1967 Political Administrations were restored in the Navy and the Air Force, and a Political Administration was also established in the Anti-Aircraft Defence arm. A separate Political Administration was set up for the Land Forces some two years later (until when the MPA had operated a special branch to look after matters in the Land Forces).

Alongside the political institutions on all levels, from the Main Political Administration down to the Political Sections, the Party set up Commissions (of Party members) to review decisions taken by the Party organisations at the base regarding the admission of new Party members and also to sit on cases of wrongful action by Party and Komsomol members. These Party Commissions are elected by and responsible to the Party Conference on the corresponding level.[2a] There are no inclusive Party Conference for the land, sea and air arms nor for the Armed Forces as a whole. In the absence of Party Conferences, the composition of the Commissions in the separate arms and in the Political Administrations themselves is settled by the Main Political Administration. The composition of the Party Commission of the Main Political Administration itself is settled by the Central Committee of the Communist Party.

[2a] These are statutory Conferences normally held at fixed intervals, comprising the elected representatives of all the Party members in the formation in question.

# SCHEMATIC STRUCTURE OF THE POLITICAL INSTITUTIONS IN THE ARMED FORCES 1960–1967

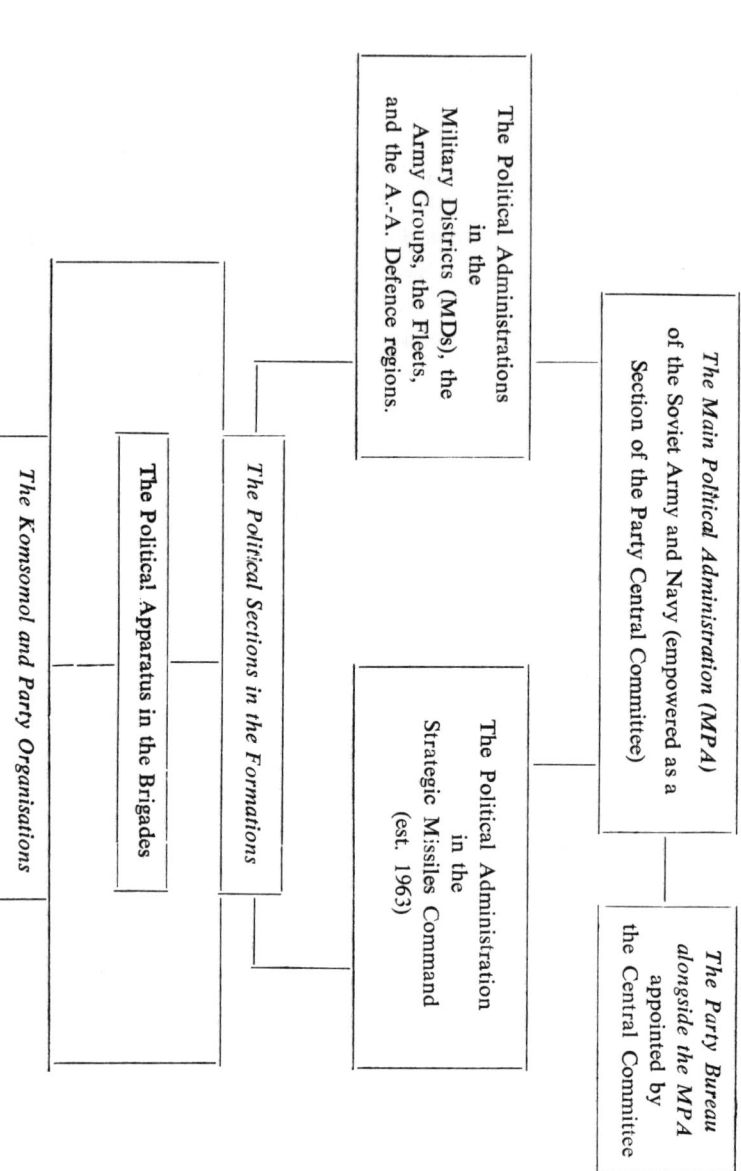

The Party Commissions are operated by the corresponding political institutions. As directed and guided by these institutions, the Commissions also take part in reviewing the proper application of Party regulations in letter and in spirit, that is, they have to see whether Party members are obeying the regulations and observing the disciplinary rules of the Party, State and Army to the full. The Secretary of the Party Commission reports on all the Commission's decisions to the head of the corresponding political institution. The Party Commission operating alongside the MPA also acts as appeal tribunal on decisions of the Party Commissions at lower levels.[3]

The striking thing about this set-up is the large gap between external form and practical content, between the appearance of democratic procedures that envelops these Party Commissions and the very exactly calculated arrangements for concentrating authority in the hands of people appointed from above and not elected. On the face of it, the Party Conference is a supreme body elected by all the Party members, but in fact the Party members in the Armed Forces vote for a list drawn up by the corresponding political institution: as Col. N. A. put it, they vote — but they have no choice. Moreover, the supposedly "elected" body, that is to say, the Conference of the arm, formation or Military District, also "elects" a Party Commission, the list of whose members was also drawn up by the political institution — and again it votes but does not really elect. It emerges therefore that the Party Commission too is directed and operated in accordance with instructions from the corresponding political institution; and even an appeal against the Commission's decisions is brought before a higher level Commission, which itself was not elected at all but was appointed by the Head of the Main Political Administration — and he too was appointed by the Central Committee of the Party.

I shall not deal here with the KGB, which has a not inconsiderable role in the political supervision of Army personnel.

I have attempted to uncover the bare bones of this network in as plain terms as possible. We shall now proceed to fill in the de-

[3] *Party-Political Action ... op. cit.*, pp. 157–58.

tails and review in turn the tasks of each of the five main components of the political apparatus.

### The Main Political Administration of the Army and Navy

The Main Political Administration (MPA) is the supreme political institution in the Armed Forces. Its authority to act is that of a Section of the Central Committee. It is through the MPA that the Central Committee operates Party policy in the Armed Forces. The MPA is responsible for administering all the political institutions, the Party organisations and the Komsomol in the Army and Navy. In accordance with decisions, it elaborates the Party structure, plans ideological action, chooses personnel, controls and reviews the implementation of Party and Government decisions and instructions by the political institutions and Party organisations.[4] The MPA watches over the state of morale among Army personnel and sees to their cultural needs.[5]

In April 1958 the Central Committee changed the name of the MPA, in the cadre of "improvements in Party-political activity" consequent on the October 1957 Plenary Resolutions. The change was no mere formality but expressed the reversal in the hierarchy of organisation. From then on it was not the "MPA of the Ministry of Defence" but the "MPA of the Army and Navy".[6] In fact the MPA was now turned into an institution parallel to or alongside the Ministry of Defence, not a part of it, responsible to the Central Committee. The Minister of Defence *and the MPA Head* now signed all instructions on questions of Party-political action in the Army and Navy. Important orders required confirmation from the Central Committee. Instructions on current matters were issued by the Head of the MPA on his own.[7]

The Head of the MPA usually had the rank of General of an

---

4 *Party Organisation ... op. cit.*, p. 155.
5 *Party-Political Action ... op. cit.*, p. 155.
6 *Party-Political Action in the Armed Forces of the Soviet Union*, p. 316.
7 *Party Organisation ...* p. 234.

Education and Political Supervision

Army; he was assisted by a First Deputy with the rank of Major-General and a whole batch of Deputies with the rank of General. Some of the Deputies were directly responsible *via* their branches for political action in the Navy and the Air Force from 1958 to 1967 and in the Land Forces up till 1969. From August 1960 on the Deputies simultaneously served as "comrades"[7a] on the Military Councils of the separate arms.[8]

The Political Administration comprises a number of branches: organisation and administration of the political institutions throughout the Armed Forces; propaganda/explanation/information; personnel; Komsomol Section and other Sections. There is also a Party Committee (to be distinguished from a Party Commission[8a]), which is "elected" by the Party members working in the MPA itself.

Alongside the MPA is the Bureau, created by the Central Committee in August 1960.[8b] Among its tasks — to ensure the collective character of the decisions taken on the most important matters of Party-political action and on problems of educating the political workers' corps in the Army in the spirit of maintaining Leninist norms in Party life and preserving the principle of Party leadership.[9] A Bureau like this alongside the MPA, in fact part of the Central Committee or rather the Central Committee Secretariat, seems at first sight superfluous, since the main task of the Political Administration itself is to watch over Party interests in the Armed Forces, but this Bureau is a prize example of the great system of "re-insurance" (*Perestrahovka*) that is such a striking and characteristic symptom of political life and of the regime in the Soviet Union. The supervisory body has to be closely supervised so as to prevent it from deviating (perish the thought) from "the line". The method of reaching decisions in the Bureau by majority vote — the main point being the right of the holders of the minority view to report the fact to the Central Committee — also shows that the

---

[7a] See pp. 187–8 above.
[8] Petrov, *op. cit.*, p. 470.
[8a] See pp. 203–205.
[8b] See p. 199 above.
[9] *Party-Political Action ... op. cit.*, p. 153.

Central Committee and the Central Committee Secretariat did not rely all that much on the Political Administration and its corps of helpers and added yet another supervisor to the corps of supervisors.[10]

The existence of the Bureau, where Secretariat people apparently also took part, presumably strengthened the status of the MPA *vis-à-vis* the Ministry of Defence: the personal connections and political "pull" of the Central Committee Secretariat members would certainly help the MPA to put through things it wanted done. To be close to the policy-shapers and decision-makers is just as important in the Soviet regime as in any other, perhaps even more so.

The authority of the Political Administration is of course influenced by the internal political situation in the State — the changes in the relative weight of the different power foci — and by the personality of the head of State.

The MPA people at the top, as we have said, are of very high military rank but the great majority have had no military experience as commanders. The Head of the Administration, General — later Marshal — Golikov, a soldier with a high reputation,[10a] was replaced in 1962 by General Alexei Yepishev, a purely political personality.[11]

---

10 It is worth recalling an instance in the history of the relations between the Party and the Armed Forces when the heads of the MPA were suspected of supporting the senior commanders although their job was Party political supervision. I am referring to Ian Gamarnik, who committed suicide, and many of his helpers, who were executed, at the time of the Stalinist purges in 1937.

10a See above, Chapter 7, footnote 25.

11 In 1938 Yepishev graduated from the Army School of Mechanisation, but from then on he held many different positions, none of them military. During the war he was not given a military command but only political posts such as that of "accredited representative" on the Military Council of a Front or "comrade" on the Military Council of an Army. After the war, he was made one of the Secretaries of the Central Committee of the Party in the Ukraine, responsible for cadres. Before his appointment as Head of the MPA, which he has held

Education and Political Supervision

*Personnel Training*
For the MPA and all its branches to be able to perform its tasks it has to train a cadre of political workers and see to their postings and promotions. A number of special MPA institutions, headed by the Lenin Military Political Academy, function for this purpose. The increasing sophistication of weapon-systems made it harder for the political officers to keep level with their military opposite numbers and a great effort was therefore made in the years under review to transfer combat officers to the political workers corps, giving them additional political training in the institutions referred to above. The MPA made parallel efforts to enable the political workers to acquire military and technical knowledge, and first and foremost in the Strategic Missiles arm.

MPA supervision and training of its personnel is done in a variety of ways. These include a whole range of publications; reports from the subordinate levels of the branches to the MPA Head; visits by heads of the branches and by senior political workers to the Administrations in the M.D.s and the formations; meetings of political workers and Secretaries of the Party organisations ("consultations") held in the MDs and at the centre; and "invitations" convoking the heads of the Administrations in the MDs (who were also the "comrades" on the Military Councils) to meet to discuss the situation of the troops in the MD or Army in question.

Discussions on the situation of the troops generally review the entire sphere of military and political action, from military training, combat preparedness and military discipline to all forms of Party-political action. The survey of the *rapporteur* (who is at the same time the "comrade" on the Military Council and the Political Administration head in the MD) is put forward for criticism and sometimes criticised by the *rapporteur* himself. When the deliberations are summed up, he is generally asked to be stricter with himself and with the MD commanders and political workers so as to

up to the time of writing (1979), he served as Ambassador in Rumania and Yugoslavia. In 1964 Yepishev was elected a full member of the Central Committee and a member of the Supreme Soviet.

209

improve discipline, combat preparedness and familiarity with new weapons and to step up alertness. The main purpose of the whole performance is of course to improve Party-political functioning. Members of the Presidium are sometimes present at these "consultations" at the centre, and the summing-up and the decisions are often made public. These decisions are cited as binding, though their content is mainly propagandist, full of repetitive references to previous decisions of the latest Party Congresses or the Central Committe Plenaries such as the October 1957 Plenary.

*"Criticism and Self-Criticism"*
The Administration and its Head do not spare the rod of criticism even regarding the political institutions under them, including the Political Administrations of the MDs and their heads. One of the ways of reprimanding an officer or expressing dissatisfaction with his work is to criticise him by name and in detail in an article or at a "consultation" of Secretaries of the Party organisations in the Armed Forces. Thus, for example, Golikov made use of the first issue of *Armed Forces Communist* for criticism of this kind, which is worth reproducing here as a sample of the genre:

> The Political Administration of the Leningrad MD has shown itself shockingly ignorant of what goes on sometimes in the units, and the worst of it is that this did not disturb Comrade V. Chebenko, then Political Administration Head in the MD, in the least from the political point of view and did not shake his self-confidence and lack of self-criticism. When the MPA recently reviewed the work of the Political Section in the advanced tactical courses for the infantry and the work of the Section Head, Lieut.-Gen. Yashkevitch, it emerged that they were very far behind in solving problems of cadet training and education. Moreover, Comrade Yashkevitch did not even voice any self-criticism or any recognition of his responsibility for the defects that were uncovered.
> At the Political Administration of the Kiev MD, we reviewed important problems regarding the composition and situation of the MD and Party organisation. We sat with the Heads

of the Political Sections and we uncovered a whole series of errors and cases of negligence, of lagging behind [the targets] and failure to attend to things needing attention. There was also a lack of strict control of lower level political institutions. All this was accompanied by self-satisfaction and an uncritical approach.[12]

*Control at the Top*

The higher the military rank, the closer the political control has to be. The MPA established offshoots in the Defence Ministry and the General Staff. In August 1960 Party Committees began to operate in these extensions instead of Political Sections. The official explanation for this change of structure was that it would "improve the form of organisation of Party action so as to maintain Leninist norms."[13] This official contention did not prevent the restoration of the previous state of affairs in 1967 and the re-establishment of the Political Sections instead of the Party Committees. The official contention this time was the need for uniformity of structure.[14] There was no difference whatsoever in the function of these extensions in the different organisational structures. On a number of occasions when the Secretaries of the Party Committees of the General Staff Headquarters and the Land Forces Headquarters were convoked to the MPA for "consultations" and the content of the summing-up of these "consultations" was made public, it was evident that the Political Administration was doing its utmost by means of these "consultations" to supervise the top ranks of the central military institutions in the closest way.

The First Deputy Head of the MPA, Major-General P. Yefimov, was present at one of these "consultations" in March 1962 and

---

12 P. Golikov, "Let us carry out the principles of action of the political institutions and not hold back," *Armed Forces Communist*, No. 1, October 1960, pp. 20–24.
13 *The Communist Party of the Soviet Union and the Development of the Soviet Armed Forces, 1917–1964*, Voyenizdat 1965, p. 440.
14 *Party-Political Action in the Armed Forces of the Soviet Union, op. cit.*, p. 318.

General Yepishev himself was present at another, in August 1962. A great deal of severe criticism was to be heard at this time, based on a review of the activity of the political workers' Committees at General Staff Headquarters. At the August "consultations", Lieut.-Colonel F. Mozhayev, Deputy Head of the political institutions organisation branch, asserted that the Party Committee was not exerting sufficient influence on the method, quality and style of work of the Party central apparatus alongside the General Staff in criticising the staff's conduct of the Armed Forces. In his opinion representatives of that General Staff made too many short visits — no less than eleven separate commissions and thirteen Generals had visited the Carpathian MD in the course of only four months. He criticised the lack of proper planning, excessive paper-work, delays and bureaucracy. The programmes for combat preparedness arrived too late, in his view, and there was not always the necessary follow-up of the execution of the instructions of the Command and the political institutions. Marxist-Leninist studies were not organised properly nor were the propaganda personnel adequately trained. Yepishev summed up: for a whole year the MPA had reviewed Party work in the General Staff, in the rear Commands of the Ministry of Defence, in the Staffs of the Strategic Missiles arm, the Air Forces and the A.-A. Defence, and the conclusion drawn was dissatisfaction with the level of organisational and Party action of the Party Committee. Their activity was not commensurate with the demands voiced by the XXII Congress, particularly as regards promoting troops fitness and combat preparedness.[15]

This report brings into high relief the official sense of the MPA's right and duty to criticise the General Staff even in details of the purely military conduct of the Armed Forces, and all this by virtue of the famous Resolutions of the last Party Congress, although these Resolutions had in fact not dealt at all with how Generals should act in the branches and the MDs.

15 *Armed Forces Communist,* No. 15, 1962, pp. 36–41.

Education and Political Supervision

*Armed Forces Appointments and Promotions*
The selection of officers, their posting, and confirmation of the appointment or promotion are supposedly part of the functions of the senior officers in the Armed Forces Personnel Section, but the political supervisory apparatus makes its appearance here too and takes a very active part. The MPA has a direct share in appointing officers to senior posts and it handles the appeals reaching it from the political institutions (mainly from the "comrades" on the Military Councils) against appointments that are not to the comrades' liking. The MPA extensions are given directives on the qualities it is important to look for in officers when deciding on promotions, and the political institutions are constantly being called in to show more vigilance in this matter.

The increased influence and even direct intervention of the Party political supervisory apparatus in the Armed Forces Personnel Section was of course a result of the deposition of Zhukov and the decisions of the October 1957 Plenary. Thus, for example, Major-General A. Belobrodov wrote in 1962:

> In the past the selection of military personnel, postings and promotions were marred by serious errors stemming from the cult of personnality. No little harm was done to our [political] work with the officers because of former Defence Minister Zhukov's rotten way of running the Armed Forces. In order to reach an objective solution of problems in promoting officers. it is laid down that candidates for the post of Brigade Commander and higher ranks have to be discussed at Military Council meetings. Where there is no Military Council, the Commanders must consult their Political Deputies (*Zampolits*), their Staff heads and the Secretary of the Party Committee or Bureau before an appointment is finally settled on and the officer posted. ... A new arrangement was introduced in 1959 in the matter of the authority of the officer corps. ... Commissions were set up to confirm [appointments], comprising the Head of the political institutions, the Secretaries of the Party Committees and of the Party Bureaus. ... Organ-

isation was improved as well as the style of work of the personnel institutions. These last tightened up their connections with the political institutions and the Party organisations.[16]

On this subject Golikov affirmed that the most important quality for a Soviet Commander was a sound Party attitude, based on ideological conviction, limitless devotion to his people, to the fatherland, to the Communist Party and Communist construction. He said that the political institutions should take a more active part in the selection of officers, their posting and their confirmation and that this held good for Generals and Admirals too.[17]

On various occasions the MPA repeatedly stressed the importance of the active role of the political institutions in the Personnel Sections. In a leading article in *Armed Forces Communist*, "The Vital Problems of the Selection, Posting and Training of Military Cadres", we read:

> The Personnel Sections have to have firm contact with the political institutions, the Party Committees and organisations, and must give due weight to the candidates' opinions and evaluations. ... The selection and postings of the cadres, their education and ideological moulding are decisive factors for success in every undertaking. This is the central problem of the Military Councils, the commanders, the political institutions and the Party organisations.[18]

### *The Political Administrations and the Political Sections*

A Political Administration is a political institution functioning alongside the Command of a Military District, a Fleet and an

---

16 Major-General A. Belobrodov, *Armed Forces Communist*, No. 2, 1962, pp. 20–21.
17 P. Golikov, "Party Political Action on the Plane of Present Problems," *Red Star*, 27 May 1959.
18 *Armed Forces Communist*, No. 24, 1963, p. 7.

### Education and Political Supervision

Army Group, headed as a rule by a political major-General or Lieut.-General, who also serves as the "comrade" on the Military Council of the Command where he is Head of the Political Administration. In Soviet publications it is customary to put his title of "comrade" first, before that of Administration Head, which indicates that the post of "comrade" is the senior one, seen as having precedence over the other. The Political Administration alongside the Command is responsible for all the political institutions throughout the Command and for the doings of the Party organisations there. Authority is vested in the Command Administrations and their Heads not only for political supervision. They have a large influence in many other spheres of military activity. The standing of an Administration Head is very solid, both because of his double function and because he is linked directly to his superiors in Moscow.

The Political Sections in the formations, military colleges and other military institutions direct educational and Party-political action — in the units, on the ships, in the various courses given in the schools and academies. They also direct the Party and Komsomol organisations and are responsible for the doings of the *Zampolits* in the units. The man in charge at the head of the Political Section is at the same time the *Zampolit* of the Commander of the formation.[19]

The tasks and responsibilities of the Political Section officers as shown in the diagram are very clearly defined. The *Zampolit* directs the work of the Section instructors, elaborates their work programme and supervises its execution; the chief instructor of the organisation for Party action assists the Party organisations in the units in their work and directs the Party *"aktiv"*; the propagandist organises the information services for the whole formation, directs the propaganda workers in the units and gives systematic assistance to the heads of the groups for Marxist-Leninist training and for political studies in general; the chief instructor for mass cultural activity directs the work for the clubs and libraries in the

19 See diagram p. 216.

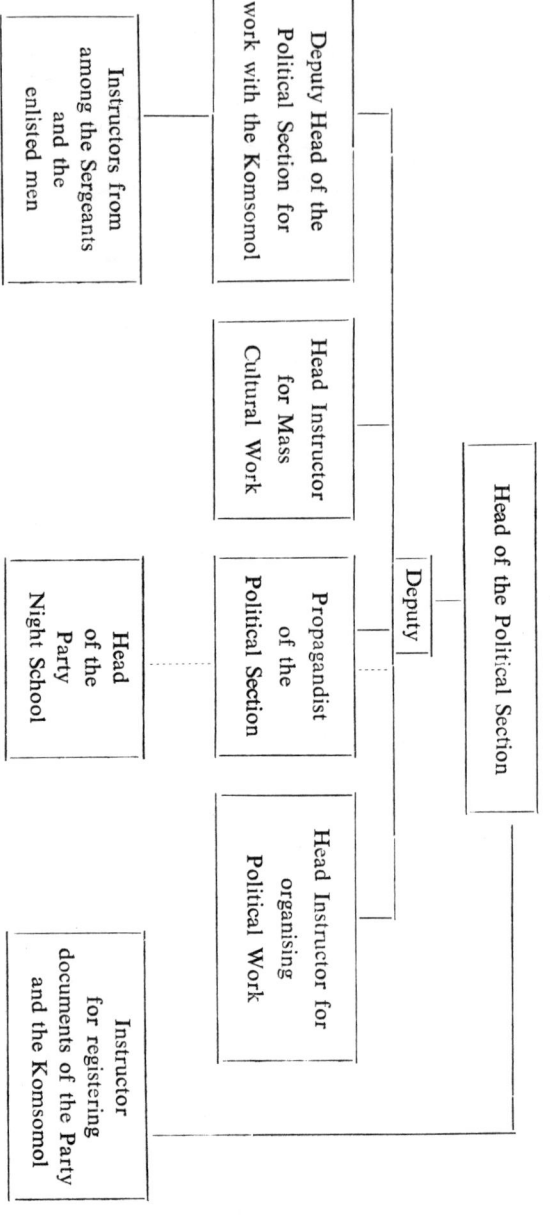

SCHEMATIC STRUCTURE OF THE POLITICAL SECTION (*POLITOTDEL*)

Education and Political Supervision

## STRUCTURE OF THE POLITICAL APPARATUS IN THE BRIGADE

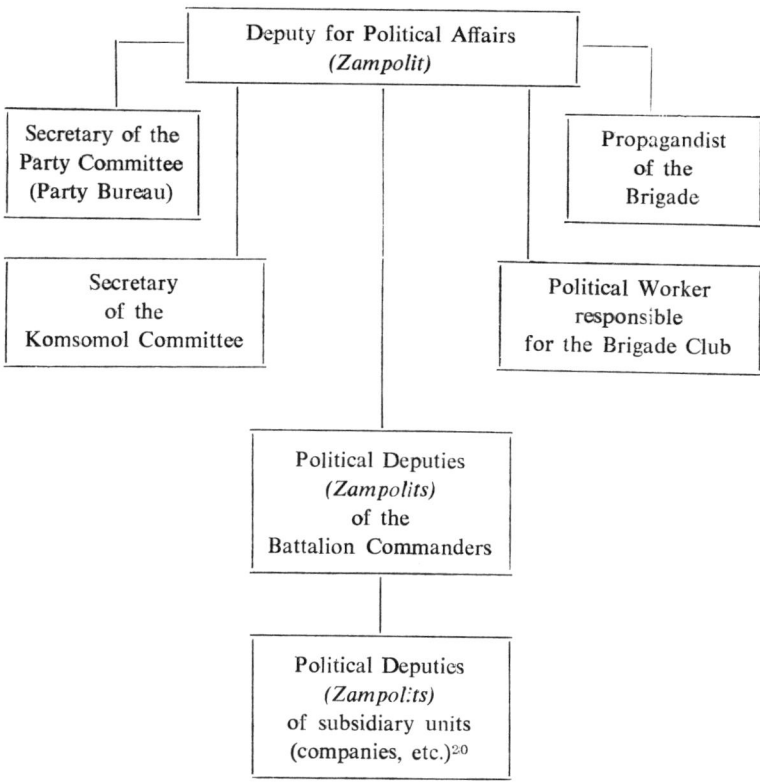

units and supervises the correct use of the technical propaganda means available for political education. There is also a Political Section Supervisor, who visits the units in the Section, reviews the work of the political institutions functioning there, tries to correct such defects as he may find and reports to his superior.

The Brigade *Zampolit* must personally conduct at least one of the Marxist-Leninist study groups for officers; he is responsible for

20 This post was abolished and re-introduced by turns: re-introduced in 1950, abolished in 1955, re introduced in 1967.

choosing the heads of the groups for political studies and he supervises the ideological content of these studies. He also sets the subjects for political information.

The propagandist assists the *Zampolit*. He must himself conduct one of the Marxist-Leninist instruction groups and must deliver lectures to the soldiers.

## The Party Organisations

The entire activity of the Party organisations in the Armed Forces is conducted in accordance with the Programme and Standing Orders of the Communist Party of the Soviet Union and with the Resolutions passed at Party Conferences and Central Committee sessions. Standing Orders lay down: "The Party organisations in the Army and the Navy must ensure the implementation of Party policy in the Armed Forces, unite the men in the service around the Communist Party, educate the combattants in the spirit of Marxism-Leninism for boundless devotion to the Socialist fatherland, concern themselves with military discipline ... and see to the execution of the orders and instructions of the Command."[21]

The practical activity of the Party organisations is based on the instructions given them, as confirmed by the Central Committee, and on instructions issued jointly by the Minister of Defence and the Head of the Main Political Administration. The instructions detail the tasks and duties of the Party organisations and of Party members in the Armed Forces. Over and over again the instructions stress the imperative obligation to ensure that all the Communists in the Forces take an active part in educational-political activity and in explaining the policy of the Party and the Government to all the soldiers. The organisations must strictly observe the moral principles of upbuilding Communism according to the Party programme and must influence non-Party soldiers in this sense.

In a leading article in the first issue of *Armed Forces Communist*, the Party organisations in the Armed Forces are defined as "com-

---

21 *Programmes Rules and Regulations of the CPSU, op. cit.*, p. 304.

mando units of the Communist Party of the Soviet Union".[22] The Political Section conducts the work of the Party organisations in accordance with Party instructions. Alongside the Political Section, the *Zampolits* give assistance in operating the Party organisations. The Party organisations at the base assist the Political Section of the formation in its work and must report to it regularly on their activities and be responsible to it. As defined in Party Standing Orders, the Party organisations at the base are the foundation of the Party: they are authorised to admit new members into the Party, but this has to be ratified by the next highest level, in this case, the Political Section.

The tasks and duties incumbent on the Party organisations in the Armed Forces and the fact of their coming under the political institutions mean that in addition to their internal roles they are in fact an auxiliary instrument of political supervision in the Armed Forces.

After the "Instruction" was re-drafted in 1957[22a] and annexes were issued in 1958,[22b] steps were taken in 1960 to extend the sphere of action of the Party organisations and increase their effectiveness in all their spheres of work in the Army.

*The Structure Re-organised, 1960*

In August 1960 the Central Committee resolved on a series of changes in the Party structure in the Armed Forces. This was presented to the public as the ratification of proposals brought forward at a "consultation" in May of that year with the Secretaries of the Party organisations at the base. The following instructions were issued in accordance with the new structure: Party Committees were to be set up in every Brigade or naval vessel where there were more than 75 Party members; a Party Bureau was to be elected in Party organisations with 15 or more members:

---

22 *Armed Forces Communist,* No. 1, 1960, p. 5.
22a See pp. 107–8 above.
22b See p. 181 above.

## Party Control Re-Imposed

in those with less than 15 members, a Secretary and Deputy were to be elected, and the Political Section would have to ratify the appointment of the Secretary. The Party organisation in a battalion or subsidiary unit of similar size would be accorded the same powers as those of the Party organisations at the base; in companies, submarines and subsidiary units of similar size with three or more Party members, Party organisations were to be set up with the same powers as those of a Party branch in a factory. In a subsidiary unit with only one or two Party members and a number of candidates for Party membership. Party groups were to be established, headed by a group instructor who would be nominated by the Political Section.[23]

### SCHEMATIC STRUCTURE OF A PARTY ORGANISATION AT THE BASE IN A MILITARY UNIT

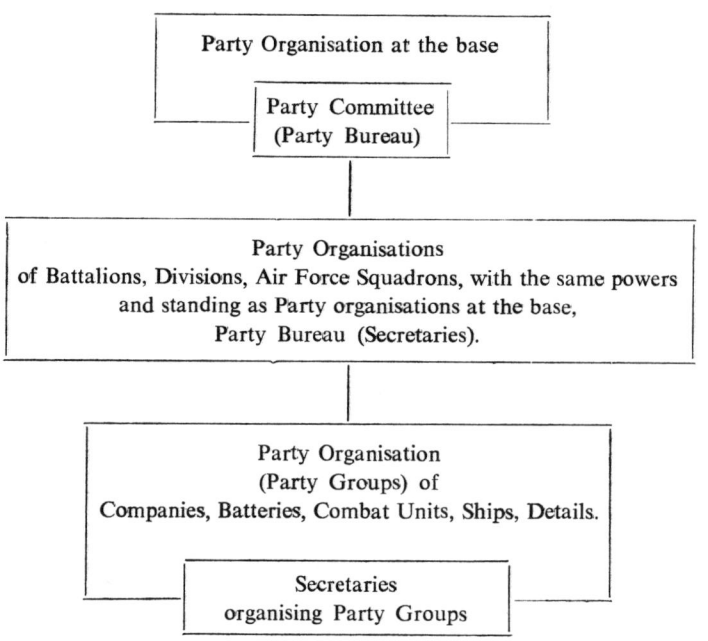

23 See diagram, of the structure of a Party organisation at the base in a military unit.

Parallel with the changes in structure in the field units, the Political Sections were also re-organised and turned into Party Committees in most of the military schools and academies. Party Committees also replaced some of the existing Political Sections in some Staffs of the MDs., the Fleets and Army Groups. The explanation given for these changes was the increased number of Communists in the field units. Golikov described the changes of structure as "a general plan of action and a source of very great new possibilities that will contribute to a big upward swing in Party activity." He did remark, however, "It is clear that the successful fulfilment of all these obligations calls for very thorough and explicit guidance on the part of the political institutions."[24]

After a year's experience with the new structure, Col. Lozovoy had this to say:

> As we know, the Party organisations in the battalions are under the direction of the (Party) Committees of the units, but this does not mean that the Political Section can stand aside and not interfere in their functioning [sc. of the Party organisations]. On the contrary — in the new conditions the responsibility of the Political Section for the state of Party-political activity in the subsidiary units is even greater than it was before. ... If previously the Political Section officers acted mainly in the Brigade, sometimes without ever reaching the battalion, they now feel greater responsibility for the activity of the Party organisations, which have been given the powers of organisations at the base; they have begun to visit the Section officers more frequently and to provide guidance for the Secretaries and the Bureau members. ... It is no exaggeration to say that with the transition to the new organisational structure, the Political Section has begun to provide the Party organisations with a more concrete lead.[25]

---

24 Golikov, *Armed Forces Communist*, No. 2, 1960, p. 24.
25 Col. I. Lozovoy, "The Political Section and the Party Organisations of the Battalions", *Armed Forces Communist*, No. 8, 1961, pp. 22–25.

*Plus ça change, plus c'est la même chose.* It emerges that we have here another example of the Soviet way of doing things, of seeking on the one hand to give the impression of democratisation and of increased powers for the Party branches at the different levels, in order to give the branches encouragement and get their members to be more active and more interested. On the other hand good care is taken to see to it that the functionaries in charge of the political institutions will lead and direct the Party organisation and will in fact retain close control in their own hands.

The political apparatus made a drive to get more commanders into Party organisational and information activity in the new structures. Many army officers were "elected" to the Party Committees and Bureaus, and this was meant to involve them in more responsibility for the branches and at the same time to encourage them to seek support from the Party organisations on the military side as well. Another leading article in *Armed Forces Communist* in 1961 referred to this hope in characteristic fashion as the fruit of "experience":

> In almost every place in the MD, the unit commanders have been elected members of the Party Committee. Experience shows that this helps strengthen unity of command and still further enlarges the commanders' authority and assists them to rely with greater assurance on the Party organisation and to guide their comrades and all the soldiers in solving their main problems. ... Successful activity by the Party Committees depends very much on alpert leadership with concrete help from the political institutions.[26]

## Party-Political Education

In the Armed Forces in the 1960's, nearly fifty years after the October Revolution, Party propaganda/information (*"agit-prop"*) was directed at the very same targets as in the '20's:

26 "The Party Committee of the Unit", *Armed Forces Communist*, No. 6, 1961, pp. 3–8

## Education and Political Supervision

1. to convince the troops that the Soviet regime is better than capitalism as regards social justice, true democracy, ethics and the economic system;
2. to inculcate a sense that constant alertness is needed to parry the danger from the aggressive tendencies of imperialist circles, whence the need for military strength and a high state of readiness;
3. to inculcate the realisation that the basic foundation for developing military strength is Party leadership of the Armed Forces, since the Party is permanently concerned to strengthen the Armed Forces, raise its level of combat preparedness, maintain military discipline and raise the morale of all who serve.

In sum, as was said over and over again, the goal of Party-political education in the Forces was to produce good soldiers from both the military and the political points of view, soldiers devoted to their Socialist fatherland and ready to sacrifice themselves in its defence. The axiom is that political/ideological education combined with military training constitutes a necessary condition for moulding the good Soviet soldier.

The educational/information/propaganda activities in the Forces are very extensive, systematic and thoroughgoing. They cover everyone serving in the Forces. Over ninety per cent of the officers are Communists and they get special, additional political "higher education", generally termed "Marxist-Leninist training".

### Publications

Party-political education has the backing of a voluminous and ramified military-political literature, which as well as books includes collections of documentary material such as, *The Communist Party of the Soviet Union on the Armed Forces of the Soviet Union,* published by Politizdat in 1958, giving documents on Party relations with the Forces from 1917 to 1958. Another collection came out in 1969 (published by Voyenizdat) with exactly the same name, with documents from 1917 to 1968. The choice of documents in the second collection was different from that in the previous one even for the same years. Another series, handbooks for political guidance, surveyed Party-political work in the Armed Forces; the names of the books in this series are all almost identical. In 1962, after the XXII Congress and the ratification of the new Party platform, Voyenizdat published a work for the Main Political Administration entitled, *On Guard for the Fatherland in Communist Constitution*, which was intended to provide directives for political studies in the light of the new programme. In 1964 Voyenizdat published the voluminous work by Petrov, *Party Upbuilding in the Soviet Army and Navy*. In 1965 Voyenizdat published a work for the Lenin Military Academy entitled, *The Communist Party in the Soviet Union and the Upbuilding of the Soviet Armed Forces*, a survey of the establishment and development of the Forces. The aim of its authors in their own words was to show that the Communist Party was the organiser, leader and educator of the Army and that leadership of the Army by the Party and its Central Committee constitutes the fundamental basis of Soviet military development.

Apart from innumerable books and this specialised documentary material, collections of articles were brought out to buttress Party action in particularly agitated periods. Two outstanding such collections were connected with the Resolutions passed at the October 1957 Plenary and with the propaganda campaign that followed; both were published by Voyenizdat, the first in 1959, *Resolutions of the CPSU Central Committee Plenary in Action*, and the second in 1960, *A Renewed Spring Forward of Party-Political Action in the Soviet Army and Navy*. Both were collections of articles written by the heads of the Armed Forces and the MPA.

There are many other publications in the form of the Army daily newspapers, fortnightlies, monthlies, quarterlies. The dailies have a very wide circulation. Some of these Army papers are devoted entirely to information/propaganda and a considerable part of the others also serve the same purpose. A special place among the periodicals devoted to political action is held by the fortnightly, *Armed Forces Communist, a military political periodical of the MPA of the Soviet Army and Navy*. It began to appear in October 1960 by a decision of the Central Committee. Its hundred or so pages are intended for Generals, Admirals, officers and wide circles of the *"aktiv"* of the Party and the Komsomol.[27]

## Lectures

In addition to the diffusion of this extensive written material, there is large-scale information/propaganda activity by word of mouth, in the form of lectures, seminars, *"aktiv"* meetings of Party and Komsomol organisations at conventions, "consultations" and Conferences, as well as regular full-time political studies and Marxist-Leninist oral propaganda. Soldiers and officers are swamped with political indoctrination in all its forms, without a let-up.

## Teachers' Training, Advanced Studies

A large network of institutions exists to train lecturers, group leaders and heads of political study circles and Marxist-Leninist studies and widen their general political-cultural education. This network was much expanded in the period under review. In 1960 there were 258 "night schools" in the Armed Forces teaching Marxist-Leninism, with some 45,000 men taking courses; in 1961 there were 126 "faculties" — 53 of philosophy, 15 of history and 14 of economics. In addition, there were Party "schools" (two-year courses) and seminars dealing largely with teaching the methodology of propa-

---

27 *Armed Forces Communist,* No. 1, 1960, pp. 3–4. The aims of the publication, as detailed by the MPA in the first issue, offer a review of the aims of the MPA: "To act for the further improvement of Party-political action in the light of the Resolutions of the XXI Congress of the Party and of the Resolutions of the October 1957 Plenary, to unite all those serving in the Armed Forces around the Party and the Government and educate them for supreme devotion to the fatherland and unqualified loyalty to the duty incumbent on the soldier. The periodical is intended to throw light far and wide on the activity of the commanders, the political institutions, the Party Committees and organisations, activity directed to increasing the vigilance and reinforcing the combat preparedness of the troops, unity of command and discipline. The periodical will foster criticism and self-criticism in Party organisations so as to correct defects; it will publish theoretical articles, material concerning the Party programme of education, both for officers' Marxist-Leninist training and for the political studies of the other ranks."

ganda, psychology and pedagogics. Study of Party history was much enlarged, about a third of all the soldiers learned this subject. Later, in 1964, political "schools" were held in the regiments and on naval vessels: these studies lasted for three years in the Land Forces and the Air Force and for four years in the Navy (the length of service in the arms).[28] All this, of course, over and above the ordinary "training" in political affairs twice a week.

Some of the lecturers and propagandists are commanders who go on with their military tasks at the same time, and others are full-time lecturers.

One must be wary of accepting terms such as "faculties", "universities", "night schools", "political schools" and even the figures given. An article in *Armed Forces Communist* on improving the quality of political training for recruits gave the figure of 400 cultural "universities" in the Army and Navy and described extensive activity in the cultural sphere, but at the same time criticised the amount of "formalism" (a term of condemnation, as is well known) still existing in the information/propaganda organisation. Herewith a passage from the article:

> At times we talk a lot about the search for new forms of activity and we fail to see the content within the form. Two or three lectures on cultural questions are sometimes called a cultural "university" or "lekturia"; an ordinary seminar or guidance session for propagandists is called a "propagandists' school" and so forth.[29]

*Forms and Formulas*

Information/propaganda activity is marked by the rigidly stereotyped nature of its content, style and symbols. Practically without exception, a lecture, article or speech on internal current affairs will be bound to include pre-established elements such as a call for greater efforts in order to attain additional achievements in

---

28 *The CPSU and the Development ... op. cit.*, p. 446.
29 Major-General of the Air Force A. Kopitin, *Armed Forces Communist*, No. 2, 1960, p. 33.

preparation for the approaching Congress or in order to carry out the Resolutions and decisions of the previous Congress or Central Committee Plenary; quotations from Lenin's writings are an iron rule, the more of them the better, and to these must be added quotations from the writings of First Secretary Khrushchev (and Brezhnev after him). Articles are for the most part long and include a great deal of repetition, both in the article itself and of things said in the past or published previously — very often actual repetition, word for word.

When the articles deal with international affairs, exactly the same standard, petrified, derogatory terms recur over and over again that have been in use in the USSR for scores of years, regardless of any changes that occurred in the world in the meantime: "imperialist, warmongering circles" as against the "peace-loving countries", "circles hankering after military adventures", "monopolists" and so on. Favourable terms are reserved for USSR supporters naturally.

The typical article is constructed in three parts. The first part recounts general or specific achievements of the Army, MD or formation and sometimes even the unit, a report sometimes accompanied by personal names and examples. The names mentioned are mostly those of devoted officers or men who have made great efforts to raise the educational and combat level of the unit or to improve Party-political activity. The second part usually begins with, "All the same...", and lists instances of neglect and defects and oversights or certain specific facts, and here too those to blame for the shortcomings and oversights are named and at times very harshly criticised. The third part of the article is in vigorous terms, stressing the need and the capacity to overcome the failings still discernible here and there and indicating present goals "in anticipation of" or "towards" or "in honour of" etc.

The range of the themes treated is not a wide one. The subject is usually an outstanding current issue demanding attention in the Army, the Party and the country at large, such as the introduction of new arms and a call for men to come forward to receive technical training or efforts to appease the widespread dissatisfaction at the time of large-scale post-war discharge of officers. In periods of particularly marked slackening of military discipline lots of speeches are made and lots of articles appear stressing the supreme importance of discipline. In periods of Party "elections" in the Armed Forces, there is a wealth of reports on current Party activity. After the XXII Congress, ideological "explanation" concentrated on the new Party platforms adopted. "Improving Party-political action" is never off the list of subjects dealt with, and after Zhukov's deposition it took first place both in quantity and in aggressive tone. Another set theme is the education of the men in the service. Other common subjects are Party history, military history, commanders' reminiscences, descriptions of campaigns, military theory, accounts of World War Two heroic deeds, biographical notes about eminent soldiers whom it is desired to honour.

Articles also appear quite often on current problems of Party theory and policy. Here is a passage summarising what is wanted of the educators:

> What is called for in education is strict maintenance of the principle of ideology and Party-ness, which naturally gives political and military education a clear Communist orientation. This principle obliges the commanders, the political workers, Party activists, engineers and all Communists to do their educational work from a strict class/Party viewpoint and to be constantly guided by Marxist-Leninist theory.[30]

*Who is at Fault?*

In the military political periodicals it is quite the accepted thing to blame shortcomings in combat training and military discipline on poor information/propaganda and educational work. Thus for example in late 1960, in an article calling for resolute implementation of the October '57 Plenary decisions, two officers write:

> At times the struggle is not waged sufficiently energetically

---

30 *Party-political Action ... op. cit.,* p. 120.

against views and states of mind still influenced by the backward past, against time-wasting futility, disrespect for law and order and vestiges of bourgeois morality and ideology. Certain commanders, political workers and heads of Party organisations make no effort to spread political enlightenment among all who serve in the army, to turn them into people with clear, settled political views, so as to get them to take part in real [sc. political] activity. How else can one explain the fact that serious defects exist in combat training and discipline in a whole series of units, and this at a time when Party-political action appears on the surface to be satisfactorily organised?[31]

This passage is sufficiently enlightening on the absence of political enlightenment fifty years after the Revolution, the failure to break down the barriers of bourgeois morality and to get those serving in the Army to "improve combat training and military discipline". Clearly, in the opinion of the writers of this article — and they are not the only ones to take this line — those to blame for these shortcomings can only be those in charge of Party-political action, that is to say, the political officers and workers in the Armed Forces. On the not unreasonable assumption that the commanders are interested in improving combat preparedness and military discipline, the conclusion has to be drawn that it is the political workers who are mainly responsible for the shortcomings described. It follows that all the measures taken after Zhukov's deposition and as a result of the Resolutions of the October '57 Plenary had simply failed. Zhukov's heavy hand had done far more to improve combat preparedness and military discipline than the political workers' increased powers and enhanced status, more than all the efforts to provide more and more explanation/propaganda/education.

---

31  Col. P. Chegodar, Lt.-Col. A. Kalachnikov, "Let us Carry Out the Resolutions of the October Plenary of the Central Committee and not Hold Back", *Armed Forces Communist*, No. 2, 1960, p. 39.

*Discipline, Discipline ...*
In mid-1961 all the Party branches in the Army held meetings to hear reports and to make appointments to new Party institutions. The main subjects to be discussed and "explained" at these meetings, in accordance with instructions from the supreme political institutions, were "raising military fitness and combat preparedness" and "enforcement of army discipline". The need to strengthen discipline is the main thread running through all the explanation/propaganda activity for the whole of this period. One can hardly avoid the impression that the top echelons failed to overcome the slackening of discipline that resulted from Zhukov's deposition and the weakened status of the officers. Articles, sermonising, criticism of the Command and of the political institutions continued to be written and voiced, with quotations from Lenin's writings and Khrushchev's speeches — and Malinovsky's — on the subject. Here are some examples of apt quotations for use in these circumstances: Lenin: "If we think over what was in fact at the bottom of the historic miracle of the Red Army's victory over the interventionists, it emerges that it was centralisation, discipline and self-criticism." Khrushchev: "Military discipline they call the mother of all the victories."

Among the many articles on discipline was one by Lieut.-General N. Yegorov, published in *Armed Forces Communist* in October 1961, headed, "The Communist Party of the Soviet Union on Strengthening Discipline in the Soviet Armed Forces".[32] A leading article in February 1962 was actually entitled, *"The Most Important Problem*[32a] — further strengthening of discipline".[33] The decline in military discipline was apparently felt most acutely in the military academies. Here is an observation from an article of June 1962 on MPA action, "Improving political action in the military schools and academies":

> One of the most important measuring-rods for the effective-

---

[32] *Armed Forces Communist*, No. 20, October 1961, pp. 32, 33.
[32a] My stress — Y.A.
[33] *Armed Forces Communist*, No. 4, February 1962, p. 38.

ness of educational-ideological action is the state of Army discipline. ... It is noted that in the current year many commanders, Party Committees and Party organisations, making use of the decisions of the XXII Congress, have succeeded in securing *a certain improvement*[33a] in discipline. ... But the state of discipline in a series of military schools still does not meet the great demands made by the Party. ... General of the Army A. Yepishev has again reminded those participating in "consultations" that the Central Committee demands a fundamental strengthening of military discipline. It is incumbent on the commanders of all ranks, the political institutions and the Party organisations to take the most concrete measures in order to introduce proper, strict order and stamp out breaches of discipline.[34]

The MPA, itself in large measure to blame for the undermining of morale through its policy regarding the powers of the military command, was now forced to harness itself to the propaganda campaign against breaches of discipline. It did not and perhaps could not reach the simple conclusion that was reached under Zhukov, and on this account the propaganda battle, fought as usual in double-headed fashion, was no more successful than previous ones.

*Educating the Senior Command*
Education activities took in the senior command, which also stood in need of enlightenment. Minister of Defence Malinovsky himself wrote explicitly in 1962:

It must be remembered that the main link in educational work and the condition for its success is education of the leaders and educators themselves. Officers — Generals and Admirals — are in need of constant education, and let us say clearly that we mean Admirals and Generals of high rank. Day in and day out they have to study how to lead

[33a] My stress — Y.A.
[34] *Armed Forces Communist*, No. 12, June 1962, p. 41.

their men, never to forget criticism and self-criticism and self-education, since without these they have no moral right to hold their high positions. The Generals and Admirals are first and foremost leaders and educators of all under their command. This makes it incumbent on them to possess high Party qualifications, to rely on revolutionary Marxist-Leninist theory in their work and to be active Party fighters for the implementation of the Party's general line in their own sphere.[35]

Malinovsky saw political studies as the basic form of political *and military*[35a] education for the men in the ranks and he therefore demanded officers to head the study groups who would be enthusiastic proponents of Marxist-Leninist ideology. As Lieut.-Colonel Mozhayev, the Deputy Head in the MPA whom we have already met,[35b] wrote so pithily, "A Soviet officer is not only a military expert but also a political activist."[36]

## Historiography

A trend emerged after the XXII Congress to be more lavish in using political explanation/propaganda in the sphere of military history. More stress was laid than previously on the need to study and do research on the military-theoretical heritage of Lenin. There was also a new outbreak of criticism of Stalin in this respect: his cult of personality "resulted in subjectivism in the evaluation of historic events, insufficient development of the science of military history and inadequate research into the heritage of Lenin in this field." The historians were called on to reveal the heroic deeds in the past of the Russian people and of the peoples of the USSR as a whole.

In an article in the *Journal of Military History* in 1963 entitled,

---

35   R. Malinovsky, "Vital Problems in Educating those Serving in the Armed Forces of the Soviet Union," *Armed Forces Comnunist*, No. 11, June 1962, p. 27.

35a  My stress — Y.A.

35b  See p. 212 above.

36   *Armed Forces Communist*, No. 12, June 1961, p. 27.

"Military History is the most important field of ideological action", Yepishev launched a trenchant attack on Stalin for his many and varied shortcomings, including the havoc he wreaked in the Armed Forces by the unjustified execution of Marshals, Commanders and many political workers, and the setbacks at the beginning of the war. He called for the preparation of historical works devoted to the analysis of the Russian art of war and its representatives, the giant commanders of the past.[37]

*Drawing up the Balance Sheet*

The apparatus of supervision and political education kept up its unrelenting struggle to improve Party-political ideological educational action. Reviews of the results achieved submitted by the apparatus heads continued to take the form of stereotyped tallies of achievements, balanced by criticism and ending with emotional appeals in rhetorical language for further efforts to correct defects, remedy shortcomings, and carry out the historic Resolutions of the Congress and the Plenary. Here is an example from 1963, an article by the "comrade" on the Military Council and Head of the MPA in the Southern Group of Armies, Alexandrov, an article entitled (like so many others). "Let There be no Slackening in Attending to Ideological Action." The writer pointed out with satisfaction that the programmes for the year of 1962 had been carried out in full in the Marxist-Leninist training network for officers, in the political studies for the men in the ranks and in the schools and circles for political enlightenment. He gave lots of details: six hundred appearances by members of the information/propaganda "collektiv" to explain various questions. He even remembered to mention the activity of officers' wives. He recalled the names of soldiers who had distinguished themselves, awarding them the usual praise, if in unusual flights of eloquence: "How splendid are the deeds and accomplishments of our fighters, deeds that grace the beauty of Soviet man and show to one and all how Communist ideas combine with Communist deeds." He then proceeded as usual to the second part, the criticism. Not everything was perfect.

37 *Journal of Military History*, January 1963, pp. 3–7.

This year too there had been a decline in the level of the studies and in military training in some of the units. Breaches of military discipline were being overcome at too slow a rate. After discussion of the situation in ideological action in the Southern Groups of Armies, the MPA found that there had been serious failings in the education of recruits. This article too, like practically all the articles intended to "improve ideological-educational action", closed with a finale in a major key:

> The Party offers a challenge — to fundamentally improve ideological action in every sphere of constructing Communism, strengthening the education of Soviet man in the spirit of high ideas and flaming patriotism, and to refuse to acquiesce in bourgeois morality and ideology. All possible means are at our disposal for this purpose — we are equipped with the great theoretical heritage of Marx, Engels and Lenin, as well as with new and important documents — the data and decisions of the Congresses.[38]

A scrutiny of authoritative Resolutions and instructions made public in the first half of the 1960's shows clearly how much energy and attention both the political and the military leadership devoted to dealing with ideological-educational action. Two apparent reasons for this are to be discerned in the Soviet publications themselves: one is the introduction of modern, sophisticated weapon-systems unparalleled in earlier periods, mainly nuclear arms, including strategic missiles; the other is the notable rise in the general educational level of a considerable proportion of those serving in the forces. These two reasons were of course interconnected — the introduction of modern arms called for better-educated men to use them, and the level of general education had risen in the country. It is reasonable to suppose that the political leadership saw that they had to ensure that better-educated soldiers, controlling more sophisticated arms systems, should be better armed ideo-

---

[38] General N. Alexandrov, "Constant Attention to Ideological Action", *Armed Forces Communist*, No. 9, 1963, pp. 2–15.

logically too to strengthen their loyalty to the regime. Parallel with and combined with this ideological immunisation, it would be necessary to maintain secure political supervision over the new men in the Armed Forces, so as to forestall any threat of crystallisation of an independent focus of enormous power.

## The Military Councils

The Military Councils are without question to be classed as belonging to the political supervisory apparatus in the Armed Forces, because of the notable role they fill in the functioning of the apparatus. The Military Councils in the MDs and the Navy were first set up in May 1937 by decision of the Central Committee — in fact by Stalin — in the period of the worst persecution of senior Army commanders. The Councils comprised the MD Commander and two "comrades". At first one of the "comrades" was the Head of the Political Administration in the MD; he was later replaced by the Secretary of the Party in the Republic or region. The Armies and Flotillas were also endowed with Military Councils, shortly after the MDs and the Navy. The creation of Military Councils was described at the time as renewing "collective" leadership in the Army on the operational, tactical level. The same May 1937 session of the Central Committee Plenary also reintroduced the institution of Military Commissars (*Polítruks*) in all units, formations, staffs and other institutions in the Army.[39] The institution of Military Commissars was again abolished in October 1942, when the wartime situation put a premium on "unity of command", but Stalin still maintained the powers of the Military Councils all through the war years and even increased them.

The Military Councils in fact played a highly important role during the war. Chief of General Staff V. Kolikov wrote an article on "The Strategic Conduct of the Armed Forces", in which he recounted, *inter alia*, that the entire activity of the Fronts and the Armies had been directed by the Military Councils. "Their conduct of the

39  Petrov, *op. cit.*, pp. 305-6.

forces clearly reflected not only the method of working collectively but also the combination of political and strategic-operational functions. The Military Councils conducted military actions directly and were closely linked to local State and Party elements".[40]

Stalin was in direct contact with the "comrades" on the Military Councils of the Armies, Fronts and Front High Commands. They were his political emissaries and trustees. He kept in close touch with them the whole time when decisive campaigns were being planned and while they were fought. Without question, political supervision was also part of the tasks of the "comrades", Stalin's "remote control" over the commanders and the morale of the troops. There were commanders bold enough to criticise the role of the Military Councils and propose their abolition. General V. Gordov, Commander of the 33rd Army, was an outstanding instance. He wrote to Stalin and Zhukov to advise that an end be put to the Military Councils in the Army as "a superfluous institution that serves no purpose". He also proposed turning the Political Sections into Staff Sections and abolishing their right to communicate independently with higher levels of the political institutions. He stuck to his opinions even after the war, when he was commander of the Volga MD. It was presumably no surprise when he was removed from his command in August 1946 because of his "deviationist" views.[41]

In 1947 the powers of the Military Councils were indeed reduced, and they were turned into purely advisory bodies alongside the MD Commands. The post of full-time "comrade" was also abolished and a Political Deputy (*Zampolit*) was appointed instead. The seesaw of the balance of forces continued, however, and later on the powers of political supervision of the Military Councils were again enlarged, in two stages: first in 1950, when by decision of the Central Committee the Councils were turned into responsible

40 General of the Army V. Kolikov, First Deputy of the Minister of Defence, Chief of Staff, ' Strategic Conduct of the Armed Forces", *Journal of Military History*, No. 6, 1975, p. 17.
41 Petrov, *op. cit.*, p. 377.

collective institutions, and then after Zhukov's deposition, when the Central Committee and the Council of Ministers decided in April 1958 to rein in the senior command. Amongst other measures to tighten political supervision over the senior command, there was an increase in the number of Military Councils and very considerable extension of the powers and responsibility vested in them. This is the text of the Resolution:

> In order to enlarge the role of the Military Councils in the life of the troops and to increase their responsibility for the combat preparedness of the Soviet Union Armed Forces, the Central Committee of the Communist Party and the Council of Ministers resolve as follows: to lay down that the Military Councils are vested with authority to deliberate and decide on all the most important matters of Army and Navy life and activity, and that they are responsible to the Central Committee, the Government and the Ministry of Defence for the situation of combat preparedness of the troops.
> 
> The decisions of the Military Councils are binding on all the members and are carried out by order of the Army Headquarters or of the Commander. All the members of the Military Council must act to execute the decisions taken in the Military Council. In case of disagreement with a decision that has been taken, the "Comrade" on the Military Council has the right to report on his view to the Central Committee, to the Government and the Minister of Defence. The existing Military Councils alongside Headquarters of the Armies, and the Military Councils of the Land Forces, the Navy, the Air Force and the A.-A. Defence are to be re-organised.[42]

It is a proof of the importance that the Central Committee attached to the Military Councils of the MDs at this time that in mid-1958 the Secretaries of the Party in the Republics and Regions were also added to their members. The post of "comrade" on the Military Council was merged with that of the Head of the Political Admi-

---

42 *The CPSU on the Armed Forces ..., op. cit.*, p. 353.

nistration in the MD, the Army Groups, the Navy and the Flotillas.

No changes were made in the tasks and powers of the Military Councils in the first half of the 1960's.

In summing up this Chapter is it worth repeating and re-emphasising what was stated at the beginning — that the main task of the whole apparatus of education and political supervision has been to inculcate loyalty to the Party and its ideology and to Soviet policy and ensure complete obedience to the political leadership. It can be said that the conjoined action of all the various elements in the network contributes to attaining the desired end.

# PART IV

## THE BEGINNING OF THE 1960's

## CHAPTER IX

## THE IMPACT OF STRATEGIC WEAPONS

When the debate over re-assessing the military doctrines of Stalin came to its close in 1955,* the factor of surprise, it will be remembered, was rated far higher than it had been previously. There was even open recognition that in certain circumstances surprise might settle the outcome of the whole war and not only of its opening phase. It was the appearance of nuclear arms at that time that had made a revision of doctrine necessary, with the burgeoning of the crucial problem of the nuclear first strike underlining the unequalled importance of surprise.

In his speech to the XX Party Congress, less than a year after the close of the theoreticians' debate, Zhukov took a step forward into the atomic era:

> The next war will be different from the last one. It will be characterised by extensive use of air forces, a whole range of rocket-borne arms and various means of *mass destruction*** — atomic and hydrogen weapons, bacterial and chemical warfare. All the same, we do not believe that these means will lessen the *decisive value of the Land Forces, the Navy and the Air Force.*** Modern war cannot be fought without them. A range of atomic and hydrogen weapons is now at the disposal of our Armed Forces, various kinds of very powerful rockets and jet arms, including long-range rockets.[1]

A cautious statement on balance: very important new weapons

---

\* See Chapter 3.
\*\* My emphasis — Y. A.
1 *Pravda,* 20 February 1956.

had been added to the Soviet arsenal, but for the time being no more than this.

Marshal Sokolovsky added a shade more emphasis by declaring that long-range rockets offered a safe way of launching the atomic and hydrogen bombs to reach any spot on earth.[2] He was making it clear that the launching systems could send the atom bombs right to the enemy's bases. This was in February 1956. Were such rockets actually at the disposal of the Soviet Union at that date? At all events it was in the autumn of 1956, during the Suez crisis but when the actual fighting was over, that the USSR for the first time threatened to launch missiles against Britain, France and Israel, in Notes to the heads of the three governments. (The missiles were not mentioned explicitly in the Note to Israel, which was couched in coarse and insulting language.) In order to magnify its repercussions, the threat was given early publication in the media, when it was clear that the end of the fighting precluded the necessity of putting the threat into effect.

Only a year after the declarations of Zhukov and Sokolovsky cited above, evaluation of the place of atomic arms in a future war had become far more affirmative. In an address to assault troops on 16 March 1957, Zhukov said: "Since atomic arms will increasingly replace conventional arms, it is inevitable that in a future war atomic arms will serve as the basic means in the conflict."[3] In August of the same year, Tass news agency surprised the world with the following announcement:

> An intercontinental ballistic missile[3a] has recently been launched. The tests were successful. ... The missile rose to a height never reached before, covered a great distance and landed in the target area. The results achieved indicate the possibility of delivering missiles to any area on the earth's surface. ...
> This will make it possible not to be dependent on strategic aviation, which is today vulnerable to A.A. defences. A series

2 *Pravda*, 23 February 1956.
3 *Pravda*, 20 March 1957.
3a Henceforth ICBM.

> of atomic and hydrogen arms explosions has recently been carried out in the Soviet Union. The tests were successful. ... The Government of the Soviet Union is bound to take every means in order to defend itself on account of the negative attitude of the Western Powers to disarmament proposals.[4]

The reference to the possibility of not needing strategic aviation was a tactful reminder that the USA was dependent on this vulnerable arm, since she had not yet overcome the difficulties of launching the ICBMs.

This Tass announcement created a sensation in the West, and a fortnight later, presumably in order to exploit the impression caused, Marshal Vershinin, Commander of the Air Force, told a Press conference (in reply to certainly pre-arranged questions by the *Pravda* correspondent):

> The American monopoly of atomic and hydrogen arms has long been abolished. We have a large enough capacity ... to return blow for blow — and in double measure — with this same type of weapon. This cancels out the possibility of a lightning annihilation of the Soviet Union, which is what the aggressive Generals are planning to carry out by means of air strikes with the forces and the arms at their disposal. The Americans' calculation that in the event of a world war, their distant territory is safe from military blows is not realistic. ... The means for delivering the most terrible of weapons — hydrogen ones — are now such that by means of ICBMs they will swiftly reach the farthest confines of any continent on this earth.[5]

Soon after this blustering declaration by the Air Force Commander, the Soviet Union sent up the first Sputnik in the world, to the amazement of the West, which did not believe the USSR capable of overtaking the USA in launching a satellite into space.[6] This

4 *Pravda*, 27 August 1957.
5 *Pravda*, 8 September 1957.
6 I was in the USA when the first Sputniks were sent up, and I wit-

convinced the West that the Soviet Union had succeeded in developing the rocket engine needed for ICBMs and it was assumed that in the near future they would also possess suitable launching vehicles.[7] In the Soviet Union itself, the flood of self-congratulation overflowed its banks (helping to sweep away Zhukov at the same time).[7a]

The launching of the Sputniks[7b] was the occasion for much speculation in army circles on the changes in military strategy bound up with long-range missiles. In March 1958 the well-known military theoretician, N. Talensky, published an article on military strategy and foreign policy — and disarmament:

> Not for nothing is the Sputnik called "Sputnik for Peace". ... The creation of the long-range missiles with the help of which the Soviet sputniks were put into orbit has ensured the Soviet Union very important advantages. The USSR desires to take advantage of her control of decisive modern arms in order, first of all, to promote her aims of strengthening peace and security. ... The ICBM has changed military strategy and its possibilities to a much greater extent and in a much shorter time than did, for example, the introduction of firearms or the invention of the airplane. ... The main

---

nessed the bewilderment of the thunderstruck public. On my return to my post in Moscow some time later, I found the general public there less enthusiastic. One heard people say that it would have been better to tackle the housing shortage or the bad distribution and shortages of consumers' goods rather than launching Sputniks.

[7] The major authorities on this subject, Horelick and Rush, analysed in great detail the "elaborate deception" by means of which the Soviet leaders succeeded in creating "politically exploitable uncertainty", and persuading the West that they were producing quantities of first generation ICBMs. See Arnold H. Horelick and Myron Rush, *Strategic Power and Soviet Foreign Policy,* University of Chicago Press, Chicago and London, 1965, Part 2, The Politics of Soviet Missile Deception, 1957–61, esp. pp. 35–41.

[7a] See p. 163 above.

[7b] The Second Sputnik weighed 508 kilograms and was launched in November. The first Sputnik had weighed only 83 kilograms.

value of the long-range ballistic missile is that it makes possible to hit the enemy and bring about his defeat anywhere in the world — no matter what the quantitative and qualitative relation of forces and the means for operating them in inter-continental warfare. ... With the ICBMs in existence, a war that the imperialists start will necessarily spread to the whole world. ... In existing conditions, local wars can only be the first stage of a world war. ... Thus the results of any war — local or total — will be absolute destruction, particularly in the thickly-populated countries of Western Europe.[8]

This analysis was not enough by itself to change military strategy on the ground. The progress of the USSR in developing atomic armament and even its success in getting the West to believe that it had solved the problem of launching ICBMs did not as yet permit application of the proposed changes in Soviet military strategy. First it was necessary to build up a certain reserve stock of the new arms, and simultaneously work out the technique and mobilise and train the manpower needed for their operation. Plans for whole new cadres had to be made and then implemented. It took two more years for the new strategic doctrine to be accepted and for its application to begin, with all that this involved in a new and different distribution of resources and a changed structural set-up in the Armed Forces. And there were also consequences for relations between the Party and the Army.

## The Khrushchev Doctrine

The drive and impetus to get the new doctrine adopted and the necessary changes effected in the make-up of the Armed Forces came from Khrushchev. He got his proposals for the reforms ratified at the Central Committee session of December 1959, and in January 1960 came his resounding declaration to the Supreme

[8] Major-General M. Talensky, "Military Strategy and Foreign Policy", *International Life*, Gosaizdat, Moscow, 1958, No. 3, pp. 34–40.

Soviet: "The Armed Forces of the Soviet Union were reduced by 2,140,000 men between 1955 and 1958, and today they number 3,623,000. The Government now proposes to reduce this number by another 1.2 million. ... We have gone into this with the General Staff and we find that it fully meets the needs. We first made a review and calculated the basis for this reduction. Thanks to the knowledge and the labours of our scientists, engineers, technicians and workers, great successes have been attained in the production of atomic and hydrogen weapons, in rocket technique and all the other means that have made it possible to raise the defence capacity of our State to such an extent that we can now reduce our Armed Forces. The Soviet Union has produced and stocked the necessary amount of atomic and hydrogen weapons. As long as no Convention exists prohibiting these arms, we are bound to go on producing them. We now have very powerful equipment at the disposal of the State. In the present conditions of development of military technique, aviation and the Navy have lost their previous importance. Aviation has been almost entirely replaced by missile technology. We have cut down and perhaps we shall even stop production of the older-type bombers and equipment. In the Navy the importance of submarines has risen greatly: surface vessels are no longer able to perform the functions they fulfilled in the past. Our Armed Forces have in large measure passed over to atomic missile weapons. ... We have sufficient atomic and hydrogen arms and the means for delivering them everywhere in the world, so that if any madman whatsoever decides to attack...we can literally wipe that country off the face of the earth. ... Reduction of the scale of our forces will take from a year to eighteen months."[9] Defence Minister Malinovsky supported this proposed reduction of the Forces, relying to some extent on the lessening of international tension. Addressing the Supreme Soviet, he dilated upon the features of missile weapons and their various operational-tactical uses. He gave details of the types of missiles capable of delivering nuclear warheads at the speed of sound, in all weathers, simultaneously to

9 *Izvestia*, 15 January 1960.

## The Impact of Strategic Weapons

numerous targets anywhere, no matter how far away. By massive blows, the missiles would be capable of effecting a decisive change in the course of the war. He quoted calculations of experts to the effect that a hundred warheads could turn a country of 3 to 500,000 square kilometres into a poisoned desert and highly developed industry into a junk-pile. He concluded:

> Taking all this into account, since we dispose of modern means of tremendous fire-power in the form of missiles with atomic warheads, it is definitely possible to reduce the number of men serving in the Armed Forces without damage to the defence capacity of our State. A reduction by 1.2 million men is definitely a wise and timely act.[10]

Not surprisingly, in view of Khrushchev's and Malinovsky's persuasive advocacy, the "Law regarding a further, considerable reduction of the Armed Forces" proposed by the Government was accepted by the Supreme Soviet, which found it both desirable and possible to effect this reduction, which would of course contribute to strengthening peace in the world. The Law provided that the Armed Forces would be reduced by 1.2 million men; the corresponding number of formations and military schools would be dissolved; armaments would be reduced and financial outlays cut down.[11] Therewith began the real and effective transition of the USSR to the age of nuclear weapons.

To back up the impression made in the West by the leaders' announcements regarding Soviet nuclear power, about a week after the end of the Supreme Soviet session, the media published a report of the successful launching of a very powerful ballistic missile over a trajectory of 12,500 kilometres to land less than two kilometres from its target.[12]

The entire emphasis in Khrushchev's address to the Supreme Soviet was on the USSR's capability to deliver such terrible blows

---

10  *Red Star*, 15 January 1960.
11  *Pravda*, 16 January 1960.
12  *Pravda*, 22 January 1960.

that no country unless led by madmen would even attempt to attack her. In short, his real aim was deterrence.

The change-over to the new era was beginning in earnest. It would have to be a fairly lengthy process, calling for production of adequate stocks of the new weapons, production of the means of delivery, training of technicians, new installations for the weapons systems — and re-organisation of the set-up of the different arms in the Forces. Not until all this had been done would it be possible to talk seriously of a "Revolution in the military sphere". It was only later on that it emerged — as everyone now knows — that at the time of Khrushchev's resounding declaration the number of Soviet ICBMs in existence was very small indeed. The evaluations in the West in 1960 of the quantity of Russian missiles that would be operational by mid-1961 were eight times too high.[13] The deception succeeded for four whole years behind the smoke-screen, in the meanwhile the transformation proceeded energetically, with demonstrative encouragement from the leadership. At the end of June 1960, the Central Committee organised a formal reception for the graduates of the Military Academies with most of the Party Presidium and the senior command present. Khrushchev's speech on this occasion again stressed the Soviet demand for disarmament, while Malinovsky addressed himself more directly to the graduates:

13 Horelick, *op. cit., loc. cit.*, and see pp. 66–68. Horelick lists three probable main objectives of the Soviet deception:
1) to conceal the decision not to engage in a large-scale deployment of the first-generation ICBM despite apparent capability to do so, hoping to reap whatever benefits might have accrued had they actually engaged in a buildup;
2) to help deter a US attack on the USSR by claiming that a US surprise attack could not incapacitate the Soviet strategic force and that the USSR would be able to inflict "a due rebuff";
3) to deter the West from political or military exploitation of its superior strategic power.
Horelick makes a remark relevant to our main concern: "Certainly, Soviet military leaders would be more willing to exaggerate Soviet ICBM capabilities in order to conceal weakness than to bluff a superior opponent in an open confrontation." *op. cit.*, p. 69.

We have to train experts in the new types of weapons and primarily for all kinds of missiles. I can now attest to the successes we have achieved in this matter. In the course of their studies, the graduates present here have been given a thorough enough grounding in questions of utilising the newest means of armed conflict in the battle and in the campaign and they will know how to handle the missiles. The problems connected with operating missiles are very complex and we expect you too to bring forward proposals for improving the technique and methods of warfare in the new conditions.[14]

In 1960, alongside the training of the manpower needed, a special arm of the Forces was established. The Strategic Missile Forces.[14a]

## *The Doctrine — and the Military Theoreticians*

The doctrine presented by Khrushchev and ratified by the Supreme Soviet in January 1960 was based, as we have seen, on the one hand on the lessening of international tension and on the other on the deterrent power of nuclear arms — the missile and the delivery systems supposedly at the disposal of the Soviet Union. As a strategy, Khrushchev's conception was limited to one sole option: preparation for atomic war by means of a minimal deterrent strategic force. The basic principle of balanced development was overthrown.[15] This conception met with a good many reservations on the part of the military theoreticians and the senior commanders.

---

14 *Pravda*, 29 June 1960.
14a The Russian term for "strategic missiles" is literally "missiles with strategic uses" or "for strategic purposes".
15 According to N. Galay, Khrushchev's declaration of January 1960 opened the new phase of the development of Soviet strategic thought that eventually led to the revolution in theory and in practice in the military sphere, precisely because he overthrew the basic principle of balanced Soviet military development in favour of the nuclear missile forces. N. Galay, "The Soviet Approach to the Modern Military Revolution", *The Military Technical Revolution*, ed. John Erickson, Frederick A. Praeger, New York, 1966, p. 22.

The Soviet professional soldier was accustomed to having military theory put to him combined with or even subordinated to Marxist-Leninist theory (even if in the last analysis this was hardly more than lip service) and tied in with the political "general line" prevailing in a given period. Hence too the quest for a "uniform" military doctrine. There had been a theoretically "uniform" military doctrine in the 1920's, it will be remembered, and a great deal of debate and friction over it as well.[15a] Fundamental problems of military doctrine emerged again after Stalin's death, and the debates in the years 1953 to '55 over Stalin's petrified "operative factors" were conducted and summed up entirely within the military set-up, while the Party leadership refrained from interfering (openly, at least).[15b] Now in the '60's, here was the Secretary-General of the Party (together with the Presidium) initiating revolutionary changes in strategic doctrine. The importance of the change of doctrine was multiplied many times over by the destructive power of the new arms. The advent of the nuclear era unavoidably had a decisive effect on policy, and military strategy had to fit in with and be subordinate to the political decisions even more than previously. A new and "uniform" military doctrine had to be framed to correspond to the technical revolution taking place in the military sphere. It had to be based on Marxist-Leninist theory and — in practical terms — on the new Party Programme accepted at the XXII Congress in October 1961, when the foundations of the doctrine were laid.

A senior military theoretician, Professor and General N. Lomov, write in *Armed Forces Communist* in May 1962:

> The foundations of military doctrine are laid down by the internal and the foreign policy of the Communist Party and of the Soviet State, in accordance with the nature of the period we are living in and its problems. Hence it is not possible to grasp the substance and content of military doctrine correctly except against the background of theoretical and

[15a] See Chapter 1.
[15b] See Chapter 6.

political conclusions in the data of the XXII Congress and in the new Programme of the Party. Working out Soviet military doctrine is done under the lead and the direct supervision of the Central Committee, on the basis of the theoretical and methodological principles of Marxism-Leninism. Hence the inestimable value of the elaboration of modern military doctrine in the speech of Khrushchev at the 4th Session of the Supreme Soviet (i.e. in 1960), in the documents of the XXII Congress and the new Party Programme.[16]

Apparently military theoreticians can be politicians too, when necessary.

Defence Minister Malinovsky formulated the close connection between Party policy and military doctrine at a general "consultation" on ideological problems in October 1962:

> In the present stormy conditions of developments regarding armed conflict, military-theoretical action assumes special significance. Thanks to the manifold exertions of the Central Committee headed by Khrushchev and thanks also to the efforts of our men of learning, we now possess a military doctrine profoundly rooted in and stemming from the political character of our State. Soviet-military doctrine, based on "the politics"[16b] of our Party and supported in its main recommendations by the conclusions of military science, assists us in penetrating the nature of war today and of its opening phase; it also makes it possible to settle on the most purposeful ways of action in the next war and to decide on the needs in Armed Forces organisation, development and training.[17]

All this talk by Malinovsky and others about their basing themselves on the Party and the political nature of the regime did not

---

16 General Professor N. Lomov, "Soviet Military Doctrine", *Armed Forces Communist,* May 1962.
16b *"Politika"* in Russian, meaning in effect "political policy".
17 *Red Star,* 25 October 1962.

prevent differences of opinion precisely on the subject of the strategic doctrine involved. General Zhilin, editor of the *Journal of Military History*, wrote in the spring of 1961:

> Uniformity of outlook on all the most important problems of the art of war and activation of the troops is needed now more than ever in the past. The political side of Soviet military doctrine has been defined with the greatest possible clarity in a series of Party documents, but in the technical-military aspects of the doctrine... there still remain propositions that are not clear and on which different opinions exist.[18]

One thing at least is clear here — that the desired uniformity of outlook on military theory was absent. When the article was published, international developments and growing internal criticism were combining to stop the reductions in conventional arms. The theoreticians were still reluctant to see the progress made so far in atomic armament as "Revolution in the military sphere".

Production and stock-piling of nuclear arms and production of means of delivery went ahead, however, as did the re-structuring of the Forces. In 1962 the Army heads and the theoreticians were at last prepared or constrained to admit that these changes did amount to a revolution. Khrushchev had been characteristically a bit previous when he used the phrase "Revolution in the military sphere" in his October '61 speech to the XXII Congress. Yet no more than a year later, "Military Strategy", the extensive and important collective work of fifteen officers headed by Marshal Sokolovsky, would affirm:

> The distinguishing feature of weapon development under current conditions is the appearance of *qualitatively new types of weapons and military equipment*[18a] and their rapid and massive introduction into the armed forces. This has led to a pronounced improvement in the latter's combat capa-

---

18 Major-General P. Zhilin, *Journal of Military History*, No. 5, May 1961, p. 73.
18a The authors' stress.

bilities, a radical break in the organisational forms of armed forces and methods of conducting military operations on every scale. *Military strategy and the art of war as a whole have undergone a revolution.*[19]

After this book came out in 1962, the Soviet military started using the expression, "revolution in the military sphere", in all the relevant papers and articles. It was in 1962 that the processes summed up in this passage, previously comparatively gradual, produced the "radical break in organisational forms".

In 1965, looking backwards, the writers in *The Communist Party of the Soviet Union and the Development of the Soviet Armed Forces* enumerated the following necessary pre-conditions for the technical revolution:

1. mass production of nuclear missile arms, based on a high level of economic development, science and technology;
2. the re-armament of the Soviet Army and Navy with nuclear missile arms and other new weapons;
3. re-structuring of the organisational set-up in the Army and Navy in accordance with the needs of modern war;
4. re-elaboration of the theory of the art of war, as well as of military regulations and instructions, in response to these needs;
5. changes in manpower training and educational methods in the armed forces;
6. elaboration of a Soviet modern military doctrine.

They contended that all these elements constituted a dialectical unity, were connected with and dependent on each other, but they went on to affirm that the first two on the list — the production of the nuclear arms with their delivery systems and the re-arming and equipment of the Army and Navy — were the main thing, and all the rest followed.[20]

It is not surprising that the military hierarchy, essentially con-

---

19 My stress — Y.A. Marshal V.D. Sokolovsky ed., *Military Strategy*, Voyenizdat, Moscow, 1962. Translated and published by Rand Corporation, titled, *Soviet Military Strategy*, 1963, p. 295.
20 *The CPSU and the Development* ..., 1965, p. 381

servative like all hierarchies everywhere and especially so in the Soviet Union, was reluctant to commit itself wholly to the atomic armaments revolution, a revolution not only in technology, but in organisation and doctrine. In the meanwhile, the technical revolution was progressing outside the universe of discourse of Marxism-Leninism and beyond the reach of the boldest political bluff though spurred on by it: by 1962, when the USSR was at last deploying considerable quantities of operational ICBMs, US nuclear capacity had grown much faster.[21] This realisation finally hit home with the Cuban missile crisis in mid-1962.

## The Cuban Missile Crisis

The myth of the "missile gap" had collapsed as a result of American intelligence re-evaluation of Soviet strategic capabilities.[22] Khrushchev felt impelled to seek some swift and dramatic means of buttressing his government's position, militarily, diplomatically and psychologically, on various issues and especially in the matter of Berlin. He thought he had found the solution in his rash decision to deploy strategic missiles in Cuba. The swift and energetic riposte delivered by the Americans — the naval blockade — accompanied by the firm demand that the bases be dismantled and the missiles removed, brought the Soviet leadership face to face with US supremacy in the region and US overall military superiority. At first they tried to deny the reports that their assistance to Cuba included the establishment of bases for launching nuclear arms. When it was clear that the US would wipe out the bases if they were not dismantled and the missiles returned to the Soviet Union, Khrushchev had no alternative but to yield.

A great deal has been written on the Cuban crisis — five days when the world held its breath, and so on — and its development

---

21 Horelick, *op. cit.*, p. 155. Galay affirms that even at this stage, mid-1962, Soviet military theory had not accepted the concept of revolution as part of its terminology. *Loc. cit.*, p. 22.
22 Horelick, *op. cit.*, p. 127.

and dénouement have been carefully analysed from different points of view. We shall confine ourselves to giving the central passage of the Note from Khrushchev to Kennedy "closing" the crisis, handed to the U.S. President on 28 October 1962 in answer to a note from him of the day before: "I regard with respect and trust your statement of 27 October that there is no intention and will not be any intention of invading Cuba; if this is so — then the reasons are removed that led to our furnishing assistance to Cuba. An order has therefore been given to our officers (and as we have already stated those missiles are in the hands of Soviet officers) to take the necessary means to stop construction of the aforesaid objects, to dismantle them and return them to the Soviet Union. ... If we base ourselves on your assurances and on our orders to dismantle — then all the conditions are thereby in being for closing the conflict."[23]

To sum up the lessons of this tense confrontation, we can hardly do better than cite the magisterial comment of John Erickson:

> In that Faustian fashion which he made so distinctively his own Nikita Khrushchev tried repeatedly to achieve too much with far too little, not least in the critical area of Soviet strategic policy: he bridged the growing gap between Soviet objectives and Soviet capability with a combination of bluster and rhetoric, he transmuted (if only verbally) "inferiority" into "parity" and even "superiority" if the whim took him. He insisted that his own version of "minimal deterrence" maximised Soviet security and proceeded to fasten both strategic doctrine and the Soviet armed forces within a single "incredible" option — nuclear war. This was a style and these were mistakes which his successors were bent on avoiding.[24]

There could be no more attempted short cuts and no more bluffing.

---

23 *Pravda*, 29 October 1962.
24 John Erickson, "Soviet Military Power", *Strategic Review*, Spring 1973, Special Supplement, p. 1, U.S. Strategic Institute, Washington, D.C.

For the USSR to become a nuclear Power to be reckoned with needed more than readiness to allocate large resources and changes in military doctrine. There had to be sufficient time for the production lines to produce an improved second generation of missiles in sufficient quantity to constitute a respectable reserve; the trained manpower too had to be "operational" and the military set-up re-organised and functioning reasonably well. Only then would the Soviet Union compete as a Super-Power in practice and not only in theory.

## CHAPTER X

## THE ARMED FORCES RE-MODELLED

The "revolution in the military sphere" that resulted from equipping the Armed Forces with nuclear weapons alerted the political leadership to the need to look carefully at the relations between the Party and the Army. The new armament with its tremendous destructive force called for the ability to take swift, fateful decisions on their use, and above all it put the question of where the effective control of this new force finally lay.[1] As nuclear arms were progressively introduced in the late 1950's and early '60's, revolutionising military organisational structure and the allocation of State resources, the Party leadership was constantly concerned to strengthen the officer corps' responsibility to the Party and its bond of loyalty to the Party. The leadership took the only path it knew — strengthening supervision by the Party apparatuses in the Army over all ranks of the command, and especially the highest. These considerations probably already contributed to the famed October 1957 decisions of the Central Committee Plenary. It was

---

1 The military theoretician, Morris Janowitz, puts forward an analysis, centred on US political strategy, which also applies to the turn taken by developments in the USSR. The growing importance of strategic deterrence, he writes, meant that the top military became more and more involved in political and diplomatic as well as military affairs, whether they were prepared for it or not. The specific contribution of the military to deterrence is of course the reality of a threat that has to be taken seriously because of its potential force. Effective deterrence is in part political strategy and in part a question of purely military decisions on how to create and maintain an effective structural organisation of combat forces prepared for hostilities. Morris Janowitz, *The Professional Soldier,* The Free Press, New York, 1965, p. 34.

on good grounds that the Plenary Resolutions were relied on as authoritative throughout the following years, for they were from then on the cornerstone of the whole edifice of Party control of the forces. The transition to the atomic era must be seen as reinforcing all the other calculations that led to the passing of these Resolutions.

It will be remembered that this was the period when the news was announced that a Soviet ICBM had been tested (August 1957) and when the first Sputnik was launched (October 1957). Khrushchev was making every effort to get the West to believe that the USSR was ahead of the USA in missiles with atomic warheads, and the Soviet war industry went into high gear to develop atomic capability for the forces in fact and not only in fiction. As an indispensable condition for this revolutionary increment of force to the Army, the leadership saw it necessary to reduce to an absolute minimum the possibility of any focus whatsoever of military power's coming into being which might conceivably be more independent than any such focus in the past, one that would be less perfectly interlocked with the Party's organs and over which the Party might have less than complete control.

Against this background, the figure of Zhukov stands out in high relief. He would clearly be a stumbling-block in the path of reinforced Party supervision.[1a] He was absolutely the wrong man to be at the head of the Army in the new conditions, in view of the measures that the leadership felt bound to take. "Zhukov showed himself ... inclined to adventurism both as regards understanding of the major problems of Soviet foreign policy and as regards his manner of directing the Ministry of Defence"[1b] — this passage in the October 1957 Resolutions states clearly enough the leadership's judgement on Zhukov in the new conditions. Thus to all the other reasons that the leadership found good and sufficient for deposing Zhukov[1c] must be added the effect of the introduction of nuclear

[1a] See Chapter 5 above.
[1b] See pp. 168–169 above.
[1c] See Chapter 6 above.

arms on Party-Army relations. The unswerving application of the October '57 Resolutions, despite their untoward side-effects,[1d] and the other measures taken in this field in the late '50's and early '60's are unquestionable proof of the Party's firm determination to reinforce its hold on the Armed Forces in the nuclear era.

The main problems centred on the relative weight of the army and the political leadership in the elaboration of military strategic doctrine — and the incurable inclination in top army circles to put military professionalism before ideological values. The ability of the military men to stand up for themselves against pressures from Khrushchev went through variations, and in the last two years that Khrushchev held office the struggle took on the character of a rearguard action.

## Khrushchev Reduces Armed Forces Effectives

The outstanding practical problem was the resistance on the part of the army to a large reduction in the scale of the conventional forces. In Khrushchev's view, strategic deterrence made possible a very considerable cut in manpower in the main three traditional arms, which would also mean very considerable savings. The funds and the manpower thus released could be directed to serving important and urgent economic needs.

Khrushchev's conception and the firm decision to implement it produced open differences of opinion between the political leadership and a good part of the senior command over the military needs and the allocation of resources to satisfy them. Was it possible to rely on the nuclear deterrent in peace-time, since the enemy would not dare attack, or did the danger of a sudden enemy attack continue to exist all the same, so that it was necessary to maintain large forces in constant readiness to launch a pre-emptive strike or a counter-stroke? If the latter were a possibility that had to be taken seriously, there ought not to be a drastic reduction of forces. The differences of opinion over this central issue produced

[1d] See Chapter 7 above.

a complicated and protracted conflict, which brought a number of after-effects in its wake.

*Bitter Resentment Over the Mass Discharges.* Bad feeling and resentment over the reform of the '60's and the main resistance to it in the Army stemmed from the dismissal of some 250,000 officers. The wounded Army command's sense of grievance was directed against the Party leadership and mainly against Khrushchev. The decisive majority of candidates for discharge were men whose only vocation was arms and whose absorption into the Soviet economy was a matter of great difficulty. Khrushchev called on them to fit themselves into agriculture and industry, but his call fell on deaf ears: the officers regarded manual labour as an unacceptable loss of status according to usual Soviet social standards. The Party leadership started right away on a campaign of persuasion, appealing to the officers' patriotic feelings.

Only three days after the Supreme Soviet passed the Law for the Limitation of the Armed Forces, a meeting of the Party's *"aktiv"* of officers of the Moscow garrison was called together in the Kremlin. It was attended by a number of members of the Party Presidium, eleven Marshals and a batch of Generals. The main speaker was Marshal Malinovsky, who explained the policy and the new Law:

> This Law effects a considerable reduction in the number of men serving in the Forces. There are some 250,000 officers, generals and admirals among those dismissed. ... If we have not met with any very great difficulties in fixing up the other ranks in jobs in industry and agriculture—about a third are discharged each year—there will be some difficulty connected with the 250,000 dismissed officers. The Army and the Government are therefore taking steps to see that they find work, and to give officers vocational training so that they acquire a civilian calling and can find employment in civilian life. ... They also have to keep up their military calling. ... We have a lot of experience in settling officers in civilian jobs ... but along with the successes, we have to remember that in not

a few instances in the past the local authorities did not ensure full employment for all officers discharged and the arrangements took a long time. The officers suffered from difficulties in arranging housing. The Central Committee is now taking steps to see to it that all this doesn't happen again. We are taking count of the difficulties facing us that we must overcome. Remember that we are patriots here ... and that it does not befit a Soviet officer to bear a grudge over the need to change his calling and to leave the military service before the end of the period needed to give him pension rights. I am sure that officers will prove their patriotism and comprehension as regards doing their duty.[2]

Malinovsky, as Minister of Defence responsible for the practical execution of the Law, provided detailed information on the grants accorded to discharged officers. He said that the officers themselves would have to set about finding work and should not be too choosy, because time passes in the meanwhile. After him the Chief Marshal of the Air Force, Vershinin, Generals and others spoke in similar terms, and the appropriate resolutions were passed.

All the explanations and exhortations and the resolutions passed at meetings were however of little assistance in solving the practical problems: the discharged men were suffering, and their embitterment grew. It soon became clear that the civilian labour market could not offer the masses of discharged officers suitable employment that would even partially come up to their expectations of what was their due as a special class in Soviet society.

*Central Committee and Government Regulations for providing employment* and ensuring economic and other conditions *for discharged Armed Forces personnel* in accordance with the Law for the Limitation of the Armed Forces of the Soviet Union were published on 26 January 1960. Their main provisions are as follows:
1. Priority is to be given to arranging work for the discharged

---

[2] *Red Star,* 20 January 1960.

men in industry, building, transport and agriculture; special attention to be paid to directing the men to the regions in the North and the Urals, Siberia, the Far East and Kazakhstan, as well as to *Kolkhozes* [agricultural collectives] and *Sovkhozes* [State farms] in the virgin lands.

2. The Councils of Ministers in the Republics and the Councils of Representatives of the Toilers must give officers transferred to the reserves or to retirement first priority housing not later than three months after their arrival.

3. In order to assist officers transferred to the reserves to acquire a productive occupation, the authorities concerned must give them priority in admission to the appropriate schools and courses for learning a suitable trade. During their studies, officers transferred to the reserves are to be paid 75% of the wages they would be earning in the occupation they are training for, but not less than 400 rubles a month, except for pensioners.

4. Dismissed officers who have no pension rights will be granted bursaries when admitted to special technical and high schools, if their attainments in their studies are satisfactory.

5. The Ministry of Defence will be authorised to award grants to officers transferred to the reserves or to retirement who have no pension rights. The grant in each case will be equivalent to one month's salary for those who served for 5 to 10 years; two months' salary for those who served for 10 to 15 years; three months' salary for those who served for more than 15 years.[2a] The grant is to be paid when the discharged man arrives at his fixed place of residence.

The Central Committee and the Government later requested the Party organisations, the various soviets, the Komsomol organisations and the heads of Ministries and Departments and *Sovnarhozes*[2b] and of the different economic undertakings to give their attention to the need to show the greatest possible concern over

---

[2a] Pension rights accrued after 20 years' service.
[2b] National Economic Councils.

## The Armed Forces Re-Modelled

arranging work and housing for the men discharged and vocational training as well.[3]

It appears that drafting and promulgating instructions was easier than putting such a complicated programme into effect. The discharged officers were thrown into the civilian labour market without sufficient preparation, the profession of arms all they knew, and over 100,000 of them remained without employment for a whole year. Many found it hard to learn a new trade on account of their age or for other reasons, and it is not surprising that the civilian labour market found it hard to absorb them. Those who had no pensions were in serious material straits — the grants allocated were very small. In many instances there was the added feeling that the civilian institutions concerned were not exactly in a hurry to find them suitable work, and there were many complaints on this score.

*"Comrades of Khazan!"*. As embitterment deepened among masses of men who had for years devoted themselves to the service of fatherland and Party, the military press organs and the appointed propagandists in the High Commands and in the Party apparatus were mobilised to prod the civilian bodies into dealing more efficiently with the problem and to encourage the discharged officers to find a place for themselves in the civilian economy and be less difficult about it. The main purpose was to calm people down. In September 1960, *Red Star* published an anonymous article with the headline, "Comrades of Khazan! Pay greater heed — Show more concern!" The obligatory opening of satisfaction did not even last a whole sentence:

> The discharged men have received a warm welcome in Khazan, but it is clear that here too a lot of things are missing: there is no contact between the different institutions. The officers are kept waiting and go on suffering. Local Commissions of the Army must bring this matter before the City

[3] *The CPSU on the Armed Forces of the Soviet Union,* 1969, *op. cit.,* pp. 356–61.

Council and get some coordination between the City Commission for Employment and the Housing Commission: the situation is especially bad as regards housing. Over 70% of those needing housing have not yet received it. The City Council allocates too few of the apartments whose construction has been completed to the officers transferred to the reserves. The military institutions are not providing sufficient guidance directives to the dismissed men. Many of these officers think that their place is behind a desk in an office and they do not understand that what we need now are working hands and not clerks in offices.[4]

There was no lack of rosier accounts, for all that. Here is a passage from an article by Admiral Kastanov in *Armed Forces Communist* a month later:

Many dismissed officers have already proved themselves outstanding production workers. Officer Danilovich was quick to learn the new occupation of locksmith in a tyre-factory in Dniepropetrovsk. He became a model of high productivity and of the culture of labour. The factory management appreciated to the full the talents and the efforts of the new production worker and sent him on a course for operatives. Danilovich was also signed on for a correspondence course in one of the institutes.[5]

Presumably Kastanov would have cited more such examples of successful adaptation if he had had any, but it looks as if the case of Danilovich was exceptional enough. The difficulties experienced by the majority, together with their feeling that their past contribution was not valued, left a sediment of bitter resentment against the regime, and mainly against the head of Government and Secretary-General of the Party who had initiated the reform and put it

4 *Red Star*, 22 September 1960.
5 Admiral V. Kastanov, Commander of the Black Sea Fleet, "The Decisions of the Fourth Session of the Supreme Soviet of the USSR", *Armed Forces Communist*, October 1960, p. 13.

through. Khrushchev's blunt, contemptuous references to those who refused to take up manual labour did not add to his popularity among the officers — including those who were not candidates for discharge.[6]

*"Serving the Fatherland in Lenin's Way".* A generalised sense of opposition to the reforms, well beyond anything foreseen, and the resentment in broad sectors of the Army over the mass discharges spurred the Party leadership into taking renewed steps to tighten Party control and supervision of the Armed Forces — a process that was in any case accompanying the introduction of nuclear arms. It was decided to launch an extensive propaganda campaign to hammer home how vital it was, in the interests of the Army itself, that it be led by the Party. The decision on this campaign was already taken in principle, it seems, in April 1960. The guideline that was energetically pushed was that the Party Central Committee always scrupulously consulted the Army heads before laying down lines for Army organisation and development. The first sign was a keynote article by Malinovsky in *Red Star*, shortly before the 90th anniversary of Lenin's birth, entitled "Serving the Fatherland in Lenin's Way"; it was probably not by chance that the opening shot in the campaign came from the head of the Army and not the MPA head nor even a member of the Central Committee, appeals from whom would certainly have had a cooler welcome.

Malinovsky expatiated on the way Lenin established the Army and on the principle of the Army's necessary and complete subordination to the political leadership. At every stage of the development of the Army and Navy, it was the Leninist Central Committee that had laid down the line along which the Forces were to be built up and educated. This was also the case now, asserted Malinovsky. In the current phase of development of the Army and Navy. "Before a decision is taken on questions of organisation and

6 Kolkowicz considers that a majority of the officers began to view Khrushchev's policy on the Armed Forces as a threat to part of their rights and interests. *Op. cit.*, p. 157

military development and of strengthening the Armed Forces' combat power, the Central Committee and Presidium with First Secretary Comrade Khrushchev make a thorough study of the state of affairs and the concrete conditions in the Army and Navy, in consultation with the Army heads. ... This enables the Party and its Central Committee to reach correct, well-thought-out decisions on the most complicated questions of military development in Lenin's way. We stress this most particularly so that our military cadres should once more be imbued with the realisation that if the Army were not led by the Party, we should not be able to live and work: we could not conceivably succeed in developing and improving the Armed Forces. Leadership by the Party is the sound Leninist basis of Army and Navy development."[7]

Malinovsky reverted to the theme of the October 1957 Plenary Resolutions, recalling their truly historic value in enhancing the leading role of the Party in the Armed Forces more than ever and in strengthening Party influence "in all spheres of Army life". It was in this article that Malinovsky made it known that the Central Committee had decided to convoke a "consultation" of the Party organisations in the Forces to review the way the commanders and the Party-political institutions in the Forces were implementing the Plenary Resolutions and the instructions issued according to the decisions of the January 1960 Supreme Soviet session and other relevant decisions.

*The "consultation" in the Kremlin from 11 to 14 May 1960* took place in the presence of three members of the Party Presidium, Brezhnev, Ignatov and Suslov, and of Army heads and commanders. Party Committee Secretaries, Party organisation Secretaries, heads of Political Sections, Political Deputies (*Zampolits*), Members of the Military Councils, heads of MD Political Administrations and representatives of Defence Ministry departments were all present, as well as representatives of the Moscow Party and Komsomol organisations. No "consultation" on this scale had

[7] *Red Star*, 14 April 1960.

taken place since the one in 1938 after the great purges in the senior ranks of the Army.

The first speakers were Malinovsky and MPA Head, Golikov. Brezhnev spoke in the name of the Central Committee. The report of the meeting took up a whole page of *Red Star*, with a photo of the dais and Brezhnev on his feet in the centre making his speech. (Three weeks later he was elected President of the Supreme Soviet.) The actual content of the speeches and deliberations, however, was very hazy and — something very unusual — there was nothing at all of what Central Committee representative Brezhnev said in his speech. It was stated that he was listened to very attentively and was very warmly applauded.

Malinovsky spoke on the prospective development of the Forces and on raising the level of combat preparedness. Golikov dealt with the tasks awaiting all the Party activists in the Forces; in the little that was given of his speech, there was again a reminder of the important effect of the October '57 Plenary decisions "in all spheres of Army life and activity". There was no report on the content of the decisions reached at this "consultation", beyond the brief statement that appropriate Resolutions on the questions discussed were adopted unanimously.[8]

Additional information on this "consultation" is given in the official publication (1965), "The Communist Party of the Soviet Union and the Development of the Armed Forces", already cited in these pages. The book stated in what had practically become code phrases that the Resolutions passed at this consultation indicated that the Military Councils had been more active in recent years and that their task had been accorded additional validity by virtue of their authority to "deliberate on all the most important questions in Army life and activity" and through their responsibility to the Central Committee, the Government and the Minister of Defence for the situation and combat preparedness in the Army and Navy. Summing up, the book stated that the participants in

8  *Ibid.*, 15 May 1960.

the consultation supported the MPA proposals in the organisational sphere of Party-political action.[9] Thus the substance of these exceptional deliberations and the decisions taken remained veiled in secrecy. There is no doubt however that the instructions issued in accordance with these decisions meant intensive measures to tighten Party control and supervision in the Forces.

In the period following this "consultation", there was an exceptionally concentrated flood of articles in the military press and in special pamphlets, all dealing with relations between the Army and the Party. Most of them called for increased Party action, propaganda and political education. There was endlessly repetitive emphasis on the need for more Marxist-Leninist studies and for action on Marxist-Leninist principles.

*Organisational changes in the Party apparatus,* which had been hinted at in the reports (such as they were) on the "consultation" of May 1960, were not long in arriving. There were changes in the structure and the authority of the Party organisations in the Forces. Party Committees replaced Political Sections in the Ministry of Defence and in a series of central Army bodies.

One means of buttressing Party control was the dismissal of officers less politically dedicated or less active in Party work, and this naturally led to advancement of younger officers of undoubted loyalty to the Party. The characteristic reaction to increased pressure on officers from the Party political apparatus was a certain degree of negligence with its usual and inevitable concomitant, a slackening of military discipline. We find references to this in statements coming from the highest ranks. Thus, for example, Colonels A. Tarasov and S. Ilin, in an article in *Armed Forces Communist* in December 1960:

> In some military academies, Party instructions calling for a fundamental improvement in military discipline are being

---

9 *The CPSU and the Development of the Armed Forces,* 1965, *op. cit.,* pp. 437–38.

carried out very slowly. Gross deviations are to be found from the requirements of the regulations.[10]

According both to the military literature and to the testimony of the officers we interviewed, the well-known effects followed the well-known causes, and discipline went from bad to worse. The commanders found it hard to impose discipline as a result of interference by the political apparatus (particularly the *Zampolits*) in purely military matters, and they raised more and more insistent demands for stronger "unity of command". They cited the need for swift decision in modern warfare, arguing that unlike the situation in the past, the commander hadn't much time to consult his *Zampolit* or to devote to lengthy "collegial" deliberations. It is safe to say that quantities of "criticism and self-criticism" did not appeal to the military either.

*"Every means to strengthen the Command"* was the title of an interestingly devious article by General of Army Krilov. He started off of course by praising the expected new Programme of the Party, which would be brought before the forthcoming Congress, and did not fail to recite that the main source of strength of the Army and Navy lay in their being led by the Party. He then came to the point:

> The most important principle of organisation and development of the Armed Forces is — unity of command. It is no mere chance that unity of command has been included in the draft new Party Programme. ... With us, unity of command is built on a Party basis; this means that the commander is there representing the Party and he imbues the entire Armed Forces with the Party ideas. ...
> In fostering criticism and self-criticism, it is necessary to exercise wisdom in the use of this sharp instrument. ... We need criticism that is directed towards getting rid of negative phenomena, enhancing the authority of the commander corps and strengthening the Armed Forces. Everything that inter-

10  *Armed Forces Communist,* December 1960, p. 31.

feres with this — *has to be brushed aside.*[10a] I particularly wish to emphasise the exceeding importance of having officers develop the ability to take the right decisions as a matter of habit. Some commanders lose a lot of time because they think they are bound to consult *all their deputies*[10a] (*Zampolits*). ... Collegial decision must be restricted to the necessary minimum and should never interfere with reaching a swift and firm decision.[11]

This criticism of "criticism and self-criticism" and of "collegial" deliberations was of course directed at the obvious targets — the Party-political apparatus and the political workers.

*Calling a half.* In mid-1961, the reduction of forces and dismissals of officers were temporarily suspended. The official explanation given was the tension over the question of Berlin.

## The Reform Faces the Traditional Structures

Formal ratification of the new doctrine and the start of its application as regards the structure and roles of the different arms led among other things to a polarisation into two groups of officers at the opposite ends of the possible gamut of views concerning the new conception. At the one end were extreme conservatives, who could not reconcile themselves to the great changes taking place and clung to the older, formerly authoritative views—mainly commanders of the Land Forces, rear services and Navy. Over against them at the other end were extreme "progressive" officers, who pressed for speedy and complete application of the reform, downgrading the importance of conventional forces and the worth of the traditional command. They were mainly officers and engineers of the cadre of the strategic and technical arms (who also had a direct interest in upgrading the value of their particular arms), senior commanders loyal to Khrushchev, trusty pillars of the Party, and

10a My stress — Y.A.
11 *Red Star*, 27 September 1961.

finally and as a matter of course the people of the Party apparatus in the Army. All these interested parties harshly criticised the conservatives in articles in the general press and in the military organs.

The higher echelons could be pontifical. In the article by General Lomov on the new Soviet Military doctrine, already cited,[11a] we find:

> The changes taking place in our day in the nature of world war, its means and its methods, make it imperative to introduce significant amendments in the content itself and the methods of armed conflict. ... This is expressed in the theory of the art of war, on the basis of which are elaborated methods of troops training and of improving operational-tactical and military-technical preparation of generals, admirals and officers.[12]

On a lower level, the debate sometimes had the air of a confrontation between youth and age. Thus for example, a Technical Senior Lieutenant wrote to *Red Star* about the contemptuous attitude of the young towards experienced veterans, quoting a conversation he supposedly overheard between two young lieutenants in a tram:

> "The views of the old are completely out of date."
> "Here we are with sputniks and missiles all around us, and they talk about the importance of Army routine and they go on about their experiences at the front."
> "Nowadays who needs experiences at the front!"
> "That's all hopelessly out of date — they're writing about it in the newspapers."
> "We're living in the atomic age — war today is a matter of pressing buttons, rockets, hydrogen bombs, electronics. What it was like in the past is over and done with."
> "Why do they teach one how to fire mortars? You'd blush even to go out hunting with a mortar!"

---

[11a] See pp. 250–251 above.
[12] *Armed Forces Communist,* May 1962, p. 20.

The writer of the letter summed up: "All the views of these young officers seem evidently absurd — this thing can do our affairs nothing but harm."[13]

*Malinovsky — "There's no Retarding Progress"*. At the big "consultation" in October 1962 devoted to ideological questions[13a] Minister of Defence Malinovsky addressed a special reproof to the conservatives:

> We must exert ourselves to promote the further development of military-theoretical thinking and to impart it to the corps of commanders. We have to give due consideration to the fact that in our generation — the generation of electronics and nuclear physics — the instruments of warfare are being improved with unprecedented speed. Points of view and conditions that we thought advanced yesterday can have become outdated overnight. If people who do not acknowledge the new developments go on clinging to outdated views and even applying them — then this puts a brake on our progress. The further promotion of military science and the fight against conservatism — these are problems it is vital to solve.[14]

Innumerable articles in the press and the military organs called on the officer in the conventional forces not to rest on his laurels but to learn, to advance, to bring himself up to date. The writers of these articles included Marshals Zakharov and Biryuzov.

*"Extremism is harmful"*. In time another tone was also to be heard — "Let us not exaggerate". Three high-ranking commanders collaborated in an essay in *Armed Force Communist* of October '64 putting forward a "balanced" view:

> In Party-political activity [sc. *in* the Armed Forces] extremism is dangerous and damaging both in underestimation and overestimation of the value of nuclear arms. Underestimation

---

13 *Red Star*, 4 March 1961.
13a Treated in detail later in this Chapter.
14 *Ibid.*, 25 October 1962.

> can lead to results pregnant with disaster, while overestimation can beget a feeling of being fated to annihilation, whence apathy and lowering of combattants' morale. Those who serve in the Armed Forces must be given a correct picture of the real danger and they must also be reassured as to the strength of the blows which we can deal the enemy, blows which are capable of clearing the way for us to attack and defeat the enemy physically and morally.[15]

*The many new engineers and technicians* who had been specially mobilised, trained and attached to the officer corps were not surprisingly among the extreme modernists. They were posted to the Strategic Missiles Command, A.A. defence, the submarine arm and also to the Land Forces, whose armament had been very extensively modernised with the introduction of tactical atomic weapons and with the proliferation of electronic equipment for signals, target location, general control and the rest. The engineers felt that every consideration was due to them because of their expert contribution to these decisive branches and arms. Professionally they were less dependent on military service than an officer graduate of a military academy, for whom there was no demand in the civilian economy. These potentially independent engineers, with their high opinion of themselves, were a real problem as regards their attitude to Party-political education and to military discipline: unlike officers who had spent long years in military schools and academies or in military units or services, they had not been subjected to prolonged Party-political indoctrination. Their interest in learning Marxist-Leninist doctrine by rote was of the slightest. At Party meetings their indifference was only too evident, and the political workers had the greatest difficulty in roping them in for Party-political action in the units. Marshal Moskalenko insisted:

> Every engineer and every technician must take part in the most active way in the political and military education of the

15 Lieut.-Gen. Lipodayev, Col. P. Galochkin, Lieut.-Col. A. Tarasov, "The Revolution in the military sphere and some problems of Party-political action", *Armed Forces Communist,* October 1964, p. 10.

soldiers, the sergeants and the sailors. He has to see educating armed, disciplined and courageous defenders of the fatherland as a vital concern of his and as his primary mission, for without them the officer-expert cannot succeed in carrying out the responsible and honoured task he is charged with.[16]

*Trop de Zèle.* In the official cadres in general and in the military Personnel Sections in particular, when given categories of manpower were accorded preference in postings, the stage was usually soon reached of overdoing things. It looks as if this is what happened now with all the "modernisation" in the Army, when perfectly suitable officers and even technicians among them were also being discharged to make way for younger men, so that the Minister of Defence himself had to intervene:

> The cadres Sections are exerting themselves to get rid of experienced technicians, mainly because they have reached the age of 35, as if they had too long been in their jobs and therefore have no chance of promotion. ... Even Brigade Commanders have no certainty that they will remain in their posts: if they have no academic qualifications, the Personnel Section workers are not prepared even to talk to them. Keeping on older officers will not block promotion for younger men — no-one, even if he wants to, can block the path to promotion of talented and hard-working young commanders. ... They "appoint themselves" to higher posts, even if they lack military higher education.[17]

The engineers were becoming something of a special group, distinct from the traditional officer corps. In studying the military literature of the early '60's one is struck by references to three groups of army people (instead of the traditional two) — commanders, engineers and political workers.

16 *Armed Forces Communist,* November 1961, p. 42.
17 Marshal Malinovsky, "A renewed spring forward ... " *October Plenary Resolutions ...,* pp. 12–13.

## The Web of Conflict

There had to be place for conventional forces even in the nuclear era, even in nuclear war. Khrushchev had got his emphases wrong. This was finally the opinion not only of a retrograde "old guard" but of the decisive majority of the High Command which set out to do battle for its views. The Party on its side opened a new, long-term, properly orchestrated campaign to get the whole officer corps and indeed the entire forces imbued with the consciousness of the Party's necessary supremacy over the Army. It also set about tightening the reins of Party supervision and re-affirming total control, while simultaneously trying to get the Army heads to take part in the propaganda effort, despite their bones of contention with Khrushchev and the grounds of complaints many of them had against the MPA.

In this conflict, with its many interwoven strands, Defence Minister Malinovsky was a key figure. He supported Khrushchev's proposals in public but he had his reservations over some of them. As the campaign went on, he joined in the attack on the extreme conservative opponents of the new conception, but at the same time his opposition to the extreme "progressives" gradually affirmed itself. At the first signs in the Army of resistance to the reforms, Malinovsky threw all his weight into making the officer corps acknowledge that the Army could not live and work if it were not led by the Party; but he grew increasingly uneasy over the line of the Party First Secretary and began to speak out in favour of massive armies numbering many millions. To a large extent he acted to moderate the attitudes of the extremists on both sides. He made speeches and wrote articles galore at this stage in the conflict. He consistently called on the officers to recognise the fact that the Army had to be led by the Party, and at the same time he attacked the MPA for the heavy yoke it imposed on the commanders, and the expressions he used on this issue came more and more to resemble those of his deposed predecessor, Marshal Zhukov.

The Army marked up considerable gains in its battle with Khrushchev. Because of the opposition in command circles and developments in the Great Powers arena, Khrushchev was constrained to withdraw temporarily from some of his more extreme positions and to reach a compromise with the Army command on the scale and importance of the conventional forces and the resources to be allocated for their further development.

Malinovsky objected to overmuch reliance on missiles and to the downgrading of traditional arms. In January 1960, in his Supreme Soviet addresses[17a] giving Khrushchev's proposals overall support, he already said:

> The Strategic missiles command of the Armed Forces constitutes without question our primary objective in the Forces, but we are of the opinion that it is not possible to solve all the problems of war by means of one single military arm. So, if we assume that the successful conduct of military actions, even in war in our day, is only possible on the basis of co-ordinated use of all the means of armed conflict and the united efforts of all the arms in the Forces — then we can take it that all the arms of the entire Armed Forces, in given quantities and well-judged proportions, and their wartime operation (its organisation and methods of conduct) will have only the slightest resemblance to what they were in the last war.[18]

If Malinovsky, as we have said, supported Khrushchev's proposals in the Supreme Soviet, his two First Deputies — Marshal Koniev, Commander of the Warsaw Pact Forces, and Marshal Sokolovsky, the Chief of General Staff — refrained from doing so, and three months later, in April 1960, they were both removed from their posts. True, they were not discharged from the Army, but Koniev remained without a post until mid-1961; Sokolovsky, like Timoshenko, who was removed at the same time from his post as Commander of the Byelorussian MD, was appointed an Inspector-General in the Ministry of Defence — generally a "sinecure" for

---

17a See pp. 246–247 above.
18 *Red Star*, 15 January 1960.

aging Marshals. (Interestingly enough, these appointments were not made public until two years later in the Encyclopaedia Yearbook for 1962). Marshal M. Zakharov, Commander of the Forces in Germany, was appointed to replace Sokolovsky — he had supported Khrushchev at the Supreme Soviet session. Marshal Gretchko, Commander of the Land Forces, replaced Koniev as Commander of the Warsaw Pact Forces. To reassure all who feared that the country's defence would be weakened by reductions in the Armed Forces, Gretchko told an Army Day gathering (end of February, 1960):

> Our unilateral limitation of the Armed Forces is a proof of our desire for peace. ... (It) also has the important aim of cutting down unproductive expenditure. While reducing the Armed Forces, the Party and the Army do not for a moment forget concern for the defensive strength of our State. Defensive strength is not measured in our day by the number of soldiers but in fire-power. The nation can rest assured that we are equipped with sufficient fire-power.[19]

*"Massive Armies of Many Millions"*? Not everyone thought the same way as Gretchko, however. In November 1960, the military theoretician, Major-General Krasilnikov, published an article in *Red Star* on "The Nature of War in our Day", which was the first open, explicit criticism of the new Khrushchev doctrine:

> If a new war breaks out, it will be fought mainly with new means of warfare of enormous destructive power and unlimited range, great speed and exact targeting. The basis of these new means is nuclear armament and missile technique. The war will therefore be of a nuclear missile type from the outset. It is inadmissible to describe this as a push-button war that can be waged without mass armies and without the active participation of the peoples concerned. The new war will undoubtedly be fought by massive armies numbering many millions, and large reserves of commanders will be needed

19 *Ibid.,* 23 February 1960.

and a tremendous number of lower ranks. The new war will present greater problems [sc. than in the past] for the moral and physical forces of individuals and of entire peoples. ... Nuclear missile forces will become our main arm, but in no way whatsoever does this mean a reduction in the land forces. Soviet-military science believes that it is only possible to gain the victory by the correct use of missile arms in coordination with other means of warfare.[20]

This flat assertion on the need for armies numbering many millions to secure the victory was made here for the first time. Krasilnikov went on to argue that though a surprise attack would certainly have a serious effect, it would not necessarily be decisive for the conduct of the war and its outcome. This was a clear challenge to some of Khrushchev's main contentions. It is worth remarking that this article did not evoke any counter-attack. Without question Krasilnikov was voicing the views of many commanders who saw the reduction in conventional forces as a danger to the country's defensive strength. It also seemed to them that Khrushchev was over-optimistic as regards the lessening of international tension.[21]

*The Lines Converge — Temporarily.* In preparation for the XXII Congress, Khrushchev somewhat narrowed the gap between his

---

20  *Ibid.,* 18 November 1960.
21  In the opinion of Kolkowicz, Khrushchev did not foresee any real opposition from the Army or special problems in getting his reforms through. After Zhukov's deposition, he relied for acceptance of his doctrine on the loyalty of the senior command, made up mostly of his "Stalingrad group" as well as on the supervision and indoctrination to which the Army had been subjected since 1957. He underestimated the officer corps' capacity for swift internal recovery, and his efforts, open and concealed, to diminish the officers' authority and cut down military allocations met with obstinate resistance. Abandoning the traditional Party policy of controlling the Army by "divide and rule", he neglected effective operative means of supervision. He harmed the interests of several different army sectors, so that they joined together to oppose his policy and his reforms and, if need be, his leadership as well. *Op. cit.,* pp. 152–53.

## The Armed Forces Re-Modelled

position and those of the Army people concerning the role of the conventional forces. On the anniversary of the Nazi invasion of the Soviet Union, Khrushchev appeared in his general's uniform for the first time in many years, and his address on this occasion marked his shift on the issue of conventional forces: "Strengthening the defence of the Soviet Union," he said, "depends on improving all the arms and all the armies in our Forces: the infantry and the artillery, the engineers' corps and the signals corps, the armoured divisions and the Navy and Air Force and the Missile Forces."[22] This list represented a considerable concession to the position of the Army heads, but it marked what was only a temporary tactical move on Khrushchev's part. He continued to press for large savings in manpower in the army. At the Congress itself in mid-1961 and for long after, differences of opinion were not at an end. The long-awaited new Party Programme, ratified at the Congress, stressed the need to unite the Armed Forces round the Party, and the drafting of this section clearly reflected the still fresh effort to get the military (and civilians as well) to acknowledge the leading role of the Party.[23]

In his speech to the Congress, Malinovsky was lavish in his praise of the Central Committee and Khrushchev, but for all that the spirit of his words ran counter to Khrushchev's views on the subject of conventional forces. Malinovsky said:

22 *Pravda*, 22 June 1961.
23 The Section of the Party Programme dealing with the Armed Forces stated: The Party sees as absolutely necessary that the corps of commanders possess a firm grasp of Marxist-Leninist theory and have a superior military-technical formation, that it meet all the requirements of modern military theory and practice, and that it enforce military discipline. The fundamental basis of military organisation and development is the leadership of the Armed Forces by the Communist Party and the strengthening of the role and the influence of the Party organisation in the Army and Navy. The Party devotes constant attention to reinforcing its organising and guiding influence in all spheres of life and activity in the Army, the Aviation and the Navy and in uniting the cadres of the Armed Forces around the Communist Party and the Soviet Government. *Programmes of the CPSU, op. cit.,* p. 189.

> In order to counter the increasing war-preparations that are under way on the pretext of the Berlin crisis, the Central Committee and the Government have had to carry out a series of actions for the purpose of strengthening the defensive power and the security of the Soviet Union. The reduction of the Armed Forces, which was being effected according to plan, has been temporarily suspended, and defence expenditures have been somewhat increased; routine transfers from the Army and Navy to the reserves of soldiers, sailors, and N.C.O.s have been temporarily postponed. Nuclear arms tests are being carried out. ...
> Despite the fact that in the next war the decisive weapon will be nuclear rockets, we have nevertheless reached the conclusion that final victory over the aggressor can only be secured as a result of combined action by all the arms in the Armed Forces. ... We are likewise of the opinion that under present conditions, the next war will be conducted, despite heavy losses, by armed forces numbering many millions.[24]

Clearly Malinovsky's reservations about over-reliance on nuclear forces were now even stronger than those he had voiced at the Supreme Soviet session eighteen months' earlier — the passage about armies of many millions was in flat opposition to Khrushchev's conception.

Wording practically identical with Malinovsky's at the Supreme Soviet appeared in an article by Marshal Moskalenko in *Armed Forces Communist* shortly after the XXII Congress. "It is well known", wrote Moskalenko, a loyal supporter of Khrushchev's, "that it is not possible to solve the problem of war simply with one arm or force alone. The Communist Party and the Soviet Government and Comrade Khrushchev personally are ceaselessly preoccupied with seeing to it that all the military arms be developed in the right proportions and be equipped with the most advanced weapons and techniques."[25] This formulation of Moskalenko's, it seems to

---

24 *Pravda*, 22 June 1961.
25 Marshal K. Moskalenko, "Perfected Control of all the Means for De-

me, marks the shift that had taken place on Khrushchev's part towards the position of the military.[26] A factor that I feel ought not to be overlooked and which may well have contributed to this narrowing of the gap was the collapse of the legend of Soviet missile superiority, the bluff that had taken in the West successfully for

fending the Fatherland", *Armed Forces Communist,* November 1961, p. 37.

26 This is also the view taken by the US editors in their preface to *Soviet Military Strategy,* the translation into English of the Soviet work, *Military Strategy* referred to in our text, pp. 252-253. The US commentators give the following factors as leading to "a narrowing of the gap between Khrushchev's strategic formulations and the prevailing outlook of the military" (pp. 19-20): 1) The U-2 episode in May 1960, which raised questions as to how seriously Soviet military security may have been compromised by loss of secrecy. 2) General deterioration of the international situation following the abortive summit meeting in Paris in May 1960, which probably strengthened the hand of elements in the Soviet bureaucracy favoring sterner economic and defense policies than those with which Khrushchev had identified himself. 3) Resentment and morale problems within the armed forces, notably in the officer corps, which accompanied initiation of the troop-cut policy in 1960. 4) Status of the Soviet ICBM program, which in light of both technical and operational difficulties often associated with early generation systems may have raised doubts about over-reliance on such weapons and helped undermine Khrushchev's one-sided emphasis on them. 5) Technological developments leading to new evaluation of manned aircraft systems, such as Soviet development of a "stand-off capability" to deliver missiles from aircraft, and of very large-yield weapons, which in their early configuration might require delivery by aircraft. 6) U.S. reaction to revival of the Berlin crisis, taking the form in 1961 of U.S. defense budget increases, expansion of Polaris and Minuteman programs, measures to improve survivability and control of strategic forces, strengthening of conventional forces, etc. — all of which provided further pressure on the Soviet leaders for reappraisal of their military posture. 7) Concern within elements of the Soviet bureaucracy lest resource reallocation to improve consumer welfare and relieve such probems as the agricultural crisis be accomplished at the expense of defense requirements, with consequent pressure on Khrushchev to shift his policies. (A Rand Corporation Research Study published by Prentice-Hall Inc., New Jersey, 1963).

four years. In his farewell address to the American people in January 1961, President Eisenhower said that there was every indication that the missile gap had been the product of — imagination.[27]

*A "Notorious Theory".* A weighty publication on military strategy that appeared at this juncture went very thoroughly into methods of warfare, to structure of the forces and the tasks of the different arms. It is worth quoting from this book, published precisely in the period when there was this measure of *rapprochement* between the views of the political leaders and the military, and when the debate on these issues was still continuing inside the Armed Forces. In the passage on "the basic direction of their (the Armed Forces') organisation and development", the editors affirmed:

> The appearance of missiles and nuclear weapons and the developments in aviation and other instruments of armed combat ... again revived the notorious theory of the possibility of waging war with small but technically well-equipped armies. The advocates of such armies fail to consider that the new equipment, far from reducing the requirements of the armed forces for personnel, increases them. For this reason, massive armies of millions of men will be needed to wage a future war. ... No matter how great a role strategic missile troops play in a future war, they still cannot carry out all the mission of the war. To triumph in war, it is not sufficient to destroy the military potential of the aggressor. ... Only modern ground forces, adequate in size, armament and organisation, can execute these mission (defeating the enemy's armed forces and capturing his military bases). ... Theirs is the extremely important role of achieving the final war aims. For this reason, the ground forces remain the largest of the various branches of the armed forces and to them falls the execution of many war missions in ground theaters.[28]

27 *New York Times,* 12 January 1961.
28 *Military Strategy, loc. cit.,* pp. 338–41.

## The Armed Forces Re-Modelled

This work, published in May 1962 with the approval of the Minister of Defence and his Ministry, can be considered as an official document emanating from the Armed Forces heads. Its affirmations without question deviated considerably from the spirit of Khrushchev's strategic conception as it was presented in 1960. The passage averring that advocates of reliance on small armies notoriously "fail to consider" that the new weapons do not reduce but rather increase manpower requirements can only be understood as a shaft aimed directly at Khrushchev himself. It is also not irrelevant that the editor-in-chief was Marshal Sokolovsky, who it will be remembered, had been removed from his post as Chief of General Staff in April 1960.

In the same month that this work on military strategy went to press, Marshal Malinovsky himself published an article in *Communist* along basically the same lines. His intention, it seems, was to impress on the paper's readership of Party activists the supreme importance of the Armed Forces for the Party's efforts to prevent a world war or, if the imperialists (perish the thought) were to spark off a war, to ensure their defeat. He also presented his views on the value of the different arms in executing their various missions. True, he referred to Khrushchev's January 1960 address to the Supreme Soviet as the first presentation of the bases of modern Soviet military doctrine, but he went on to stress that analysis of the doctrine showed that however large the role of nuclear arms and their effect on the course and final outcome of the war, this did not cancel out the need for other means of warfare and for the existence of massive armies. Victory in modern war, Malinovsky echoed the theoreticians, is to be achieved only by the united means of all the forces and arms, which have to be developed accordingly. Furthermore, given the permanent threat of the imperialists' sparking off a war, the Party was forced to adopt the principle of maintaining a standing army capable, by virtue of its size, composition and preparation, of repulsing an attack and defeating an aggressor at the beginning of the war.[29]

---

29 *Communist*, No. 3, May 1962, pp. 11–12.

Rotmistrov took the same line in an article (October 1962), "The modern tank and nuclear weapons." He was one of those who fought against Stalin's petrified military formulas in the early '50's, and now in the early '60's, as Chief Marshal of Armoured Troops at the time of writing the article, he was fighting against underestimation of the ground forces. After starting his article with the usual bow to the power of nuclear weapons and their undoubted effectiveness in the hands of the Air Force and Missile Force for securing strategic results at the very beginning of future hostilities, he proceeded to add the inevitable, "All the same ... ":

> In order to secure final war aims, an important role pertains to the ground forces, also armed with nuclear weapons and the means for delivering them. Moreover, the use of nuclear arms raises the value of ground forces sharply and offers them new possibilities in the execution of active offensive missions. ... Nuclear weapons, powerful though they are, do not conquer territory. The soldier has to get there in order to do this, he has to advance in depth and wage battle boldly — this is what armoured troops are suitable for. In cooperation with the Missile Force and the Air Force, they are capable of annihilating the enemy in short engagements and parachute actions. No less important is the improved tank, shielded against radiation and radioactive dust and against blast from atomic explosions. In view of the danger of imperialist attack, the State has equipped its army with first-class tanks, and the troops are kept in a state of high alert.[30]

The military press kept on publishing articles that supported the need for large, strong, well-armoured ground forces, equipped with modern arms, and for a strong Air Force. It is worth citing two of these articles, published in January 1963. The first was by the Land Forces Chief of Staff, Lieut.-General Ztemenko: "The Land Forces in Modern War and their Preparation." To back up his

---

30 P. Rotmistrov, "The Modern Tank and Atomic Weapons", *Izvestia*, 20 October 1962.

assertions on the need for strong ground forces, he wrote that the West had reached the absolutely certain conclusion that strong, and mobile ground forces would be needed in the next war, and the USA was therefore devoting extra attention to a many-sided development of the Land Forces.[31] The other article, by Brig.-General Kruchinin, was supposedly an answer to the question addressed to the editor of *Red Star*, "What are massive armies for nowadays when we have nuclear arms?" Kruchinin had the answer. Soviet military science was based on the position that in present-day conditions, there would be a need for massive armies differentiated from earlier armies by their superior technical equipment and tremendous fire-power.[32]

## *Tension Rises in the Aftermath of the XXII Congress*

Khrushchev's temporary concessions to the military on questions of doctrine and reform brought no concomitant improvement at all in the tense relations between the commanders and the political apparatus in the army. The XXII Congress with its Resolutions and its ratification of the new Party Programme reinforced the efforts of the Party leadership and the MPA to tighten their grip over "every sphere of Army life and activity". This line was not exactly calculated to raise the morale of the commanders or improve their performance. As a matter of course the consequence was a continued decline in discipline and the spread of the "don't care" attitude in the officers corps. And once more we find an article in the *Armed Forces Communist* on this "most important problem of all".[33] In the next month's issue, March 1962, an MPA notice appeared on a "consultation" that had taken place of Secretaries of the Party Committees of the central direction of the Defence Ministry: there had been sharp criticism of the work of the Party Committees and organisations at the General Staff and

---

31 *Red Star*, 3 January 1963.
32 *Ibid.*, 13 January 1963.
33 *Armed Forces Communist*, February 1962, pp. 3–8.

the rear administration of the Ministry. The report stated that those concerned had failed to improve military discipline and had not succeeded in executing the orders and instructions of the Defence Minister and the MPA, and it concluded that the source of these shortcomings was in the new information propaganda organisation.[34] This criticism was in fact directed not only at the Party Committees but also and indeed chiefly at the central direction of the Defence Ministry itself and at the General Staff.

In April 1962 a meeting was called of senior personnel of the political apparatus in the Armed Forces in order to lay down the measures needed to reinforce the Party's role in the Forces. The Army commanders came in for the strongest conceivable criticism: they were accused of putting up a pretence of acquiescence simply in order to silence the politicals, or else of using the methods of "You take care of me and I'll take care of you", nor were generals and admirals exempted from blame. Officers were accused of pursuing personal benefits, economic and social. Instructions of the MPA and the Ministry of Defence were not being carried out. Senior commanders had even attempted to prevent the Party institutions from investigating the personal files of friends of theirs. The Political Administrations were ordered to put an end to the prevailing arrogance in officer circles — and to foster "criticism and self-criticism".[35]

These criticisms were answered by Malinovsky himself. An article of his appeared in *Red Star* at the end of May and then — but not until a fortnight later, perhaps by mere chance — in the *Armed Forces Communist*. The title was, "The vital problem of educating those serving in the Armed Forces of the Soviet Union." The article afforded the MPA and its offshoots the benefit and privilege of learning Malinovsky's views on its educational work. The Minister of Defence started off as usual with high praise of the XXII Congress Resolutions and the new Party Programme, which would serve as a light to guide the footsteps of educational action in the Armed

---

34   *Ibid.*, March 1962, pp. 55–57.
35   *Ibid.*, May 1962, pp. 22–28.

Forces. He then went on to say that the standard of political studies in a whole series of units and formations was very low indeed and very far from meeting the demands of the day. Sometimes, he wrote, the group leader will come to his group unprepared and negligently attired, and will get through the hour with boring and tiresome verbiage that simply sends the soldiers to sleep. "It is incumbent on the MPA, the Military Councils and the Political Administrations of the formations," wrote Malinovsky, "to find a way to make decided improvements in the content of political studies. ... Only what is most important for combat training should be kept — and only what can be properly carried out. ... We have to teach the Army only what is needed for war. To do this, we have to cut out of the programme of studies all out-dated material and everything that does not absolutely meet the needs of our time".[36]

Malinovsky's style may indeed have differed from Zhukov's — he was not quite so blunt — but what he had to say was much the same. Both these Marshals of the Soviet Union, Ministers of Defence in their day, demanded concentration on the essential — combat training. When they spoke of better education, they meant reducing political studies to their most important elements alone. Malinovsky's criticism of "boring and tiresome verbiage" in fact outdid even Zhukov's written expressions in his time.[36a]

Tension between the officer corps and the political elements did not ease off — it even worsened. Both sides entrenched themselves in their positions and their criticisms of each other. In October 1962 an all-Army "consultation" was called on ideological problems, the main participants being Malinovsky and MPA Head Yepishev. The declared intention of the meeting was "to improve Marxist-Leninist and military-theoretical training for officers and generals".[37] If it was also hoped to use this opportunity to reduce the prevailing tension between the Defence Minister and the MPA, it emerges

---

36  *Red Star*, 24 May 1962; *Armed Forces Communist*, no. 11, May 1962, pp. 3–15.
36a Perhaps this was why the *Armed Forces Communist* held up the Defence Minister's article for two weeks.
37  *Red Star*, 25 October 1962.

from a reading of the published speeches that this purpose was not achieved. Yepishev's speech, published in the *Armed Forces Communist*, raised the banner of the October 1957 Plenary Resolutions — now as then, five years' before, the guiding line for all the "sole commanders", the Military Councils, the political institutions and the Party organisations. As regards educating the educators (that is to say, the commanders), Yepishev admonished his hearers:

> There are Party-political workers who for some reason think that only the high-ranking people in charge should educate the senior corps. Is it not clear that the political institutions and the Party Committees and organisations are equally responsible to the commanders whose concern it is and to the political workers for the education of the whole ensemble of those serving in the army, including the senior corps? ...
> While supporting strict officers, it is necessary at the very same time to firmly root out cases of rudeness, arrogance and showing off. The well-tested means for countering any and all negative phenomena — and amongst them the problems of unity of command — is Party criticism and self-criticism.[38]

A very different note was struck in Malinovsky's address at this "consultation". He went a step further still in criticising the MPA:

> All the means, forms and methods of ideological action ought to be directed towards educating the soldiers in the spirit of fulfilling and executing the orders of the commanders exactly and conscientiously, and also towards educating the commanders themselves in the spirit of Lenin's demands regarding the style of conducting the Army. ... Support should be given by every possible means to strictness on the part of the commanders and it is necessary to burn out at white heat every instance of negligence and failure to obey orders. It is

---

38 Yepishev, "Carry out the Party's policy in the Armed Forces with decision and energy." *Armed Forces Communist*, October 1962, pp. 2–15.

at times a question whether it is permissible to criticise a commander for his shortcomings and failings and whether this does not undermine the commander's authority and whether it does not go counter to the unity of command. You are certainly aware of Lenin's teachings on the role of criticism and self-criticism and their educational importance is tremendous. The Army is a very special kind of organism: it is built on a highly centralised basis, on discipline and unity of command, and there is no room for criticism of the commander's orders and instructions. ... Shortcomings are often to be found among us and sometimes even disgraceful acts, and these have to be fought against. ... We do not need all sorts of criticism, but only criticism on matters of principle, directed towards improving the state of affairs and strengthening the Armed Forces.[39]

Malinovsky's remarks on the need to have the men obey orders not only bore a striking resemblance to Zhukov's way of thinking and feeling — in a number of sentences the wording was actually identical with things that Zhukov had said.

Comparison of the speeches of Yepishev and Malinovsky with their very different emphases shows that the gap between the channels of military command and the political channel in the Armed Forces had in fact widened. The pattern repeats itself. The same actions produce the same chain of reactions: pressure from the Party-political apparatus; decline in discipline; a certain negligence in carrying out the military assignment; counter-attack against the Party-political apparatus by the Army head in the attempt to restore discipline, the commander's standing and authority and the combat preparedness of the forces.

In the meanwhile, a plan was being worked out, apparently on Khrushchev's initiative, which in the later stages brought the world dangerously close to the brink of atomic war, the plan to set up a Soviet missile base in Cuba.

39 *Red Star*, 25 October 1962.

## Cuba

There is no certainty over the exact date when this venturesome decision was taken.[40] The motive, as we have already said, was to get round the Soviet inferiority in nuclear armament, which had only recently become known. One of the consequences of the decision was an increase in the differences of opinion between Khrushchev and some of the Army heads in a number of spheres.

We witness a number of important events in internal developments at this time. Marshal Koniev was removed from his post as commander of the Group of Armies in East Germany. Marshal Golikov was replaced at the head of the MPA by General of Army A. Yepishev, and Marshal Moskalenko was replaced by Marshal Biryuzov, Commander of the Strategic Missiles Force. Why Marshal Koniev was removed from his post for the second time is not clear. Yepishev's appointment marked the leadership's decision to clamp down Party-political supervision on the Army. The Party leadership was deeply concerned over what practically amounted to the failure of political action in the Armed Forces ever since the beginning of the reforms early in 1960, a failure that had crystallised into the chilly attitude of many of the Commanders. Golikov as the man mainly responsible for Party-political action had to go. The man who replaced him was not a combat officer like him but had had a purely political career.

The replacement of Moskalenko by Biryuzov raises the question whether this may not have been connected with the decision on Cuba, which Moskaleno may have disapproved of.[41]

Another sphere of differences of opinion had been that of allocation of resources. The Cuban venture certainly necessitated expenditures that had not been budgeted for. In order to forestall any possible intention of taking the funds needed for that from the

---

40  Tatu cites Sorensen for his view that the decision was taken as early as April. *Op. cit.*, p. 249.
41  Tatu suggests that Moskalenko as Commander of the Missile Forces may well have had doubts about the Cuba plan. *Op. cit.*, p. 252.

budgets of the conventional arms and to ensure the continued development of these arms, the military stepped up their pressure over massive armies and their contentions that only with properly developed conventional arms for combined forces would victory in war be possible.

The formal demand to proceed to develop the conventional forces was presented as such for the first time in the article of Malinovsky's in *Communist* in May 1962, already cited.[41a] It is my view that the timing of this article can be seen as a move in the struggle for additional allocations of resources to the conventional arms. Another article by Malinovsky in the same month, on the occasion of the anniversary of the victory over Germany (*Pravda*, 9 May 1962) also treats the same subject.[42]

The collapse of the Cuban venture at the end of October 1962 was of course a blow to all concerned, putting an end to the hopes of bridging the missile gap with the USA quickly by establishing a missile base close to US borders. It seems certain that doubts gnawed at the hearts of the senior commanders and others in the army and that a sense of insecurity lodged in their bosoms over the wisdom of the whole Cuban episode. A dose of persuasion was clearly needed.

In the communications media in the Soviet Union a sudden concentration of information/propaganda on a given issue or issues is likely to be evidence of the existence of serious problems in those fields. Precisely in the conditions of the Cuban anti-climax, the leadership launched yet another propaganda campaign to convince the officer corps of the decisive importance of the Army's being led by the Party (as well as of the need to reinforce discipline, of course, and to improve political action in the Army, equally of course). This time it was Marshal Chuikov, one of Khrushchev's closest associates, who was chosen to expound the role of the Party in the Army. *Red Star* published an interview with him in mid-November: "The fundamental basis of military organisation and

---

41a  See p. 280 above.
42   *Pravda*, 9 May 1962.

development." Chuikov brought forward four "new" points that in his view demonstrated the need for leadership of the army by the Party in the age of modern war.[43]

A Plenary Session of the Central Committee in November 1962 was followed by a meeting of the Party *aktiv* of the Defence Ministry. The report published in the Press was headed, "Improving the style and the methods of the leadership." The meeting was addressed by Malinovsky, Bagramyan, Rotmistrov, Yepishev and others. Among the subjects discussed were defects in the style of work and demands for improved ideological action in order to reinforce military discipline, have instructions carried out and intensify the activity of the Party Committees and Party organisations in the Forces.[44]

The information/propaganda offensive and the efforts at persuasion went on without a pause. Of the great quantity of articles published and speeches made and reported, we shall cite the joint effort of two Colonels, O. Baranov and Y. Nikitin, senior lecturers in historical science, in April 1963, entitled, "Leadership by the Communist Party of the Soviet Union — the fundamental basis of Soviet military organisation and development." As befits men of learning, they presented scientific arguments, divided into chapters with appropriate sub-headings, and studded with quotations, lots of quotations, from Lenin, from Party decisions and Resolutions and from the new Programme. The main theme was that the role of the army was now larger than ever before precisely in the modern army and in the nuclear era.[45]

[43] *Red Star*, 17 November 1962. Marshal Chuikov's four "new" points were: (1) The greater complexity and larger scale of the problems of developing the country's defence capability. (2) The widening range of international problems and the Soviet Union's commitment to the Socialist States. (3) The considerably increased weight cf the factor of political morale. (4) The serious danger of nuclear war's being launched by the aggressors. These causes, according to Chuikov, had enlarged the role and the responsibility of the Party in the lead of the Armed Forces.

[44] *Red Star*, 8 December 1962.

[45] *Armed Forces Communist*, April 1963, pp. 17–25.

Military theoretician General Professor Lomov went to the length of a two-part article, published in *Red Star*. He affirmed:

> Soviet military doctrine recognises nuclear missile weapons and especially strategic ones as the decisive means for the defeat of the enemy. *At the same time*,[45a] since armed conflict, even under conditions of nuclear war, will be characterised by the many-sidedness and complexity of its missions and ways of carrying them out, to triumph over a strong enemy will demand the exertions of an army of many millions. A most important principle of Soviet military doctrine lays down that securing final victory will call for the exertions of all the Armed Forces, supported by the decisive role of the nuclear missile weapon.[46]

The wide differences of opinion we have surveyed here were not bridged over in the whole period from the beginning of the '60's to the deposition of Khrushchev late in '64. This issue of the relative weight of nuclear weapons systems as against ground forces was not the sole nor even the chief cause of the tension between the Party and the Army but unquestionably constituted one of its main sources.

---

[45a] My stress — Y.A.
[46] *Red Star*, 7 January, 10 January 1964.

## CHAPTER XI

## THE ARMY CHIEFS AND KHRUSHCHEV

### 1953–1957, Honeymoon

The honeymoon period between Khrushchev and the Army chiefs that began early in 1953 ended late in 1957. During those four years the Army's interests coincided with Khrushchev's declared positions, and they were together on the same side in the internal struggles in the leadership and in the conflicts between power focuses in the State. There were three main conflicts in that period:

1. The arrest of Beria in mid-1953 and his execution: Khrushchev apparently played a part here, though not a leading one, while the Army, interested in getting rid of Beria, assisted in the entire operation.

2. The removal of Malenkov from his position as Head of Government. Here Khrushchev played a more important part, supported by the Army chiefs, who, like him, opposed Malenkov's views on reducing budget allocations to heavy industry and the Armed Forces.

3. The removal of the "anti-Party group" in mid-1957, where Khrushchev took the lead and was very much indebted to the help he received from the Army chiefs.

### Those October 1957 Plenary Resolutions

The deposition of Zhukov and the Resolutions of the October 1957 Central Committee Plenary, as we have said, closed this honeymoon period. True, the Army was now headed by one of Khrushchev's closest adherents, Marshal Malinovsky, and there were also

## The Army Chiefs and Khrushchev

other supporters of his at the tcp. Nevertheless the sustained effort of the leadership to apply the Plenary Resolutions strictly and alter the relations between the Party and the Army led step by step to accumulated resentment in the officer corps and mainly among the senior commanders. Their resentment was directed against the political leadership and more especially against Khrushchev.*

The reform of the Armed Forces proposed by Khrushchev and ratified by the Supreme Soviet in January 1960 led, as we have seen in the foregoing chapters, to renewed criticism of Khrushchev and even to two Marshals' being removed from their posts on this account in April 1960.

### May 1960, a Watershed in Military Conceptions

The incident of the US reconnaissance plane, U-2, on 1 May 1960 probably caused a measure of confusion in political circles, and it must have confirmed many of the Army chiefs in their distaste for Khrushchev's line.[1] In the month of May we witness apparently paradoxical attitudes on the part of the Army heads: they delivered themselves of numerous and forthright declarations and instructions on strengthening the Party's leading role in the Army and securing complete compliance with the Party general line,[1a] but this large-scale propaganda activity of theirs did not mean any improvement in Khrushchev's authority among the Army men or greater support from them for his military conceptions. On the contrary, the main weight of their pronouncements in May 1960 was clearly against Khrushchev's plans to lower tension with the West, reduce military effectives and raise the standard of living plans which he put to the Supreme Soviet session at the beginning of May 1960. In his key address, the proposed abolition of taxes on workers and officials, in order to leave more money in their hands, and a large

---

\* See chapters 7 and 10 above.
1  Tatu, *op. cit.*, p. 74. This observant analyst says that "political confusion" may have "spread" to military circles as well.
1a See Chapter 5 above.

295

expansion of the production of consumption goods for them to buy. On foreign affairs, he expatiated on the summit meeting of the "Big Four" that was about to take place later in the month in order, he declared, to lay firm foundations for peace and make coexistence possible between States with different regimes. He called for general and complete disarmament and for an end to the cold war, warned the US over the spy-plane incident and stressed the will to put an end to international tensions.[2]

In the debate on this address of Khrushchev's to the Supreme Soviet many representatives took part but only one spoke for the Army, Marshal Gretchko, and he did so in a very different vein and tone of voice from Khrushchev's. As was to be expected, he exploited the U-2 incident to buttress the Army's demands:

> We are at the present time carrying out the Supreme Soviet decisions on a further reduction of the Armed Forces, but the Soviet State will in no way permit any weakening whatsoever of the capacity to defend the Fatherland. ... We shall teach the aggressor a lesson. ... The plane was downed with the first shot. ... As long as complete, general disarmament is not achieved and as long as the peace-haters are not reined in, Soviet fighting men will defend their country. ... We are sure that Khrushchev will know how to defend the cause of peace with honour and how to uncover and foil the plots of the aggressive circles. We wish him success in his difficult negotiations in Paris.[3]

It seems certain that in addition to these pointed remarks of Gretchko's in public, the Army heads were stubbornly defending their hard-line position in closed deliberations, questioning the wisdom of appeasing the West, demanding more allocations for armament and proposing to slow down the tempo of reducing the forces if not to actually increase their overall number.

Khrushchev's summing up at the close of the Supreme Soviet

2  *Pravda,* 6 May 1960.
3  *Ibid.,* 7 May 1960.

session included a reply to Gretchko and to the Army's demands in general: "The incident of the US spy-plane is certainly not helpful for reaching a peaceful settlement of the problems in the conflict," he admitted, "but it must not force us to change our plans and increase allocations for armament and the army. We must not halt the process of reduction of the forces. We shall continue to take our stand on our Leninist peace policy of co-existence."[4] The Soviet delegation to the Paris summit meeting included the Minister of Defence, which was something unusual. (It is true that Zhukov took part in the 1955 Geneva summit, but his presence there was probably occasioned by his personal friendship with Eisenhower.[4a]) A possible explanation for Malinovsky's participation is that the hard-liners in the political leadership as well as in the Army sent him as their representative to keep a watch on Khrushchev and restrain him from going too far in appeasement. This summit meeting, it will be remembered, was torpedoed by Khrushchev, who demanded that Eisenhower flatly condemn the American act of espionage as a condition for the Soviet Union's participation in the conference. This fiasco can perhaps be construed as an achievement for the hard-liners.

In the last week of May 1960 there was a large all-Soviet Union gathering of the "winning trail-breakers" in the competition of the Communist Workers' Brigades. It lasted for several days and was given wide publicity. Long speeches were delivered by Khrushchev and other central personalities. Malinovsky attacked the USA and sharply criticised the "Camp David policy".[4a] He even went so far as to refer insultingly to US Secretary for War Forrestal, "Who went out of his mind and jumped from the fourth floor". "Sane men are what is needed," said Malinovsky, and went on.

> History teaches us that it is forbidden to believe a promise of the imperialists even if its sounds sweet. Camp David[4b] has

4 *Ibid.*, 8 May 1960.
4a See Chapter 5 above.
4b The reference is to Khrushchev's visit to the USA in September 1959 and the attack is of course on his appeasement policy.

finally given us a lesson too sharp for us to be able to ignore history. ... No! — we do not trust the imperialists! We can be sure that they are waiting for a convenient opportunity to fall upon the Soviet Union and the other Socialist States. The only thing that prevents them from doing so is the danger of the destruction of capitalism as a social system. Comrades! The men serving in the Armed Forces and the entire Soviet people wholeheartedly support the foreign policy of our Government and the Leninist Central Committee.[5]

It should be noted that Malinovsky refrained from support of Khrushchev along with "our Government and Leninist Central Committee" and instead made this transparent attack on "Camp David". His aim was clear: he was calling for more Soviet power, distrust of "imperialist" intentions and a harder line in relations with the USA. Here we have part of the explanation of the apparent contradictions in the Army chiefs' attitudes towards the Party — on the one hand, they demanded of the Army greater loyalty to the Party leadership, and on the other hand they did not spare criticism of the First Secretary, who was also Head of Government. I am inclined to accept the interpretation that at this time Khrushchev was already in a minority on the Central Committee Presidium and did not represent the "general line". Accordingly the Army chiefs saw declarations of loyalty and support for the general line as in some measure identifying them with the position of the majority of the Presidium in favour of a stiffer attitude towards the USA and all that this involved. The Army chiefs were in fact expressing their own reservations regarding Khrushchev's conceptions in this way.[6]

The to-and-fro of the conflicting pressures from this point on has been traced in the preceding Chapter[6a] and we need only

5  *Ibid.*, 31 May 1960.
6  Tatu, *op. cit.*, pp. 78–79, putting forward the above interpretation, adds that this attitude of the Army heads may well have prefigured Khrushchev's deposition at the critical moment in October 1964.
6a  See p. 269 *et seq.* above.

pause to remark how very long it took until the various power focuses were all completely entagonised.

## Cuba — the Real Beginning of the End

The setting up of the missile base in Cuba in mid-1962 seriously affected the attitude of several Army chiefs to its initiator, Nikita Khrushchev, even before the venturesome project went wrong. The end of the matter in October sharpened their criticism of the man mainly responsible for the project and whom they saw as to blame for the surrender to the US demands to dismantle the base and return the missiles.

Differences of opinion had led in the past to the removal of some of the highest-ranking commanders in the forces. Now, in April 1963, Chief of General Staff Marshal Zakharov was replaced by Marshal Biryuzov. The reasons for Zakharov's removal are not clear — Khrushchev charged that he was inefficient. Zakharov had supported Khrushchev's military doctrine in January 1960 and in April of that year he had replaced the Chief of General Staff, Marshal Sokolovsky, who had reservations over Khrushchev's proposals. After Khrushchev's deposition, his criticisms of Zakharov's inefficiency were shown to be baseless — or at least not accepted by others, for when Biryuzov was killed in an air crash, Zakharov was restored to his post. It therefore seems reasonable to assume that Zakharov was among Khrushchev's critics after the failure of the Cuban operation. It is also worth recalling that when Biryuzov was appointed Chief of General Staff, he left the post of Commander of the Strategic Missiles Force, which he had held for only a year and to which he had been appointed in place of Moskalenko; at that time Moskalenko was apparently replaced because he too had had reservations over the preparations for the Cuban affair.

## Chiefs-of-General Staff — and Chemicals

In this same month when the Chief of General Staff was replaced, April 1963, Khrushchev was still constantly advocating and pressing on with the development of the chemicals industry. At an "Industry and Building" Conference of the Russian Federative Socialist Soviet Republic, he delivered a speech that took up five-and-a-half pages of *Pravda,* contending that unexploited reserves of premises and equipment in the machinery and metallurgical branches should be better utilised, instead of having more new concerns established. The chemicals industry, Khrushchev argued, was far less developed than it could and should be, given existing capacity in the economy. Nor did he spare his criticisms of the defence industry:

> There are large reserves for increased production even in the defence industry, but they are little used because these factories are absolutely closed off — and they're also closed to criticisms of shortcomings and negligence. (Movement in the hall and applause.) But there's nothing to be done about this — these factories will remain immune whatever happens; nevertheless, certain neglectful persons who work in these concerns must not be allowed to profit from this immunity. Comrade Ustinov has now been appointed Chairman of the Supreme Economic Council; he is well acquainted with the defence industry and has been responsible for it. Let us hope that he will introduce better order in this sphere. (Applause.) The defence industry has fulfilled tasks assigned to it successfully and produced modern means of warfare, but this could have been done even more successfully at less cost. The Supreme Economic Council of the State will have to do a thorough investigation into how the productive capacity is utilised in the defence concerns and must promote better utilisation.[7]

An attack like this on the defence industry, in front of representatives of other industries and economic branches, coming from the First Secretary of the Central Committee and Head of Government — and the applause which it evoked — was something utterly out

7   *Pravda,* 26 April 1963.

of the ordinary, and it no doubt made its contribution to the Army chiefs' "reservations" regarding Khrushchev.

Throughout 1963 Khrushchev continued to fight for priority for the chemicals industry and other consumption goods industries in order to raise the standard of living of the general population.

## Khrushchev Cuts the 1964–65 Military Budget

We have related how in 1961, on the eve of the XXII Congress, Khrushchev temporarily gave way on the issues of the scale of the armed forces in general and the role of the conventional forces in particular. By now, however, he had the bit between his teeth in his fight to raise the standard of living. In preparation for the December 1963 Central Committee Plenary, to be followed as usual by a Supreme Soviet session to pass the budget for the year 1964–'65, the press (and *Pravda* in particular) was swamped with articles demanding investment of additional resources in the chemicals and consumption goods industries: funds for this purpose could be diverted from heavy industry and defence expenditures. The Plenary met from 11 to 13 December. In his summing up speech Khrushchev said: "The fight for a developed chemicals industry has to be turned into an important issue for the whole people. By developing chemicals we shall expand the capacity of many industries to supply the material and spiritual needs of the population. The main thing is to produce more goods and raise the standard of living." Then came a statement that did not appear in *Pravda* on the morrow and was only published twelve days later in *Red Star* on 25 December, over a week after the close of the Supreme Soviet session. Khrushchev affirmed that the development of the chemicals industry had been carried out without detriment to the strengthening of the country's defence. This may have been considered (by the *Pravda* censor) too controversial a statement — perhaps a controversy as to whether the country's defences had or had not been weakened had better not be aired in public.

*Pravda*'s readers were allowed to know that later in this speech Khrushchev said: "Thanks to our exertions, we have recently been successful in securing a certain lowering of international tension; the Supreme Soviet's [sc. forthcoming] ratification of our Government's proposal to reduce expenditure in the military clauses of the 1964 budget represents yet another Soviet step in the direction of lowering this tension." Then came the crucial sentence: "I wish to inform the Plenary that we are now weighing up the possibility of a further reduction in the scale of our armed forces." The reduction had been made possible, he said, by the lowering of international tension, a process which had received an impetus from the agreement banning certain nuclear tests. The reduction in conventional forces and the budget cuts would themselves in turn constitute a new contribution to furthering the process. "Let us direct our efforts not to the arms race but to disarmament, to peaceful competition and the solution of international problems by means of negotiation." This final pacific flourish was hardly calculated to appease the military. What the reductions would really mean could be seen in an admission of Khrushchev's that appeared in the later *Red Star* account: in the new conditions, the accomplishment of historic (combat) missions would call for greater exertions on the part of the Armed Forces in general and of every individual combattant.[8]

The Supreme Soviet ratified the State budget put before it by Finance Minister V. P. Gorbuzov totalling 91.3 milliard rubles, an increase of 4.8 milliard over the estimates for 1963. (For the 1965 budget an increase was foreseen of 10% over the 1964 figure.) Gorbuzov cited Khrushchev's statement to the Central Committee Plenary about solving international problems by means of negotiation, which was why the Government found it possible to reduce the 1964 military allocations by 600 million rubles. The defence budget for 1964 would constitute 14.6% of the overall budget as against 16.1% in 1963.[9]

The Army chiefs reacted angrily to these proposed new cuts. The first sign came from Marshal Chuikov in the pages of *Izvestia* on

8 *Pravda*, 15 December 1963; *Red Star*, 25 December 1963.
9 *Ibid.*, 17 December 1963.

22 December only a few days after the close of the Supreme Soviet session that ratified the budget with its cuts. Under the headline, "The Land Forces in our Day", he wrote:

> To ignore the objective laws of balanced development of all types of weapons and of the different branches in the Forces and their coordinated use in warfare necessarily has catastrophic consequences. An outstanding example is the bankruptcy of Hitler's forces, when he banked basically on tanks and planes. ... The US Command has now begun to pay greater attention to developing the land forces with ordinary as well as nuclear armament, alongside increasing their nuclear-missile potential. ... Soviet military science holds the view that victory in a future nuclear war can be secured only by means of the joint efforts of all the arms in the forces. The Strategic Missiles Force will undoubtedly play a decisive role in attaining the main goals in the war, but under modern conditions the land forces continue to be not only a necessary but a most important integral component of the forces. This means that they have to be strong enough, mobile enough, properly armed and organised.[10]

It also meant of course that they would have to be properly financed.

The decisions had in fact been taken at the Central Committee Plenary and the cuts had been ratified by the Supreme Soviet, but the public debate continued to an extent very unusual in the Soviet Union.

*February 1964, Plenary Extraordinary.* This unheard-of state of affairs of continued public questioning of a decision already taken and ratified necessitated the convocation of another Central Committee Plenary only a short while after the December one. Implementation of the Supreme Soviet's decisions had apparently met with what almost amounted to passive resistance. Khrushchev convoked a Plenary extraordinary in February 1964 with the not very

10   *Izvestia*, 22 December 1963.

convincing explanation that the December Plenary had not finished working out the details of his projects. At this Plenary, Khrushchev heatedly defended the previous December's decisions as a whole and the priority given to the chemicals industry in particular. He argued:

> The December Plenary plan for the chemicalisation of the State economy covers the fields of production and of consumption at one and the same time, and it is not possible to argue that it refers only to group B or only to group A. One thing is clear: chemicals — figuratively speaking — successfully synthesises the interests of the State and of the people too. The State is interested in developing heavy industry and Soviet men and women are interested in consumption goods. Only backward dogmaticians can regard this as a deviation from the general line. No! This is the development to come of the general line, which takes into account the possibilities of science and technique and the demands that life faces us with now, in order to create better conditions — to satisfy the great needs of our people. ...[11]

## Khrushchev Circumvented and Ignored

The February Plenary apparently did not help change the minds of Army chief and others who were against giving priority to "chemicalisation" and what it involved. In a *Pravda* editorial of 3 March we find an attempt to calm fears of discrimination against heavy industry. The article stated: "The Party has accorded first priority to development of the chemicals industry. Steel and iron-rolling are needed in increasingly large quantities everywhere: our metallurgical industry continues to expand and improve its performance."[12] This is not exactly the tone of Khrushchev's pleas to satisfy the great needs of the people.

Defence Minister Malinovsky was now mentioning Khrushchev

---

11 *Pravda*, 15 February 1964.
12 *Pravda*, 3 March 1964.

less and less when he addressed the Party and the Central Committee. In an article by him (also of 3 March) dealing with the ideological and organisational action of the Army cadres, he mentionel Khrushchev only once in a short routine phrase.[13]

*Congratulations.* On 17 April 1964 the main headline in all the papers, *Pravda, Izvestia, Red Star* and others, ran "Joint Congratulations fom the Cental Committee Pesidium, the Council of Ministes and the Presidium of the Supreme Soviet for the 70th Birthday of Khrushchev, First Secretary of the Central Committee and Chairman of the Council of Ministers." To mark the occasion, Khrushchev was being awarded the decoration, Hero of the Soviet Union, one more time. The congratulatory message ran in part:

> In the Civil War years, when you were a political activist in the Red Army, you fought, arms in hand, against the interventionists and against counter-revolution and the White Guard. In the grave years of the War for the Fatherland, together with other Party activists, you yourself directly conducted the war of the Soviet combattants on the battle fronts against the Hitlerite invaders. On a series of fronts of the fighting army, you took a most active part as a member of the Military Council in elaborating and implementing the main military operations in the historic campaigns of Volgograd, Kursk, Oryol and others.[14]

Malinovsky for his part, in an article entitled, "In the Party's Leadership Lies Our Force and Thence the Fact Our Being Undefeated", seized the opportunity to belittle Khrushchev's military past. He went on at some length about Lenin, towards whom the people turned its eyes in gratitude for all the victories of the Civil War and the Great Patriotic War. He of course repeated the formula, "The Army's being led by the Party is the basic foundation of military development and organisation." Then he came to Khrushchev's part in the victories:

13  *Red Star*, 3 March 1964.
14  *Ibid.*, 17 April 1964.

The Party sent about a third of its main activists to conduct political action in the Army, among them important activists of the Party and the State, like Voroshilov, Zhdanov, Manuilsky and Shcherbakov, and activists from Party organisation of the Republics and Districts, Brezhnev, Bormistenko, Ignatov, Klederzon, Kuznietsov, Mzhuvendze, Suslov and many more. They conducted the organisational and political action of the Army together with outstanding commanders in order to ensure the carrying out of the gigantic operational plans to annihilate the invaders. Khrushchev belonged to a series of activities like these. The Soviet men and women know that Khrushchev took an active part in the battles for the sake of Soviet rule at the fronts of the Civil War. As a political worker (*Politrabotnik*) with the battle units, he encouraged the Red combattants with his fiery Bolshevik words and his personal example. In the years of the Great War of the Fatherland, Khrushchev was a member of the Military Council on a series of fronts. His tireless activity and his capacity for judging the situation and events at the front correctly was an encouragement to us, the commanders. ... We always regarded him as an organiser and leader in war, and a real Leninist-Communist. ... The combattants in the Army and Navy are imbued with profound love for their brilliant leader and Supreme Commander, Nikita Sergeyevitch Khrushchev, and send him wishes for good health on his 70th birthday.[15]

Alongside the fulsome flattery and the use of the title "Supreme Commander", this description of Khrushchev's career was clearly meant to "cut him down to size". The enumeration of so long a list of Party activists, some of them practically unknown in the Soviet Union — with the added remark that he belonged to a series of activists "like these" — robbed him precisely on his birthday of the laurels of planner and director of the decisive military campaign in the Patriotic War that he had worked hard for years to have himself crowned with and that were of the utmost importance

15   *Ibid.*

## The Army Chiefs and Khrushchev

in his eyes. It was a deliberate affront, an accurate blow dealt him where it would hurt most. This, and not the flattery, pointed to the senior Army chiefs' real evaluation of Khrushchev and their attitude to him in the spring of 1964. More, it showed the way the wind was blowing if Malinovsky could say these things in the pages of an Army paper without fear of some serious sanction. Early in 1964 these signs of what would happen were perhaps not strikingly evident to outsiders, but Khrushchev's comrades in the leadership who were beginning to weave the threads of the conspiracy to unseat him could read into these words a signal from the Army chiefs that his deposition would not have any obstacles to face from their side.

### Why Khrushchev Had to Go

We must review here, even if only briefly, the main reasons that brought Khrushchev's colleagues in the collective leadership, or the majority of them, to the difficult decision — and one not lacking in danger — to take the drastic and unprecedented step of deposing the First Secretary of the Central Committee, who was at the same time the Head of Government. We shall also have to sketch the circumstances that made it possible to carry out the *coup* successfully.

*A Different Breed.* Though Khrushchev came up all the way in the Stalinist school, together with his comrades in the leadership, he was not like the others. He behaved more openly, travelled far and wide in the country and outside it; he would appear everywhere and deliver speeches, talk to lots of people and make lots of jokes. At the many meetings he initiated with foreign visitors and with diplomats, he would launch into lively and almost free discussion. At times he permitted himself to make remarks that no other Soviet leader would have made, remarks contradicting fundamental Soviet propaganda propositions, such as his famous comment on workers in the West (as the guest of Rosabelle Gerst, in Ohio, in September 1959): "I've seen the slaves of capitalism and they live not at all badly."[16] The Soviet press completely ignored so eccentric a pronouncement. ...

I was present at scores of receptions where almost all the members of the leadership were on view, as it were — Army heads and high Government officials — but no-one else held long conversations with the diplomats like Khrushchev did; compared with him the rest of the top Soviet leadership seemed sombre men, personalities bolted and barred, while Khrushchev was outgoing, accessible. From his conversations with groups of ambassadors and his spontaneous remarks in discussions on the nature of different regimes, I personally formed the opinion that he firmly believed that capitalism was a dying system and that in the near future the Soviet Union would catch up with and even surpass the USA in productivity and wellbeing.

*Innovator:* The period of Khrushchev's leadership was full of innovations in internal policy reforms. In his foreign policy too, he excelled in adventurous initiatives, and his path was marked by much boldness and no little opportunism. He tried many experiments in his attempts to break out new paths, but he did not sufficiently calculate the cost beforehand or the results. There had been organisational changes under the Soviet regime in the past, but never at such speed as in Khrushchev's day. His decisions on organisational changes often led to a sharp struggle between him and his more conservative colleagues.

Among the bold actions initiated by Khrushchev in different fields of internal policy were the following:

1954: Programme for developing the virgin lands.
1956: 'Pandora's box' — his secret speech to the XX Congress on the crimes of Stalin.
1957: 1. Overthrow of the Malenkov, Molotov and Kaganovitch group, an operation that very nearly failed and which strengthened his standing in the leadership.

16 Thomas P. Whitney, *Khrushchev Speaks,* Ann Arbor, University of Michigan Press, 1963, p. 5, *apud* Merle Fainsod, Problems of Communism, Jan.–Feb. 1965, p. 3.

2. Deposition of Zhukov and the beginning of reinforced Party supervision over the Army.
3. Abolition of the central Government Ministries for the economic branches and establishment of National Economic Councils (*Sovnarkhozes*) — a measure led by Party elements and one that strengthened them, since they had had no direct influence in the branch Ministries. The reform strengthened the hold of the Party machine over the executive echelons of economic policy.

1958: 1. Removal of Bulganin. Khrushchev took over as Head of Government in addition to his Party post.
2. Abolition of the Tractor Stations and unification of the smaller *kolkhozes* into larger units.

1959: Ratification of the 7-Year Plan (1959–1965) instead of the traditional 5-year development plans.

1960: Ratification of the new military doctrine and the decision to reduce the scale of the Armed Forces by a third.

1961: The new Party Programme.

1962: 1. Introduction of the method of special Party-Government supervision of the economy. This reform strengthened Party influence at the level of supervision over the implementation of economic policy, since there no longer remained in the Government's hands an independent instrument of central supervision, and the Party machine became the central factor in special economic supervision.
2. Division of the Party membership into two groups, one arm dealing with industry and building and the other with agriculture. This made possible a larger measure of involvement of all levels of the Party in the two main sectors in the Soviet economy. The aim of the division was to spur on the fulfilment of the economic plans.
3. Abolition of the all-Soviet Ministry of the Interior (MVD).

*Khrushchev's foreign policy* was rich in initiatives for lowering international tension, on the one hand, but also in adventures that created situations of tension on the other. It is sufficient to recall his attempts at appeasement with Yugoslavia and the summit meeting with heads of Western States in 1955 and "spirit of Geneva" felt in its aftermath. In the same year there were efforts to extend the influence of the Soviet Union in countries in Asia and Africa. In 1956, Khrushchev elaborated the theory of co-existence of States with different social regimes, but in 1958 he himself addressed an ultimatum to the West to abolish the regime of the occupation of Western Berlin. He had already begun to work the large-scale and prolonged scheme of deception as to the size and capability of the Soviet strategic missile system. The Camp David meeting with Eisenhower in 1959 helped to decrease tension and Khrushchev made further moves in that direction — but then new tension was created over the question of Berlin and the announcement of the construction of the Berlin Wall in 1961.

The setting up of the missile bases in Cuba in 1962 marked a peak of tension. As against this came the agreement on nuclear tests and the installation of the "hot line" connection between Washington and Moscow, which may have been decided on in view of mounting tension between the Soviet Union and China.

*Frustration and Antagonism.* The balance sheet of all these contradictory moves was that Khrushchev succeeded in antagonising all the main focal centres of power and different interest groups in the Soviet Union. His favouring Party elements over Government ones antagonised the Government bureaucracy; at the same time, some of his economic reforms (the *Sovnarkhoses* and the division of Party members into two sectors) as well as the institution of special Party supervision of the economic plans cost the Party its traditional status of being outside and above economic implementation, the arbiter between different interests. Well-established existing routines were upset and the Party's authority was damaged. Many in the Party could not adjust to the changes and felt their special status affected.

All Khrushchev's efforts to kindle enthusiasm for his reforms in the Party's ranks were fruitless and ended in frustration, nor did they make him a hero in the eyes of Party members. His reforms came up against ill-will, deliberate slowing-down and even stone-walling. His pressure on members of the leadership to endorse the many changes he initiated was not always to his comrades' liking. To this was added a habit of his that angered them no little of going over their heads and appealing directly to the public. In various meetings and consultations in Moscow and during his visits in the length and breadth of the country, Khrushchev would throw out suggestions and ideas and would even go so far at times as to say that these had not yet been discussed in the leadership, but he would like to hear the reactions of the grass-roots activists. On a tour in Northern Ostya in August 1964, Khrushchev said: "Some of the comrades tell me that perhaps its not proper to publish this matter now and say ahead of time what the content will be of the address to the Central Committee Plenary. ... But if we don't talk about it now, we shall lose a lot of time. ... Maybe you'll still manage to do something about this matter before the Plenary."[17]

The Central Committee Plenary was planned for November 1964, and here was Khrushchev talking like this in August and in fact telling his listeners ahead of time the decision itself to convoke the Plenary, something simply not done. On this tour he was inviting his listeners in the agricultural regions to begin applying programmes that had not yet been accepted by the Central Committee and perhaps not even in the Presidium, an unprecedented proceeding.

## Khrushchev Settles His Own Fate

Just how and when Khrushchev's comrades in the collective leadership reached their decision to remove him from all his posts is obscure, but plausible conjectures can be framed as to the timing of the move itself. The mid-October date, in the view of Tatu, was linked precisely with this Central Committee Plenary, convoked for November, when decisions were supposed to be taken on agricultural management and on the personal status of certain leaders.

17 *Pravda*, 10 August 1964.

Tatu writes that Khrushchev planned to utilise the contention that agriculture must be made more efficient in order to deprive some members of the collective leadership of their practical responsibility in this sphere. This would have upset an administrative equilibrium that had been preserved with difficulty for the previous four years, besides being unwelcome to the persons concerned. In Tatu's opinion, this was the last straw: Suslov and the others saw that they must act, that it was now a case of Khrushchev or them. And if Khrushchev was to go, it must happen before the November Plenary. Thus in a certain fashion Khrushchev himself set the date of his own downfall.[18] He made it all the more certain by ignoring the increasing restiveness in the main focuses of power over his handling of foreign affairs as his own personal sphere (with a little help from members of his family) and over his stubbornness in pressing on with production of consumption goods in preference to heavy industry.

At the beginning of October a joint session was held of the Central Committee Presidium and the Council of Ministers, with the participation of heads of Party and Government organisations of the Republics and the people in charge of economic planning. The report took up nearly the whole of the front page of *Pravda*. Khrushchev addressed those present on "Basic Directions in working out the Economic Development Plan in the Near Future". He declared: "We shall be guided by the main objective of this Plan — an additional rise in the people's standard of living. In the period of the first 5-Year Plans and in the post-war years, we placed the main stress on heavy industry as the basis for the economic development of the whole country and for strengthening our defensive capability. Now that we possess a mighty industry and our defences have reached a proper level, the Party has set itself the objective of swifter development of the branches producing consumption goods. ... Our country has reached the stage of development where we have to put at the head of our plans for the future satisfying the growing material and spiritual needs of the

18  Tatu, *op. cit.*, p. 432.

individual."[19] The *Pravda* report said nothing about the deliberations at this session, except for a short sentence at the end to the effect that Gosplan (the State Institute for Economic Planning) was instructed to make the necessary calculations and submit proposals to the Central Committee and the Council of Ministers on the optimal period that the plan should cover, and on the basic directions of development of the State economy.

On the day this report was published, Khrushchev went away on holiday to his estate at Gagra, leaving his comrades in the leadership a clear field. His double position at the head of the two main power focuses in the State apart from the Army — the Party and the Government — meant that there had to be complicated and careful preparations for the deposition. There are no rules of procedure laid down in the Soviet Constitution or in the Communist Party Programme for the transfer of power if the leader dies or is no longer fit to exercise authority. There was moreover no precedent for the deposition of the holder of what was without question the key post in the regime that of the First Secretary of the Communist Party.

The Army chiefs' attitude to a plot like this was particularly important, as had been sufficiently proved by the June 1957 crisis in the leadership. We have seen that the Army chiefs had good grounds for wanting Khrushchev removed; his frequent pronouncements in September and October on matters affecting Armed Forces interests must have added fuel to the flames and brought tee Army chiefs still closer to the persons or groups that were lining up against him. It was probably precisely in these weeks that the opposition finally crystallised.

On 19 September Khrushchev had made a speech to the "World Youth Forum", which was a striking example of how he infuriated his opponents:

> So a few days ago I really told the Japanese delegation about the terrible weapons we have which I've seen, and the imperialists are making a fine fuss over this, as if we were

19 *Pravda*, 2 October 1964.

producing new arms to wipe them all out. That I didn't say, actually, but aren't the atomic and hydrogen arms bad enough that we are already producing? I'll tell you this too: I've been through three wars: in these wars the terror of the battlefield was the tank; and now I'll tell you in confidence — when I went along to the training grounds and saw how the tanks set out to the attack and saw the hits that the antitank artillery registered on those tanks, this upset me very much. Here we are spending so much money on producing tanks and if, God forbid (as they say), war breaks out, these tanks will go up in flames even before they reach the line fixed for them by the Command.[20]

What is really astonishing is that an experienced politician and superb manipulator like Khrushchev should have failed to realise that he was in danger and to take measures to prevent his opponents from lining up against him. There is no doubt that he could have called upon men loyal to him for support — there were still such to be found. Perhaps ten years of successes in the wrestling matches within the leadership had developed in him an exaggerated self-confidence and blunted his alertness to danger.

### The Role of the Army Chiefs

There is no certain information on whether the Army chiefs played a direct part in the political *coup*. It is however plain that this time Defence Minister Malinovsky, unlike Zhukov in June 1957, was not ready to help Khrushchev extricate himself from the trap set for him: he and his fellow commanders had no reason to wish to do so. He must have known what was in the wind and the planners must at least have felt sure of his neutrality.[21] There was certainly no sign of any opposition in the Army.

20   *Ibid.*, 22 September 1964.
21   Tatu affirms "according to different sources" that Malinovsky was invited to take part in the discussion of the Presidium when the crisis broke. I agree with Tatu's view that it would be only natural for the

## The Army Chiefs and Khrushchev

*According to Plan.* On 16 October 1964, the following announcement appeared on the first page of all the main newspapers: "On 14 October a meeting took place of the Central Committee Plenary. The Plenary responded to the request of Comrade N. S. Khrushchev to be released from his posts as First Secretary of the Central Committee, Member of the Central Committee Presidium and Chairman of the Council of Ministers of the Soviet Union, on account of his advanced age and the deterioration in the state of his health. The Plenary elected Comrade L. I. Brezhnev as First Secretary of the Central Committee." On the same page of the papers appeared an announcement of a session of the Presidium of the Supreme Soviet, which also responded to the request of Comrade Khrushchev to release him from his post as Chairman of the Council of Ministers on account of his advanced age and the deterioration in the state of his health. The announcement added that Comrade A. N. Kosygin had been appointed Chairman of the Council of Ministers. Brief and to the point, in the usual way of Soviet announcements of this kind.

An exposé of the motives for the deposition with criticism of Khrushchev's style of leadership was put before the public on the morrow in a leading article in *Pravda*, which did not even mention his name, headed: "The Stable Leninist General Line of the Communist Party of the Soviet Union." The article began by stressing the unity and cohesion of the Party. The Party would never acquiesce in any form of opportunism. It went on:

> The monolithic unity of the Party and its indefeasible loyalty to the prescripts of Lenin were demonstrated with new force at the Central Committee Plenary of 14 October. ... The Party of Lenin is the enemy of subjectivism and spontaneity in the development of Communism. It finds alien to it the use of spotlights, hasty conclusions, hurried decisions, actions cut off from reality; it finds alien to it boasting, empty

> plotters to try at the outset to secure Malinovsky's consent to the steps they proposed to take or at least to try to see to it that he remain neutral. *Op. cit.*, p. 455.

verbiage, infatuation with administrativeness, unwillingness to give due consideration to the achievements of science and to practical experience. The development of Communism is a living, creative thing and it does not tolerate decisions by one man and the ignoring of the practical experience of the masses.

The article closed with the affirmation that collective leadership was the most important of Lenin's principles of Party action, constituting the Party's well-tried weapon and its greatest achievement. The implication was that this principle had been endangered and it had been necessary to save it.[22]

*Red Star* contented itself with publishing the announcements of the Central Committee Plenary and the Supreme Soviet Presidium on the same day that they were published in *Pravda*. Therewith the name of Khrushchev vanished from the pages of the military press for a decent interval into the limbo of oblivion. It was not until February 1965 that the *Journal of Military History* endorsed the Party leadership's pronouncements, in just a sentence or two at the end of a long article (nine pages) by General Zheltov, former head of the MPA, entitled, "The Leadership of the Communist Party of the Soviet Union and the Organisation and Development of the Armed Forces in the Post-War period." Wrote General Zheltov:

> The decisions taken at the October and November Plenaries mobilised all our combattants for great new actions to raise the level of combat power of the Soviet Army and Navy. These decisions, imbued with loyalty to the prescripts of Lenin and strict observance of the Leninist principles and norms elaborated by the Party, guide the cadres of the Army as they do the whole Soviet people not to acquiesce in subjectivism, spontaneity, or any kind of hasty conclusions, hurried decisions and acts cut off from reality.[23]

---

22 *Pravda*, 17 October 1964.
23 *Journal of Military History*, February 1965, p. 11.

## "As You Were!"

The new leaders hastened to abolish most of the changes Khrushchev had introduced and which they had so disliked. The post of Chairman of the Council of Ministers was again separated, as we have seen, from that of First Secretary of the Party. The division of Party members into two economic sectors was annulled; economic administration through *Sovnarkhozes* was abolished and the central Ministries for the different branches reestablished. The Party-Government committees (headed by the Party representatives) for special economic supervision also went, and the situation reverted to what it had been before — the Party established its own economic supervision and the State a separate supervision. One more thing — criticism of Stalin and his period was again restricted.

*Budget Cuts Restored.* The Army chiefs were now able to push their own interests in the areas where they had differed from Khrushchev. In the budget for 1965, confirmed at the Supreme Soviet session in December 1964, defence allocations were indeed reduced by 500 million rubles, and the percentage of the whole State budget earmarked for defence expenditure was set at 12.9% as against 14.5% in 1964.[24] Nevertheless, given the considerable development in the Army that was already perceptible in 1965, it is difficult to accept that this ratio as published represented the real outlay on defence. To support this contention, let me quote from the opening passages of the magisterial research by Erickson, already referred to in these pages. "Within a matter of months" of Khrushchev's downfall, he writes, "(in March, 1965), the management of the defence industries was re-centralined, and it was to become clear from the evidence of deployment that a start had been made on a major build-up of strategic weapons, the results of which showed all too plainly by the late summer of 1966. ... There has been no "new" strategic policy ... but the great and growing difference with the early 1960s has been the magnitude of the military effort. ... In the spring of 1965 the Soviet military began

---

24  *Pravda*, 10 December 1964.

to exert real pressure, beginning with Marshal Zakharov's stinging condemnation of the "hare-brained" schemes of self-styled military experts, to wit, Khrushchev: this assertiveness was reinforced by Marshal Sokolovsky, who in the wake of Marshal Zakharov emphasised the need for military expertise in planning defence matters and for taking account of the necessity for large armies even in an age of nuclear war."[25]

In sum, one may say that the differences between Khrushchev and the Army chiefs over strategic conceptions and the development of the Armed Forces in the nuclear age, added to the advance immediately assured the Army after Khrushchev's removal, constitute clear evidence that his deposition suited the needs and interests of the military establishment, and it follows that the operation to remove him must have received that establishment's support in one form or another.

### Summing-Up

In every country where the Army does not control all the ruling institutions, the military authorities are subordinate to the political authority in the State. This subordinaion is in basic axiom from the conceptual point of view and it is also respected in practice from the institutional point of view, with certain differences of form in different countries.

The relations between the Armed Forces and the civil power in the Soviet Union are thus not unique in respect to the subordination of the Army to civil authority and supervision. What is unique is subordination to the lead not of the Government but of the Communist Party: the Armed Forces are led, guided and given orders under Party supervision. The Army owes loyalty to the Party and its ideology. The officers and all ranks are educated by its light, and military doctrine is elaborated on the basis of its principles. This is the open, official position, both from the conceptual and the institutional points of view. Official declarations by authorised insti-

---

25 Erickson, *loc. cit.*, pp. 1–3.

tutions, including those of the Armed Forces, refer to the conduct of the Armed Forces by the Party and do not speak of the Government as conducting the activity of the Forces. The statement recurs over and over again that their being led by the Party is the basic foundation of the Forces' organisation and development. This flat affirmation is regularly repeated by the Army chiefs themselves.

Because of this unique relation between the Armed Forces and the civil power, differences of opinion between the Army and the civil power or tensions between them are not expressed as in other countries by confrontation with the Government or its extensions. In the Soviet Union these confrontations and tensions exist within the Party set-up itself and not between the Party and an outside body. There is a special tissue of relations between the officer corps and the Party. Over ninety per cent of the officers are Party members; the Army chiefs and the vast majority of the officers see themselves as emissaries of the regime and their task not only as the defence of the Fatherland but also defence of the regime expressed in and maintained by the Communist Party. The officer is imbued with the consciousness that the "sole commander" represents the Party and the Government in the Armed Forces. He is the Party's trustee, charged with inculcating the Party line in the units and among the soldiers.

The image is fostered of the monolithic Party, united around its "wise, Leninist leadership", which is the sole and final arbiter in any instances of friction that may arise between different factors. The image also calls for fostering — at least outwardly — something like a cult of the personality of whoever is at the head of the leadership, even if he is not in fact the sole ruler and also when his proposals are sometimes rejected by the majority of the *Politburo*.

*The Party is Infallible*

The idea of "the Party" is constantly inculcated in the consciousness of "Soviet man" in general and the Soviet officer in particular as inextricably bound up with the Fatherland — the Soviet Fatherland. Just as you do not accuse your country of injustice, so you do not accuse your Communist Party. You can put the blame for injustice on "conditions", internal and external; individual persons — sometimes past leaders — are accused of being unjust, or mistaken, or of having failed, but the Party as such "is always right". Serene and securely based on the scientific Marxist analysis of the necessary course of social evolution, the Party foresees events, its teachings are true, it cannot fail, err, or be mistaken. Just as you do not revolt against your country, so you do not revolt against the Party, flesh of your flesh, bone of your bone.

The Soviet officer has deep patriotic sensibilities, and the regime is constantly concerned to strengthen the roots of his patriotism not only in love of country but also in devotion to the Party and its ideology. Let us quote Marshal Gretchko: "High political consciousness and a conviction of the correctness of the ideas of Marxism-Leninism serve as the basis of Soviet patriotism, expressed in moral-political fighting qualities, such as devotion to the Soviet Fatherland and to the Communist Party cause. ... Soviet patriotism is the source of the extreme vigilance of the combattants, aware of their personal responsibility for the fate of the Fatherland."[26]

*Why the Apparatus?*

If this is so, if the senior command and the officer corps are part and parcel of the Party and see it as flesh of their flesh and bone of their bone, if instances of friction are internal affairs which are resolved solely within the Party — then the leaders should calmly rely on the Army's absolute loyalty to the Party and to themselves as representing the Party monolith. Yet the reality has throughout been otherwise. The leaders are not light-headed and they do not rely absolutely on the blind loyalty of the Army. We see the leadership's apprehensions awakened by every sign of the Army command's entrenching itself in defence of its direct professional needs.

26 Marshal A. Gretchko, *The Armed Forces of the Soviet State,* Voyenizdat, Moscow 1974, p. 197 (Russian).

when these are opposed to the needs of the Party. Hence the constant insistence on the priority of Party needs. We have seen the investment of great and sustained efforts to establish and keep going special Party-political supervision over the officers — a supervision without parallel in other professional groups in the State.

It is fairly easy to understand some of the grounds for this state of permanent apprehension in the leadership as regards the officer corps:

*The life-style of those serving in the Soviet standing army* and their sense of military honour, with all the external symbols of gold braid, epaulettes and decorations, help create a unique professionalism in the officer corps, quite distinct from that of other professional groups. Army officers live apart, differentiated from civilian society; they and the members of their families mix but seldom with civilian families, even if they do not live far away. In senior officers' circles, it is the usual thing for sons and daughters to marry within their own circle, and it is even preferred that there should not be a marked difference of rank between the fathers-in-law.

The special professional interests beget a common outlook on affairs and a constant demand for strengthening the Armed Forces, not alway in line with the political leadership's scale of priorities. True, the Soviet Army chiefs are not unique in this respect at least.[27]

Social isolationism and common interests and a similar outlook work together to create something like a closed caste, an endogamous clan. The Party's repeated attempts to develop ties between the officers and local Party organisations did not succeed in breaking down the social barriers, and the result was certainly not in the least commensurate with the effort invested.

*Personal and national loyalty.* As is the case in other armies too, a senior officer taking over the command of a Military District or

---

[27] See *inter alia,* Bengt Abrahamson, *Military Professionalization and Political Power,* Sage Publications, Beverley Hills, California, 1972, p. 17.

a Commander transferred to a high Staff post will often want to bring with him some of the officers who worked with him previously; but the Party supervisory apparatus and the KGB command see to it that this does not develop into too much of a bond of personal loyalty to the commander and that groups do not come to being in the Army bound to a given personality.

Senior commanders frequently choose to have men around them of their own nationality and give them promotion. The Ukrainian Marshal Timoshenko, according to the evidence of former Soviet officer, N.A., succeeded in getting Ukrainian senior officers into the Command of the Belorussian MD when he was in charge there, raising them in rank. In N.A.'s opinion and that of others interviewed, this was by no means an isolated case. Junior officers too sometimes preferred to promote their fellow-nationals as NCOs in their units. It should be noted that the officer corps is on the whole more national-minded than other professional groups. Russian nationalism is in the lead.

## Is an Army Coup d'Etat Conceivable?

There have never been any signs as far as is known of senior officers organising themselves into a group of men held together by over-strong bonds of allegiance to one another. The "Stalingrad group", which has been described as something of the kind, in fact lacked any political colouring whatsoever. For a certain period the members of this group were considered loyal to Khrushchev and apparently enjoyed his protection, mainly as regards promotion, but their support for him was not unconditional: in the '60's some of them even opposed his conceptions, which led to their being removed from their posts at the centre.

Without doubt the KGB kept a specially watchful eye on any possibility of officers organising on political lines, and took steps to block any such grouping, for example, by arranging judicious postings to the remoter outposts.

What gave the leadership most cause for apprehension and called for their constant vigilance was the simple, obvious fact that the

## The Army Chiefs and Khrushchev

Army held in its hands the greatest potential capacity for utilising violence. The danger of the use of this potential for violence as a possible means of coercion in internal politics could become a real threat only if a special situation were to come into being within the Party leadership. A modest example of the possibility of this potential influence on the solution of a crisis in the leadership of the Party was the assistance rendered Khrushchev by Zhukov in June 1957. The probability of such a situation recurring is not very high, to go by experience up to now. Over the years, the leaders of the Soviet Union learnt to work as a team and to get on with each other, so that at least to the outside they have generally kept up the appearance of unity and cohesion, even when a protracted internal struggle for power or for the succession was going on within the leadership. The leaders have also learnt to compromise temporarily, until one of their number or one group overcomes the rest and externally the situation seems "as you were".

Under normal conditions in relations between the Party and the Army, when the political leadership and the bureaucratic machines are themselves functioning well — that is, there is unity and co-ordination or at least reasonable arrangements and a minimum of internal friction among members of the central leadership, supported by the main intermediate-level focuses of power, and the military command is part of the Party and is representing it adequately in the Army — it is inconceivable that any junta should form in the Soviet Armed Forces. No commander, however senior he might be and however great his influence in the Army, could conceivably try to raise the standard of revolt in the Party, overthrow the leadership and seize power, in the State in its stead. It is inconceivable that an officer corps, educated in the way customary in the Soviet Union, fundamentally loyal in its own way to the Party, seeing it as flesh of its flesh and bone of its bone, should put its hand to a revolt of this kind.

Even if a special situation should arise of a breakdown of the political leadership within the Party, while the Army remained united, it seems to me that the influence of military force could only be brought to bear through the Party and in the name of the

Party. It would be a take-over all the same, but not a military *coup* in the usual sense. True, *coups* of very different kinds take place in different parts of the world, and there is no single pattern. (In Syria, for example, Army heads apparently rise to power on behalf of the or a ruling Party, but the fact is that it is the Party that is supported by the coercive power of the Army.) In the Soviet Union, however, there would certainly not be anything like the known examples of military *coups*.

What would happen after a change had taken place of all or some of the ruling heads is another matter altogether; depending on the personality of the new chief ruler and the power focus he was supported by, the dynamics of events would necessarily produce considerable changes, perhaps even very fundamental ones, in spheres such as the composition of the ruling group and the increased influence of this new group on the internal regime and on foreign policy. It is practically certain that this hypothetical new group would not lean towards democratisation of the internal regime or to speeding up the rate of raising the standard of living of the population. The trend would probably be more nationalist than previously, and there could be obstacles in the way of lessening international tensions. To the outside world, the new ruler or rulers would certainly remain the monolithic Party of Lenin, clarifying its principles anew but continuing to set the "only correct" general line, infallible as ever.

In the Soviet Union, what is hidden is frequently more than what is disclosed. This is certainly true of the future. If I have contributed however little to the understanding of what is open and what is hidden, this will be my reward.

# BIBLIOGRAPHY

## I. RUSSIAN

### A. BOOKS

Anfilov, V.A. *Deathless Adventure.* Bessmertnyy Podvig. 'Nauka' (Science) Publications, Moscow, 1971.

Antipenko, N.A. *The Main Direction.* Na glavnom Napravleniyi. 'Nauka' Publications, 2nd ed., Moscow, 1971.

Bagramyan, A. *How the War Began,* Tak nachinalas Voyna, Voyenizdat, Moscow, 1971.

*The Communist Party of the Soviet Union and the Development of the Soviet Armed Forces, 1917–1964.* KPSS i Stroitelstvo Sovetskikh Vooruzhonykh Sil. Voyenizdat, Moscow, 1965.

*The Communist Party of the Soviet Union on the Armed Forces of the Soviet Union.* KPSS o Vooruzhonykh Silakh Sovetskovo Soyuza. Gospolitizdat, Moscow, 1958.

*Congresses of the Councils of the Russian Federal Soviet Socialist Republic and of the Autonomous Republics of the R.F.S.S.R.* Syezdy Sovetov RSFSR i Avtonomnykh Respublik RSFSR. Gosizdat Legal Literature. Vol. I, 1959.

*XXII Congress of the Communist Party of the Soviet Union,* Stenographic Report. XXII Syezd Kommunisticheskoy Partiyi Sovetskovo Soyuza. Moscow, 1962.

*Constitution (Basic Law) of the Soviet Union,* Konstitutsiya (Osnovnoy Zakon) Soyuza Sovetskikh Sotsialisticheskikh Respublik. Gosizdat Legal Literature, Moscow, 1957.

Encyclopaedia. *The Big Soviet Encyclopaedia,* Bolshaya Sovetskaya Entsiklopedia. State Science Publications. 2nd ed. Moscow, 1949–1958, 3rd ed., 1970.

Engels, F. *Possibilities and Prospects for a War of the Holy Alliance against France in 1852.* Works of Marx and Engels. Vozmozhnosti i Perspektivy Voyny Svyatovo Soyuza protiv Frantsiyi. Gospolitizdat, 2nd ed., Moscow, 1956.

Bibliography

*Foundation and Development of the Soviet Union*, Obrazovaniye i Razvitiye Sovetskikh Sotsialisticheskikh Respublik. Gosizdat Legal Literature, Moscow, 1973.

Frunze, M.V. *Selected Works*, Izbranyye Proizvedenya. Voyenizdat, Moscow, 1957.

Gretchko, Marshal A. *The Armed Forces of the Soviet State*, Vooruzhonyye Sily Sovetskovo Gosudarstva. Voyenizdat, Moscow, 1974.

Gretchko, Marshal A. *A Renewed Spring Forward in Party-Political Activity in the Soviet Army and Navy*. K. Novomu Podyomu partiyno-politicheskoy raboty v Sovetskoy Armiyi i Flote. Voyenizdat, Moscow, 1960.

*History of the Great Patriotic War of the Soviet Union, 1941–1945*, Istoriya Velikoy Otechestvenoy Voyny Sovetskovo Soyuza. Voyenizdat, 5 Vols., Moscow, 1961–1964.

*Ideological Action of the CPSU at the Front, 1941–1945*, Ideologicheskaya rabota, KPSS na fronte. Voyenizdat, Moscow, 1961.

Lenin, V.I. *Collected Works*, Polnoye Sobraniye Sochineniyi. Politizdat, 55 Vols., Moscow, 1960–1971.

*October 1957 Central Committee Plenary Resolutions in Application*: Resheniya Oktyabrskovo plenuma TSK KPSS v Deystviyi. Voyenizdat, Moscow, 1950.

*Party-Political Action in the Soviet Armed Forces*. Partiyno-politicheskaya rabota v Sovetskikh Vooruzhonykh Silakh. Voyenizdat, Moscow, 1974, A Hand-book for Use in Military-Political High Schools.

*Party-Political Action in the Armed Forces of the Soviet Union, A Historical Survey*, ed. A. Ytpishev, Partiyno-politicheskaya rabota v Vooruzhonykh Silakh SSSR. Voyenizdat, Moscow, 1974.

Petrov, Y.P. *Party Organisation and Development in the Soviet Army and Navy*, Partiynoye Stroitelstvo v Sovetskoy Armiyi i Flote. Voyenizdat, Moscow, 1964.

*Party Organisation and Development*, Partiynoye Stroitelstvo. Politizdat, 3rd ed., Moscow, 1973.

*Party-Political Action in the Soviet Army and Navy*, Partiyno-politicheskaya rabota v Sovetskoy Armiyi i Voyeno-Morskom Flote. Voyenizdat, Moscow, 1966.

*Programmes, Rules and Regulations of the Communist Party of the Soviet Union*, Programy i Ustavy KPSS. Politizdat, Moscow, 1969.

*Protocols, All-Russian Central Executive Committee*, Protokoly Zasedaniyi VTsIK. Moscow, 1920.

*Protocols, Congresses and Conferences of the All-Russian Communist Party, VII Congress, March 1918*, Protokoly Syezdov i Konferentsiyi Vsesoyuznoy Kom. Partiyi. Gosizdat, Moscow, 1928.

*Resolutions and Decisions of the Congresses, Conferences and Plenaries of the Communist Party of the Soviet Union*, KPSS v Rezolyutsiyakh i

Bibliography

    Resheniyakh Syezdov Konferentsiyi i Plenumov. Politizdat, 8th ed., Moscow, 1970.
Serbin, Evgeni, *States of Mind in the Soviet Army in the Post-Stalin Period*. Politicheskiye nastroyeniya v Sovetskoy Armiyi v poslestalinskiy period. Institute for Soviet Union Research, Munich, 1956.
    Sokolovsky, V.D., ed. *Military Strategy*, Voyennaya Strategiya. Moscow, Voyenizdat, 1963.
*Soviet Government Decrees*, Dekrety Sovetskoy Vlasti, Gosizdat, Moscow, 1957–1964.
Stalin, Y., *Works*, Sochinyeniya. Politizdat, 13 Vols., Moscow, 1946–1951.
Stalin, Y. *On the Great Patriotic War of the Soviet Union*, O Velikoy Otechestvenoy Voynye Sovetskovo Soyuza. Gospolitizdat, Moscow, 1943.
Trotsky, L. *The Arming of the Revolution*, Kak Vooruzhalas Revolyutsiya. Revolutionary Supreme Military Council, Moscow, 1925, 3 Vols.
Tukhachevsky, M.N., *Selected Works*, Izbranyye Proizvedeniya. Voyenizdat, Moscow, 1964.
Vasilevsky, A., *My Entire Life's Work*, Delo vsey Zhizni. Politizdat, Moscow, 1973.
World War II: *The Great Patriotic War of the Soviet Union, 1941–1945*, Velikaya Otechestvenaya Voyna Sovetskovo Soyuza. The Institute for Marxism-Leninism of the Central Committee, Voyenizdat, Moscow, 1956.
Yepishev, A., *Some Problems of Ideological Work in the Soviet Armed Forces*, Nekotoryye Voprosy ideologicheskoy raboty v Sovetskikh Vooruzhonykh Silakh. Voyenizdat, Moscow, 1975.
Zhukov, G., *Memories and Reflections*, Vospominaniya i Razmyshleniya. Novosty Press, Moscow, 1971.


B. PERIODICALS AND NEWSPAPERS

*Bolshevik*, Bolshevik Party organ appearing from 1924 till 1952, when it was replaced by *Communist*. Moscow.
*Izvestia*. Daily paper, organ of the Government of the Soviet Union.
*Journal of Military History*. Voyeno-istoricheskiy Zhurnal. Began publication in 1960. Published by *Red Star*.
*Military Gazette*. Voyenyy Vestnik. Publication of the Soviet Ministry of Defence. Published by *Red Star*.
*Historical Problems of the Communist Party of the Soviet Union*. Voprosy Istoriyi KPSS. Published by *Pravda*.
*Red Star*. Krasnaya Zvezda. Principal organ of the Soviet Ministry of Defence. Daily paper.
*Communist*. Kommunist. Political and theoretical periodical of the Central Committee of the Soviet Communist Party. Published by *Pravda*.

*Armed Forces Communist.* Kommunist Vooruzhonykh Sil. Published by Red Star. Moscow.
*International Life.* Mezhdunarodnaya Zhizn. Gosizdat, Moscow.
*Socialist Gazette.* Sotsialisticheskiy Vestnik New York.
*Pravda.* Pravda. Daily paper, organ of the Central Committee of the Communist Party of the Soviet Union.

II. HEBREW

A. *BOOKS*

*Khrushchev Remembers.* Translated and edited by Strobe Talbot, notes and commentary by Edward Crankshaw. Translated by Aviezer Golan. Adi Publishers for *Yediot Ahronot.*

*Soviet Military Thinking in the Nuclear Age.* Collected articles by Soviet military theoreticians, with a historical survey of 50 years of the Soviet Army by Prof. John Erickson. Published by *Ma'arakhot,* Israel Defence Forces, 1969.

*Soviet Military Power,* Prof. John Erickson, Hebrew by Meir Golan. Published by *Ma'arakhot,* Israel Defence Forces, 1972.

Chuikov, V. *The War for Stalingrad,* Hebrew by L. Merhav. Published by *Ma'arakhot,* Israel Defence Forces, 1970.

III ENGLISH

A. *BOOKS*

Abrahmson, Bengt. *Military Professionalization and Political Power.* Sage Publications Ltd., Beverley Hills, California, 1972.

Brzezinski, Zbigniev and Huntington, Samuel P., *Political Power USA/USSR.* The Viking Press, New York, 1965.

Brzezinski, Zbigniev, *Political Controls in the Soviet Army.* Research Programme on the USSR, New York, 1956.

Bauer, Raymond A., Alex Inkeles and Clyde Kluckholm, *How the Soviet System Works.* Vintage Books, New York, 1956.

Bohlen, Charles, *Witness to History 1929-1969.* Norton and Company, Inc., New York, 1973.

Conquest, R., *Power and Policy in the USSR.* New York, San Martin's Press, 1961.

Chaney, Otto Preston, *Zhukov.* University of Oklahoma Press, Oklahoma, 1971.

Dinerstein, H. S., *War and the Soviet Union.* Frederick A. Preager, New York, 1962.

Eisenhower, Dwight D., *Mandate for Change 1953-1956,* Doubleday and Company Inc., Garden City, New York, 1963.

Bibliography

*Economic Performance and the Military Burden in the Soviet Union,* U.S. Government Printing Office, Washington, 1970.

Erickson, John, *The Soviet High Command, 1918-1942,* The Macmillan Company, London, 1962.

Erickson, John, *The Road to Stalingrad,* Harper and Row Publishers, London, 1975.

Fedotoff, White D., *The Growth of the Red Army,* Princeton University Press, Princeton, 1944.

Finer, S. E., *The Man on Horseback,* Pall Mall Press, London and Dunmow, 1962.

Fainsod, Merle, *How Russia is Ruled,* Cambridge Mass., Harvard University Press, 1963.

Finkle, Jason L. and Richard W. Gable (ed.) *Political Development and Social Change,* John Wiley and Sons, New York, 1971.

Frankland, M., *Khrushchev,* Penguin Books Ltd., Harmondsworth, Middlesex, England, 1966.

Garthoff, R., *Soviet Military Doctrine,* The Free Press, Illinois, 1953.

Garthoff, R., *Soviet Strategy in the Nuclear Age,* Frederick and Praeger, New York, 1962.

Gallagher, Matthew A., *The Soviet History of World War II,* A. Praeger, New York, 1963.

Huntington, Samuel P., *Political Order in Changing Societies,* Yale University Press, New Haven, 1968.

Huntington, Samuel P., *The Soldier and the State,* Vintage Books, New York, 1964.

Horelick, Arnold L. and Myron Rush, *Strategic Power and Soviet Foreign Policy,* University of Chicago Press, 1966.

*Interest Groups in Soviet Politics,* ed. H. Gordon Skilling and Franklyn Griffiths, Princeton University Press, New Jersey, 1971.

Janowitz, Morris, *The Professional Soldier,* The Free Press, New York, 1965.

*Khrushchev Remembers,* Translated and edited by Strobe Talbot, Little, Brown and Company, Boston, 1974 (Bantam Books, London, New York, Toronto, 1971, by arrangement with Little, Brown and Company, Boston).

Kolkovicz, Roman, *The Soviet Military and the Communist Party,* Princeton University Press, Princeton, 1967.

Linden, Carl, *Khrushchev and the Soviet Leadership, 1957-1964,* Johns Hopkins Press, Baltimore, 1966.

Mackintosh, Malcolm, *Juggernaut,* Secker and Warburg, London, 1967.

Mićunović, V. *Moscow Diary,* Doubleday and Company, Inc., New York, 1980.

Rigby, T. H., *Communist Party Membership in the USSR*, Princeton University Press, New York, 1968.
Schapiro, L., *The Great Purge in the Red Army*, ed. B. H. Liddell Hart, Peter Smith, Gloucester, Mass., 1968.
Schapiro, L., *The Communist Party of the Soviet Union*, Eyre and Spottiswoode, London, 1970.
Shuman, Frederick L., *Government in the Soviet Union*, Thomas Y. Crowel Company, New York, 1961.
*Soviet Military Strategy*, ed. V. Sokolovski, Introduction by H. Dinerstein, L. Goure, T. Wolfe, Rand Corporation, 1963.
*Stalin and His Generals*, ed. Seweryn Bialer, Pegasus, New York, 1969.
Wolfe, Thomas W., *Soviet Strategy at the Crossroads*, Harvard University Press, Cambridge Mass., 1964.
Wolfe, Bertram D., *Khrushchev and Stalin's Ghost*, Frederick A. Praeger, New York, 1957.
*The Military Technical Revolution*, ed. John Erickson, Frederick A. Praeger, New York, 1966.

PERIODICALS

*Bulletin*, Institute for the Study of the USSR. Munich.
*Problems of Communism*, United States Information Agency, Washington, D.C., bi-monthly.
*Soviet Studies*, edited by the University of Glasgow, Oxford.
*Slavic Review*, American Quarterly of Soviet and East European Studies, University of Illinois, Urbana-Champaign.
*The Russian Review*, American Quarterly devoted to Russia Past and Present, sponsored by the Hoover Institution on War, Revolution and Peace.

IV. OTHER LANGUAGES

Koniev, J. S. *El Año '45*, Traducido del russo por Joaquin Rodriguez, Editorial Progreso, Madrid.
Meisner, Boris, *Russland unter Chrushtschew*, R. Oldenbourg, Muenchen, 1960.
Tatu, Michel, *Le Pouvoir en URSS*, Paris, Editions Bernard Grasset, 1966.

# INDEX

ALEXANDROV, N.
on political education in the army 233
ARTEMIEV, P.
Interior Ministry General 132

BAGRAMYAN, I.
views on Zhukov 121–122 125–126 140–141
on strengthening the Armed Forces 183
on improving style and methods of leadership 292
BARANOV, P.
on increased role of Army 292
BATOV, P.
169
BELOBRODOV, A.
on increased influence of Party on choosing Army personnel 213—214
BENES, E.
President of Czechoslovakia; communication with Stalin 47
BERIA, L.
72 138 147 171
head of Ministry of Interior and of Internal Security 49
power of, 50
conspiracy against and arrest of 50–52 53 93 132 294
BIRYUZOZ, S.
169

promoting development of military science 272
replaces Moskalenko 290
replaces Zakharov as Chief of General Staff 299
BLUECHER, V.
commander admired by Zhukov 121 162
BOHLEN, C.
U.S. Ambassador to Moscow; meetings between Zhukov and Einsenhower 136
BREZHNEV, L.
227, 266, 306
elected President of Supreme Soviet 267
elected First Secretary of Central Committee 315
BUDIENNY, S.
support for Stalin in 1936 Central Committee 46
BUKHARIN, N.
attack against Stalin 46
BULGANIN, N.
59 85 135
head of Ministry of Defence 49 132
conspiracy against Beria 51
support of Army command 54
elected Head of Government 55 83 94 134
support for "anti-Party" group 62
appointed Minister of War 72

official condemnation of Stalin 87
removal from power 309

CAMARNIK, Y.
Head of Political Administration 46
CHEBENKO, V.
Political Administration Head of Leningrad MD; criticism of 210
CHERDNICHENKO, M.
criticism of Stalin's personality cult 75–76
CHUIKOV, V.
member of "Stalingrad group"; support of Khrushchev 113
army career 120
on role of Party in the Army 291–292
reaction to cut in military budget 302–303
CLAUSEWITZ, C.
78

EISENHOWER, D.
meetings with Zhukov at Geneva, 1955 and impressions 135–137 292
on Russian missiles 282
1959 Camp David meeting 310
ENGELS, F.
67 78 234
ERICKSON, J.
123
on changes of Army tactics after 1942 127
on Cuban missile crisis 255
on development of Army after Khrushchev's removal 317–318

FRUNZE, M.
47 171
plan for reorganizing Army 16–21
appointed Deputy Commisar for War 20
on Unity of Command 36

appointment as head of Army and threat to Stalin 45
military doctrine 67

GRILEV, A.
on methodology of military-historical research 110 111
GOLIKOV, F.
214
on "Unity of Command" 184
replaces Zheltov as head of MPA 193
deposed 208 290
criticism of Political Administrations of MDs 210
on changes in Party structure in Armed Forces 221
on tasks of Party activists in Forces 267
GORBUZOV, V.P.
State Budget 1964–65 302
GORDOV, V.
Commander of 33rd army; proposal to abolish Military Councils 236
GORSHKOV, S.
169
GRETCHKO, A.
47 296
on role of Army commander 198
appointed Commander of Warsaw Pact Forces 277
on Soviet patriotism 320
GROMYKO, A.
Minister of Foreign Affairs and delegate to Geneva 135
GUSIEV, S.
Head of Army Political Administration, 1921 16 18
on military doctrine 67

HEYDRICH, R.
Head of German State Secret Service 46

334

Index

and forged documents 47
HITLER, A.
46 47

IGNATOV, N.
266 306

KAGANOVICH, L.
member of "anti-Party" group 62 154 158 177
defeat and fall from power 63 308
demands for trial of 156–157
KALEDIN, A.
White Russian Commander 23
KARDELJ, E.
58
KASTANOV, V.
on successful adaptation of dismissed Army personnel 264
KAZAKOV, V.
169
KENNEDY, J.
Cuban missile crisis 255
KHRUSHCHEV, N.
1 5 55 58 59 60 65 84 87 113 114 132 143 155 171 227 230 252 258 280 281 291 293 297 317 323
appointment as First Secretary of Central Committee 49
conspiracy against Beria 51 294
struggle for leadership 54 64 150–151 177 308
tribute to Army commanders 57
secret speech, XX Congress 57 78 106 107 130 157 308
opposition in the Party 60–63 294 308 310–311
concessions to senior officers 108
participation in Stalingrad Front Military Council 112
criticism of 115 277–278 299 315
effort to consolidate power 135

fear of Zhukov 138 157–158 159 172 174–175
plans for deposing Zhukov 147 160 165 166 174 308
deposition of 176 307 311–316
new strategic doctrine; reducing forces 245–249 251 259 279 283 297 302 309
and Cuban missile crisis 254–255 289 290 299
opposition with Army 260 265 275 290 295 298 299 313–314 318
Party guideline on Army development 266
loyalty to 270 322
compromise with Army command 276 285 301
address to Supreme Soviet, 1960 295 296
plan to reduce international tension 295 296 309–310
removal of Zakharov 299
development of chemicals industry 299–301 304
cuts military budget 302
1964 Plenary Extraordinary 303–304
belittled by Malinovsky; 70th birthday celebrations 304–307
conspiracy against 307
comparison with other leaders 307–308
innovations 308
removal of Bulganin 309
internal policy 308–309
foreign policy 309–310
KIRICHENKO, A.
support for Khrushchev 62
KLASHNIK, M.
article on "criticism and self-criticism" of commanders 161
KOLIKOV, V.
Chief of General Staff; on role of Military Councils 235

335

KONIEV, I.
65 130 162 166
trial of Beria 53
on developing heavy industry 56
on enhanced status of Army leaders 57
on originality of Soviet military planning 88
accusations against Zhukov 169 173
against Khrushchev's Army proposals 276
removal from post 276 277 190

KOPITIN, A.
discussion on military-historical research 111

KOSYGIN, A.N.
elected Chairman of Council of Ministers 315

KRASILNIKOV
criticism of Khrushchev's Army doctrine 277–278

KRILOV, N.
Army general; on "Unity of Command" 269–270

KUZNETSOV, N.
appointed Commander of Navy 50

LENIN, V.
16 20 28 34–35 47 67 71 78 82 85 90 124 169 181 195 227 265 292 305 315 316 324
on abolishing the Standing Army and arming the people 9–12
and Army's international revolutionary role 24
support of centralized control of Army 29
in favour of military experts 32–34
on Army discipline 230 288 289
military-theoretical heritage of 232 234

LOMOV, N.
on military doctrine 250–251 271
call for large Army 293

LOZOVOY, I.
on changes in Party structure in Armed Forces 221

MALENKOV, G.
56 83 86 135 147
appointed Head of Government 49
conspiracy against Beria 51
struggle for leadership and fall 54–55 94 134 294 308
member of "anti-Party" group 62 154 158 171 177
defeat by Khrushchev 63
demands for trial of 156–157

MALINOVSKY, R.
110 149 166 179–180 230 265–266 267 283 291 294 297–298
on "Unity of Command" 47 184 197
apointed as Minister of Defence 65 167
member of "Stalingrad group" 113 159
army career 120
appointed Commander of Land Forces 159
accusations against Zhukov 173
on Plenary Resolutions 1957 179–180
on reinforcing Military Councils 187 189
on insufficient discipline in the Forces and strengthening commander's authority 196 197 198 288–289
on educating members of the Armed Forces 231–232 286–287
policy for reduction of the Forces 246–247 260–261
on training experts in nuclear weaponry 248–249
on military doctrine 251 272
reservations about Khrushchev's Army reforms 275

Index

objection to too much reliance on missiles 276 279–80
comparison with Zhukov 287 289
on improving style and method of leadership 292
belittles Khrushchev 304–306 307
deposition of Khrushchev 314
MANUILSKY, D.
306
MARX, K.
67 82 124 234
MEISNER, B.
on effect of trial of "anti-Party" group 156–157
MICUNOVIC, V.
Yugoslav Ambassador 58 158
MIKOYAN, A.
62
MOLOTOV, V.
58
member of "anti-Party group 62 135 154 158 177
defeat by Khrushchev 63
demands for trial of 156–157
fall from power 308
MOSHEROV
Party Secretary of Byelorussian Republic 149
MOSKALENKO, K.
65
arrest of Beria 52 53 132
promotion 53
on political and military education of engineers 273–274
reservations about over-reliance on nuclear weaponry 280
deposition and reasons for 290 299
MOZHAYEV, F.
criticism of Party Committee 212
on educating senior command 232

NIKITIN, Y.
on increased role of the Army 292

NOVIKOV, A.
demoted from command of Air Force 72

PAVLOV, D.
122 142
PERVUHIN, M.
support for "anti-Party" group 63
PETROV, V.
Soviet historian 39 81–82 85 86 181 190 224
on role of MPA 96
accusations against Zhukov 105 164–165 176–177
on reform of Military Councils 186–187 188
POKREBYSHEV, A.
138
PEREVETKIN, S.
command of internal Army 53
PONOMARENKO, P.
59 115

RANKOVIC, A.
58
RAZIN, Y.
Soviet historian 73 78
RITOV, A.G.
article on "criticism and self-criticism" of commanders 161
ROKOSOVSKY, K.
115 143 169
Army career 120
views on Zhukov 123 141
demotion 165
ROTMISTROV, P.
87 284
on role of surprise in war 82–83
on need to develop new military thinking 85–86
on improving style and methods of leadership 292

337

SABUROV, M.
support for "anti-Party group 62
SAFRONOV, A.
opposition to Trotsky's army policy 15
SAMSONOV, A.
on methodology of military-historical research 110
SEROV, I.
support for Khrushchev 63
SHAPOSHNIKOV, B.
on role of armour in combat 123
SHEPILOV, D.
member of "anti-Party" group 62 154
SMILOV
Interior Ministry General 132
SMIRNOV, V.
opposition to Trotsky's Army policy 15
SOKOLNIKOV, G.
15–16
SOKOLOVSKY, V.
56 86 88 169
criticism of Stalin's personality cult 75–76
demand for revision of Soviet military science 84–85 318
appointed Chief of General Staff 131
on weapon development 242 252–253
against Khrushchev's Army proposals 276
removal from post 276 283 299
SPIRIDONOV, N.
Interior Ministry General 132
STALIN, Y.
1 5 16 20 21 25 28 39 40 41 47 50 51 59 79 80 81 82 85 86 90 93 107 108 109 110 122 124 125 127 128 134 137 140 143 144 147 156 172 187 191 250 284 317

support of centralized control of the Army 29
determination to destroy opponents 45 46
effect of death of 48–49
criticism of 57 58 74–75 84 87 241
praise for heroic historic leaders 70–71
on improvements in Army structure and curbing senior command 72
and the atomic bomb 72–73
personality cult of 75–76 91 106
abilities questioned 76 78
imposing Party domination over Army and Navy 92
participation in planning Battle of Stalingrad 112–114
jealousy of Zhukov 130 132
on strengthening Armed Forces 131
and the Military Councils 235–236
SUSLOV, M.
266 306
support for Khrushchev 312
SVERDLOV, V.
161
SVETLISHIN, N.
views on Zhukov 140 141

TALENSKY, A.
85 87 191–192
article on basic law of war 79–80
criticism of views of 80–82
on changes in military strategy 244
TARASOV, A.
268–269
TARENCHUK, M.
85
TATU, M.
on timing of Khrushchev's deposition 311–312
TIMOSHENKO, S.
149 169

Index

appointed Minister of Defence 38
Army career 120
removal from post of commander of Byelorussian MD and new appointment 276
promotes fellow-nationals 322

TITO, B.
58 157

TRAIANDAPHILOV, B.
123

TROTSKY, L.
21 45 120
policy on creating an Army 15 16
opposition to Frunze's Army plan 17–20
appointed Head of Supreme Military Council 23
on abolishment of Army elections and changeover to centralism 27–28 29
on tasks of Political Commissars 30–32 35
on military doctrine 67

TUKHACHEVSKY, M.
123 171
support of Frunze's Army plan 18–20
false documents against 47
Zhukov's support for 157

TUKHOVSKY, N.V.
on Soviet military science 74

USTINOV, D.
Chairman of Supreme Economic Council 300

VASILEVSKY, A.
appointment as First Deputy to Defence Minister 49 132
on enhanced status of Army leaders 57
criticism of Talensky 81
article on surprise attacks 88–89

on planning of Battle of Stalingrad 113
deposition 151

VATSETIS, Y.
First Commander of Red Army 14 34

VERSHININ, K.
Commander of Air Force; on impact of nuclear arms 243
on reduction of Forces 261

VOROSHILOV, K.
Red Army commander 18 38 306
opposition to Trotsky's Army policy 15
support for Stalin in 1936 Central Committee 46
support for "anti-Party" group 62

YAROSLAVSKY, Y.
opposition to Trotsky's Army policy 15

YEFIMOV, P.
First Deputy Head of MPA; supervizing top ranks of military institutions 211

YEGOROV, N.
article on Army discipline 230

YEPISHEV, A.
231
appointed Head of MPA; reasons for appointment 208 290
supervizing top ranks of military institutions 212
criticism of Stalin 233
participation in Army "consultation" on ideological problems 287–289
differences with Malinovsky 289
on improving style and methods of leadership 292

YEREMENKO, A.
169
member of "Stalingrad group"; support of Khrushchev 112

YEZHOV, N.
Head of People's Commissariat for Internal Affairs
attack against Bukharin 46

ZAKHAROV, G.
169
on insufficient discipline in the Forces 198
on promoting development of military science 272 318
appointed Chief of General Staff 277
support for Khrushchev 277 299
deposed 299
restored to post 299

ZHDANOV, A.
306

ZHELTOV, A.S.
164 316
MPA head; deposed 193

ZHILIN, P.
on strategic doctrine 252

ZHUKOV, G.K.
5 59 61 62 83 84 85 99 112 115 131 179 185 188 190 192 195 197 228 229 231 236 237 244 275 294 309 314
appointment as First Deputy to Defence Minister 49–50 131 132
conspiracy against Beria 51–52 132–133
full member of Central Committee 52 93 134
support of Army command 54
appointment as Defence Minister and influence 55 94–95 134 159
on enhanced status of Army leaders 57
support for Khrushchev 63 143 171 323
elected full member of Presidium 64 143 151
plans for deposition of 65 147 151 159–167
condemnation and accusations against 66 105–106 152–153 158 160 168–170 173 258
demotions 72 129–130
official condemnation of Stalin 87
restricts tasks of Military Councils 96–97 149
abolishes post of *Zampolit* at company level 103–104
on strengthening Commanders' powers 104–105 108 126–127 128 183
on planning of Battle of Stalingrad 113
childhood 117–118
Army career and rise in power 118–126 148 150
the great strategist 128
popularity 129 147
as a political figure 134–135
meetings with Eisenhower at Geneva 135–137 297
praise of 139
views on 140–143
review of career 143–144
fear of 151–152
speeches on "anti-Party" group 153–157
demand for rehabilitation of Stalin's victims 162
evaluation of Zhukov 170–178
change in official attitude to 176
on political education of the Army 181
on weakening Military Councils 187
effects of deposition 213 230
on nuclear weaponry 241 242
comparison with Malinovsky 287 289

ZHYGAROV, P.
Commander of Air Force 50

ZTEMENKO, S.
on need for strong ground forces 284–285